CITIES AND SPACE
THE FUTURE USE OF URBAN LAND

CITIES AND SPACE
THE FUTURE USE
OF URBAN LAND

ESSAYS FROM THE FOURTH RFF FORUM
By
Lowdon Wingo, Jr.
Melvin M. Webber
Stanley B. Tankel
Catherine Bauer Wurster
Frederick Gutheim
Leonard J. Duhl
Roland Artle
Charles M. Haar
Henry Fagin

EDITED BY LOWDON WINGO, JR.

PUBLISHED FOR Resources for the Future, Inc.
BY The Johns Hopkins Press, BALTIMORE AND LONDON

The Johns Hopkins Press, Baltimore, Maryland 21218
The Johns Hopkins Press Ltd., London

ISBN-0-8018-0677-1 (clothbound edition)
ISBN-0-8018-0678-X (paperback edition)

Originally published, 1963
Second printing, 1964
Third printing, 1967
Fourth printing, 1970
Johns Hopkins Paperbacks edition, 1966
Second printing, 1969

RESOURCES FOR THE FUTURE, INC.
1755 Massachusetts Avenue, N.W., Washington, D.C. 20036

Resources for the Future is a nonprofit corporation for research and education in the development, conservation, and use of natural resources and the improvement of the quality of the environment. It was established in 1952 with the cooperation of the Ford Foundation. Part of the work of Resources for the Future is carried out by its resident staff; part is supported by grants to universities and other nonprofit organizations. Unless otherwise stated, interpretations and conclusions in RFF publications are those of the authors; the organization takes responsibility for the selection of significant subjects for study, the competence of the researchers, and their freedom of inquiry.

This book is based on papers prepared by authorities who participated in the 1962 RFF Forum on The Future Use of Urban Space.

RFF editors: Henry Jarrett, Vera W. Dodds, Nora E. Roots, Tadd Fisher.

CONTENTS

CITIES AND SPACE
THE FUTURE USE OF URBAN LAND

LOWDON WINGO, JR. is director of the regional and urban studies program of Resources for the Future. He was director of planning in El Paso, Texas (1953–56) and a Littauer Fellow in the Graduate School of Public Administration at Harvard University (1956–57). He is the author of *Transportation and Urban Land* and articles on metropolitan transportation and planning problems. Mr. Wingo was born in El Paso, Texas, in 1923 and holds degrees in planning and public administration from the University of Chicago and Harvard University.

URBAN SPACE IN A POLICY
PERSPECTIVE: AN INTRODUCTION

LOWDON WINGO, JR.

THIS BOOK ADDRESSES A SET OF PROBLEMS that are pre-empting
more and more of the attention of our society and confounding its collective wisdom—the birth of a metropolitan civilization. The scope of its impact on today's citizen and the institutions which order his world, the visions of a future so vastly
different from our past, and the speed with which it is taking
place attest to the fact that this is revolution, and all revolutions
are painful. That conventional prescriptions have not eased this
transition is the core of what has become known as "the urban
problem." High on the agenda of national policy is the question
which, bidden but unexpected like Banquo's ghost, attends this
affair—can cities be planned so that this metropolitan future
will be a progression toward higher levels of material, aesthetic,
social, and even spiritual satisfaction for the urban citizen?

SOME DEFECTS OF PERSPECTIVE

During the past few years students and policy-makers on the
urban scene have had a mounting sense that their approaches to
the emerging problems of urbanization were not completely

appropriate. Like generals brilliantly prepared to fight the preceding war, our policy-makers have occasionally been trying to solve the problems of the city that was. The perspectives frequently reflect earlier concerns which still linger in the social cortex even though the sources of the concerns have long since been transformed, replaced, or dissipated. The making of policy to organize and exploit the physical environment of the city has been especially prone to the influence of such vestiges working through our conception of the phenomenon, our feelings about it, our choice of the directions in which we have sought to induce the evolution of our urban society. Consider some of these traces now—their origins and their influence.

Utopianism—society's daydreaming—is rooted in the history of western man. Its central characteristic is the persuasion that an ideal world is within reach if the energies of society are mobilized and directed along the appropriate path. Nay, more, we know what this ideal looks like and, if we have been assiduous in our public efforts, the dream will become reality when we reach the target year—2000 A.D. or whenever it is. The urban master plan—our cartoon of Utopia—is at the same time the core concept of city planning and the philosophical scaffolding upon which courts have hung the community's right to manage its space. Thus, the Utopian trace has become institutionalized in our collective psyche, and, if we would manage our spatial environment at all, we are committed to some physical end state which is to be materialized at some reasonably specific point in time and which somehow embodies in its physical extension the aspirations of some earlier community which zealously embarked on this course of development.

Closely related to Utopianism is the brand of environmental determinism that has influenced architecture. It holds that social welfare and individual behavior are closely and determinately conditioned by the characteristics of the physical environment, that social and human goals could be realized in large part, if not entirely, by an appropriate physical environment. How much well-intentioned housing reform has been carried out under the axiom that the uplifting of character would stem directly from the upgrading of shelter! To make a city a better place to live is the explicit mission of city planning, where "city" is understood to be a physical artifact, and "a better place to live" means a more congenial physical environment.

These are innocent vagaries, however, compared to the predisposition of such a point of view to understate or underrate the human and social costs of achieving the desired goal. Such a logic implies that the payoff to the community is realized only as the sought-after environment emerges. In fact, a plan begins to accrue costs and benefits from the first moment that it influences the behavior of a firm or individual. The total time stream of costs and benefits must be summed up in some fashion and the abandonment of conflicting goals appraised, if the concept "a better place to live" is to have any substance. For the critical policy question is not only how much the community is prepared to give up to realize the goals implicit in the master plan, but *who* gives up *how* much so that the fruits of the plan can be realized—quite frequently by others. This perspective has led the uncritical liberal to the implicit conclusion that the importance of the social goals realized by the planned transformations of urban environments always outweighs the current individual and group values which must be foregone. It is by no means obvious that this is the case.

A third trace that still conditions much policy-thinking about the spatial organization of the city is a distrust of the automatic processes of society in favor of conscious, central, rational determination of the community's goals and strategies. Sophisticated analyses pointing out the gross imperfections of the markets for land and housing did not begin with Henry George, but he dramatized the theoretical issues, and his ghost stalks the busy corridors of our city planning offices even today. The archvillain of this piece is the speculator, striving mightily to exploit, to circumvent, or to overthrow the plans of the community in his pursuit of the windfalls of the market. Confounding this Lucifer has become a major involvement of American local government: witness New York City's zoning ordinance with its

numerous land use classes, the increasing number of city coun-
cils who find themselves devoting over half their time to matters
of land use regulation, the proliferation of appellate and administrative institutions charged with protecting the community's interest in the employment of its space. If a casual ob-
server should find our distrust of the mechanisms of our economic life excessive, how much more dramatic must appear our
lack of confidence in the good faith and competence of our political institutions to provide for the community's future. The
coalition of politician and speculator is presented as the arch-
enemy, even though it constitutes a logical redeployment of
interests dammed up or denied by the objectives, content, and
procedures of city planning.

Although other archaisms, attitudes, procedures, and institutions have left their mark, it is the synthesis of Utopian logic,
physical environmentalism, and the custodial view of the community's future that dominates the current perspective of city
planning. These institutional residues from the problems of
other days frequently blind us to the fact that our emerging
problems are not merely old ones in new garb. The great and
continuing revolutions of our technology, our wealth, and our
institutions are constantly working their changes on the character of our wants, of our cities, of our opportunities. The resulting problems are genuinely novel, and need to be dealt with
in new ways.

The peculiar native genius of Americans for institutional innovation and adaptation is assurance that organizational arrangements, procedures, and approaches will not congeal into
a kind of Byzantine-like bureaucracy drifting away from the
realities of the constantly changing character of our metropolitan future. Significant breakthroughs are accumulating in the
analysis of urban problems which will help us to recast them in
more appropriate policy frameworks. Our ability to mobilize
public resources at local, state, and federal levels has relaxed the
constraints on the kinds of solutions which are possible. In this
book, nine scholars consider the changing nature of an aspect

of metropolitan development as a first step toward a reappraisal of our potential to plan our urban future.

THE ISSUE

These essays are concerned with space—space as a resource to meet future requirements for the growth and development of American cities, about how social and economic activities get efficiently structured in urban space. Both the *resource* and the *structural* dimensions of urban space are tied up in the bundle of issues we refer to as the urban problem. Cities exist in space; their activities occupy space; space constrains the interaction among their activities.

Space as a resource in short supply absorbs our attention with questions concerning the optimum allocation of space among competing uses, about the management of this resource. Are we using it well or badly? Is our "supply" of space, defined in terms of location, employed among activities so that rearrangement could bring about no more than a trivial gain to society?

The problem is transformed as the level of our interest changes. The national interest arises from the productivity of urban land, not the amount. Urban space represents substantially less than one per cent of the nation's area, but it houses three out of every four people in this nation and produces well over four-fifths of the total economic output. This massive concentration suggests the critical importance of urban efficiency to the national product: increasing inefficiency in the organization and functioning of our major urban areas will in short order militate against the effectiveness of our national economic establishment simply because they will affect the bulk of our economic activities. Although we are not likely to run out of space for urban activities, cities may at some scale become subject to increasing costs which can be traced back in large part to inefficiencies in their spatial organization. The national interest in the future structure and organization of the urban economy stems in part from the potential impact of the urban environment on the productivity of the national economy.

For the great multistate regions, the issue has another aspect, one associated with the subnational development of our economy. Some regions are growing rapidly in population, production, and wealth, while others stagnate or decline. The growth of the rapidly growing regions has its greatest impact on their cities, whose problems can be characterized quite justifiably as "growing pains." Los Angeles, Miami, Phoenix, and Houston are more than rapidly growing cities; they are the focal points for the growth of larger regions, and their urban problems stem from this relationship in large degree.

Supply problems occur at this level, also. Behold Megalopolis. From Washington to Boston stretches perhaps the greatest concentration of economic activity since the beginning of human history. Viewed from the window of a Boston-to-Washington airliner, Megalopolis is predominantly green open space; yet by automobile one can travel this four hundred miles and rarely lose sight of urban development. This region is far from filled up, but shortness of supply is signalled by rising land prices which tend to squeeze out marginal activities. Land-intensive and capital-extensive horticultural specialties, poultry production, and dairy farms to feed the massive markets of Megalopolis are replacing the land-extensive and capital-intensive cash crops which are being pushed out by the rising land values. This agricultural shift is in reality an urban phenomenon, since the economic condition of every parcel of land in Megalopolis reflects the increasing concentration of persons and activities in the region as a whole. The economic growth of the region and the resulting pressure on its endowment of space cannot help but move the issue of the supply of all space to the center of the policy stage.

At the State House the urban space problem has unique policy dimensions. From the states, the fountainhead of sovereignty in our system, flow the powers with which urban regions attack their developmental problems. Here reside the powers to enact laws, to launch out in new policy directions, even to intervene

mischievously in the uphill fight to bring the great urban problems under control. The problem of urban space varies tremendously among states, but in every one the job of the legislature
is to put the urban and nonurban policy claims in perspective.
This has not always been done well, but institutions are changing and states show signs of assuming new responsibilities for
urban development policies. More difficult to solve is the interstate nature of much of the urban problem; sharply differing
policies across jurisdictional lines add special factors of distor-
tion to the structure and organization of the urban economy.
The State House can help but little here. This failure, as much
as any other, is responsible for the alliance of convenience between the federal government and the cities.

At the metropolitan level, the resource and structure dimensions of urban space merge, simply because we cannot easily disentangle them. The metropolitan region is a special social, economic, and spatial entity. A substantially greater volume of
transactions takes place within its borders than across its
borders, and the larger it is, the more this tends to be true.
Furthermore, no substantial proportion of these transactions
could be isolated without doing violence to viability of the
whole.

Efficient organization of activities in space becomes an even
more critical metropolitan problem when one adds in the satisfactions which the citizens of the city derive from the web of
interactions. Here public investment in facilities and services
can militate against or facilitate the ability of the metropolitan
region to function well. Communication and transportation facilities will define the basic conditions of interaction among
firms and households; investment will flow into profitable locations and away from unprofitable ones; and the accumulation
of these effects will transform the spatial organization of the
metropolitan region.

The supply aspects of metropolitan space are dramatized by
the contrast between the intense utilization of space at the region's economic center and the scattered, diffuse exploitation of
land at the expanding metropolitan "development front." The

supply of metropolitan space is defined only in terms of relative accessibility and its implications for the costs of interaction among its people and enterprises: City X, for example, may be said to have a shortage of open space or industrial area or land for houses only if the supply is insufficiently accessible to "linked" activities. The supply of metropolitan space depends on the communication and transportation facilities, which determine relative levels of accessibility among the parts of the metropolis.

To the local municipality, urban space presents essentially a management problem. Since its boundaries envelop only a part of the web of interactions of the urban community, the municipality's control over its future is generally limited by the powerful external factor of the development of the region itself. What control it has is more negative than positive: it may zone industry, or low-income housing, out of its jurisdiction. Even then, local controls can create costly distortions in metropolitan growth patterns, unless there are institutions to moderate them in favor of the interests of the region as a whole: New York is turning itself inside out as it grows because suburban jurisdictions have held the line against the advance of rising densities and more intensive urban activities, forcing such developments to flow beyond them with the consequent loss of the economies of centralized development.

In effect, the managerial responsibility of the municipal jurisdiction for the use of its space involves not so much efficient arrangements among activities having close functional ties as the need to assure appropriate levels of public services and harmonious relations among spatially proximate, if functionally unrelated, activities.

The concept of urban space, thus, takes its meaning from the organization of the nucleated, interdependent set of activities whose characteristic form a millennium ago was the town, a century ago the city, today the metropolis, and a decade hence, perhaps, megalopolis.

Thus, the policy issues inherent in the spatial organization of an urban society exhibit varying dimensions at different levels of government. What these will mean at every level, however, will depend on the way in which the powerful forces now emerging in our cities work themselves out. It is useful, then, to get a feel for what is happening to cities under the impact of these forces. Not everyone agrees on how these forces should be ranked in importance, but few would disagree that they are all elements of the problem.

CITIES IN SPACE: SOME PROSPECTS AHEAD

Begin with the perspective that the city evolves to expedite the interactions of social and economic activities. The content of these activities is changing, and simultaneously a revolution is taking place in how these activities interact with each other. New organizational factors supplant earlier ones in the evolution of our cities, overcoming inertia and the resistance of entrenched (if vestigial) institutions—sunk capital in the physical plant of the city, legal institutions, behavior patterns. New forces are presenting us with new problems for which the conventional design solutions of the city planner are frequently inappropriate.

First, consider some projections of the main dimensions of the American economy recently carried out by the National Planning Association. Personal income per capita is expected to rise 50 per cent in constant dollars between 1960 and 1976. An increasing proportion of the nation's families will share in these gains, also: where only one out of six consumer units earned $7,500 or more in 1947, and accounted for 42 per cent of the total consumer income, by 1971 half of the consuming units will exceed this figure and account for 77 per cent of the consumer income. These projections have some important implications for changing household consumption patterns. Rising family income means less margarine, cheap clothing; more motorboats, orthodontia, education, and significantly better housing. These shifts in income and consumer demand are resulting in differential rates of growth among the sectors of the national economy. Utilities, construction, services, communication, and household sectors will grow faster than gross national product; agriculture, food processing, and trade will grow more slowly. The rapidly growing industries will account for two-thirds of the 20 million new jobs projected between 1960 and 1972, and services will account for half of those. The slow growth sector will absorb only 15 per cent.

A disproportionate share of the gains in employment attributable to the growing sectors is being realized in the metropolitan areas, and especially in those with advantages of access to large consumer markets. Thus, most large urban communities can expect some broad changes in the composition of the output and employment in their economies. Since locational requirements vary sharply among activities, these changes will influence the spatial organization of the future urban region.

Meanwhile technological innovation transforming the processes of production and advances in communication systems are reorganizing the city. Recent developments in automatic controls and information handling have revolutionized production activities: complex machine tools are now preprogrammed to carry out their operations on the production line without human guidance. The floods of paper necessary to control the economy have been tamed by electronic data processing. Closed circuit television is substituting for some kinds of face-to-face contact. All of these developments replace material flows with information flows, and operations which previously had to be spatially integrated because of the costs of moving persons or materials are finding their earlier bonds relaxed.

This revolution is creating new machines, new techniques, and new organizational arrangements. At the same time, the existing plants and machines are aging and becoming less efficient, so that the new plants enjoy the competitive advantages of both newness and a more productive technology. Somewhere in the aging process enterprises must decide whether to update themselves technologically to recapture lost competitive advantages. At some point in this process, a plant may also make a new locational choice responding to differential transportation cost and site rents to take advantage of more space or better access to linked activities. Such factors work through the economic structure of the urban community to change its spatial organization.

A substantial part of the interaction among urban activities takes place through the urban transportation system, which is also changing, through the imposition of its costs on users and on the community at large. Public costs (the expenditure of funds by public bodies for the construction, operation, and maintenance of transportation facilities) are to be distinguished from private costs (out-of-pocket money and time costs), because they measure different things. Private costs influence the trip-making and locational behavior of persons, while public costs represent community decisions about how a total transportation system should perform. In combination, these costs have a tremendous influence on how an urban region gets spatially organized. The relationship is quite simple. Public investment in transportation systems tends to reduce the private time or money costs of movement and thereby the costs of those economic linkages which take place through the movement of goods and persons.

Much of the tight concentration of urban activities around a dense urban core can be explained by the economies that existed under earlier conditions when transportation costs were relatively high and there were substantial locational differentials in the costs of transporting materials and persons. That our production technologies no longer depend so heavily on these flows is dramatically illustrated by comparing the spatial organization of the auto age cities, such as Los Angeles, with their predecessors, such as Boston. The urban concentration—the gigantic piling up of capital structures at the region's center tapering off dramatically as one moves toward the periphery—seems to be subsiding.

Substantial improvement (cost reduction) in outlying transportation can be effected at low capital costs, and the time and money costs to users may be substantially reduced by the construction of high-speed transportation channels which operate at less than capacity loads. In the center of the region, however, it would require exorbitant public investment in transportation facilities to reduce private costs per person-mile in time and money to a par with those in the hinterlands. Some of these costs will undoubtedly be shifted to users as time costs resulting from accepted congestion of the facilities at peak, with the result that public and private costs per unit of movement are now and will increasingly be higher in the vicinity of the center than in much of the rest of the region.

For centrally located activities which find themselves functioning paradoxically in an increasingly high-cost part of the region, the lower transportation and land costs of outlying locations will be appealing alternatives when new investment (i.e., locational) decisions are to be made. Retailing and manufacturing are already moving to the suburbs, and service industries are following. The growing accumulation of capital in transportation facilities, coupled with the increasing substitution of information flows for material flows, is gradually dissipating many of the advantages of economic togetherness.

The city will not, of course, fly apart explosively, no matter how dramatic these effects. Marginal activities will be spun off from the center, as sunk capital can be written off, and this may be a fairly slow process. The lion's share of new activities will find locations away from the center. Increasing specialization of the urban core by activities with special communication and transportation needs, such as frequent face-to-face contact, is certain, but this may also give way in time.

A much more dispersed urban pattern seems to be the prognosis not only because private movement costs in the core have increased, but because public investment in outlying transportation has sharply reduced private transportation costs in suburban areas and dissipated many of the economic advantages of central location. The current strategy of constructing high-volume, high-speed radial freeways articulated by sets of beltways or circumferentials will amplify these effects, and eventually we will come to a new urban pattern—no longer the centrally articulated, classical city, but a loosely knit, weakly centered, low-density urban region spread over a wide hinterland. The cause? Quite simply, the sharply reduced transportation costs outside the center make land or space even less a scarce good to be husbanded. The old pattern of a broad spread of urbanized land occasionally interrupted by scattered green spaces may be reversed, and the emerging pattern may tend toward islands of development scattered over a green landscape and linked together by transportation facilities.

As the bonds of transportation costs are relaxed, the *next* most important factors will tend to dominate the locational decisions of firms and individuals. No longer tightly bound to the urban core, the residential land market is likely to find its most intense demand focusing on the more coveted aspects of the physical environment—resources such as landscape and climate. The availability of public services such as potable water, waste removal, schools, and recreation facilities may have highly selective development effects about the region. Finally, the selective gregariousness of social groups will probably continue to influence how groups get distributed. In general, the emerging pattern is likely to be space extensive and resource oriented.

These anticipated developments pose a number of issues for a future urban problems agenda:

1. The underutilization of the capital which has been cumulatively built up in the core area. It is not enough to point to new construction in the central business district (CBD) as a symptom of good health—new construction skims the cream off the CBD real estate market. A more sensitive test is to look at what is happening to the older capital in the core area. Vacancy rates are likely to soar while rents decline. The process of decentralizing historically centralized communities will leave in its wake an accelerated tendency toward physical and economic deterioration at the center which can wash out tremendous book values.

What is our best strategy here? To marshall all of our resources to try to hold this core together when the rationale of concentration has disappeared? Are we willing to (or can we) dramatically reduce investment in new transportation facilities on the outskirts and vastly increase it at the center to redress the distribution of accessibilities over the region in favor of the center? We should realize that this strategy of conserving the investment at the core entails some severe costs and may not even be possible. Perhaps we should merely try to apply brakes to this process so that the "write down" of central area values may take place at a rate that will tolerate better adjustments.

Should we expect the public to bear the losses of the subsidence of CBD values through such mechanisms as urban renewal? Over the nation as a whole the sums involved could be gigantic. Two kinds of decisions follow. What new conditions and what kind of a center will be coherent with this emerging urban form, and be sustained by it? What are the specifications of a program for achieving the new conditions with a minimum of transitional loss?

2. We just do not have a transportation or communication technology which can long sustain a massive, highly centralized urban complex, New York notwithstanding. The transportation modes we have developed to handle massive demands in highly concentrated areas do not serve effectively a wide dispersion of trip origins and destinations; similarly the mode of private transportation that functions so effectively for decentralized travel and scattered destinations becomes highly inefficient under conditions of intense demand. We are not certain that we can effectively marry these two.

Present administrative arrangements and policies militate against mass transportation. Each new freeway undercuts the market for mass transportation—in the short run by drawing potential users away; in the long run by drawing economic activities away from the center. At the same time, we expect mass transit operations to act like private enterprises and highway agencies like bureaus. We are not technologically prepared to serve well the classical city writ large; we are not administratively prepared to integrate regional transportation activities. The private auto may have already won this competition so irreversibly that nothing can hold the center together and sustain mass transportation.

3. The management of open land in a decentralizing region is a very special issue which begins with a need to re-evaluate the purposes of land use regulations generally. The threat of misallocation of a plenteous resource is considerably less than that of a scarce one; land use regulation under these circumstances could shift purposes in considerable degree moving away from government (or planning) determinations of appropriate use and in the direction of protecting each man from the spillovers of his neighbor's use of his property, away from regulation by arbitrary use classes and in the direction of broad community standards, away from statutory implementation toward a greater exploitation of private arrangements.

The open land problem still presents us with a major issue, however. Certainly one of the effects of scattered development is that agricultural land mingled with areas of urban development can easily become unprofitable. Withdrawn land—to use Marion Clawson's term for land made unprofitable by urban development and left, unused and unlovely, interspersed among new subdivisions—may well become an important part of the environment of much of this widely scattered development. Here land use planning may well focus on environmental conservation, a new marriage of ecology and economy, not land use regulation, but urban land use management.

Our mission in this symposium is to identify, if we can, the things that are likely to count for the most in the growth and evolution of these urban regions. We need assurance that what we do now in manipulating these elements and forces will count for something positive tomorrow. We must assess our real alternatives, their costs and benefits, the gainers and the losers, and carefully weave these considerations together in our view of the future. The base alternative is always to do nothing, to ride the trends, patching a little here and there, and making the most of whatever occurs. Any other alternative can be chosen only if it nets out better than the "zero intervention" one, and to determine this we must be able to see where these forces are pushing, always with the idea in mind that it is much easier to swim with the current than against it, if it will take you anywhere near where you want to go.

THEMES FROM THE SYMPOSIUM

In March, 1962, Washington, D.C. was the site of the Fourth Resources for the Future Forum, a symposium to explore the emerging factors that are likely to influence the manner in which urban space will be used during the next generation and the alternatives available to society in laying out its metropolitan future over the long run. That is, given legal, political, cultural, and economic restraints, what is possible? The symposium was composed of the scholars whose thoughtful essays are brought together in this volume. They set out the dominant intellectual positions current in the growing debate over appropriate policies to guide the growth and organization of our cities. Each then went home, reflected on this experience, and this volume is the result. It is in the context of a nation become metropolitan, of cities growing, undoubling, dispersing over the national landscape, that their essays take on significance. Each addresses a dimension of this urban future, probes choices and consequences, suggests perspectives and directions.

Three authors found themselves deeply involved in issues that stem quite directly from the changing organization of cities in space. It is not sheer coincidence that they are city planners deeply troubled by the picture of the future which a projection of existing explosive trends suggests. While each sees the same thing in the unfolding pattern of urban settlement, each appraises its significance for tomorrow's citizen differently. Melvin Webber finds in the dissolution of the urban settlement a liberation of human energies and a proliferation of opportunity for human interaction. Cities are pouring out over the countryside as the bonds which held them tightly contained are loosened, and in the offing is a different kind of world in which the characteristics we have associated with urban life are becoming diffused throughout our whole society. Mobility, communication, and the broadly distributed fruits of rising productivity are generating a society dispersed and heterogeneous, organized by functional relations rather than proximity.

Stanley Tankel finds this a melancholy prospect indeed. The great positive values of an urban civilization stem from its "togetherness," from the concentrated variety that a Manhattan typifies, not from the endless, monotonous homogeneity which middle-class suburban dispersion has produced. Its excitement lies in the contrast of city and countryside; its humanity has stemmed from its ability to provide environments which will nurture many sides of the human spirit. If these things are lost, a special human quality of our civilization will fade. Here urban design, prescribing the organization of open space at the level of the street, of the community and county, of the region can promise some rescue: it is city planning as an enterprise in spatial design, not as an exercise in the social sciences, that will make the critical decisions.

Catherine Wurster argues that Webber and Tankel have not really posed the critical problem. The individual may be equally lost in Webber's placeless space or in Tankel's human ant hill with open spaces. We need an urbanism more to the scale of his needs for rewarding contacts, for integration, for stability, for a sense of mastery over the externals within which he lives, for a choice of life styles. There are practical alternatives, she argues, to the inhuman scales which these futures promise. The strategy to find them requires rethinking the relationships of economic activity to space, so that smaller units can be developed which can present a reasonably self-sufficient social and physical environment within which individuals may not only prosper but grow.

Frederick Gutheim picks up Tankel's theme of urban design, moves away from the question of urban form, and asserts design to be the master framework in urban policy-making and development. Here the city emerges more clearly as a work of art, not so much in its shape as in its innumerable perspectives and details. The planner is engaged with the quality of urbanism, which reflects the highest, in contrast to the barbaric, strains of this age of cities. This quality of urbanism is nowhere more dramatically present than in the perceptual dimensions of the urban milieu.

A caveat is sounded, however, by Leonard Duhl. The fruits of urban design are not synonymous with humanism nor always consistent with the social and psychic needs of urban humanity. Planners are too prone, too readily persuaded to sacrifice today's flesh-and-blood citizens on their Utopian altars, because the values which dictate their choices are those of a class rather than of urban society as a whole in all its pluralism and complexity. The welfare of individuals—not the spaces and artifacts in which they live and move—should reflect the pay-off of the planner's efforts.

Decisions about cities must concern themselves with people, argues Roland Artle, simply because the outcomes of public policies are actually the product of the interaction of the daily decisions of individuals and firms within a context defined by public policies. More sophisticated ways of anticipating outcomes will require a further development of decision models to help us test policy outcomes experimentally. Before they can be exploited fully, much of our thinking about goals and objectives in metropolitan development will have to be reviewed and recast in more operational terms. In the end, we can look forward to metropolitan policy-making much more sensitively articulated to the developmental needs of urban life.

This raises another critical issue, warns Charles Haar. Our legal and political institutions are bending before the planner and the need for more versatile policy tools with which to attack the problems of a metropolitan civilization. We are releasing ever greater social powers to alter the course of cities and regions. Unless policy-makers are clear about the objectives of their policies and their relations to the whole fabric of public and private interests, the well-intentioned misuse of such powers will be a continuing threat. Unless we have a firm, scientific understanding of the consequences of public action on the mainstreams of urban life, we may achieve limited ends at the cost of being engulfed by their side effects.

In the end, Henry Fagin surveys these portents and opportunities and concludes that new institutions for metropolitan policy-making are to be restructured from the present inappropriate constellations of government organizations, processes, and perspectives congealed in federal-state-local relations. Where policies directed at regional problems have traditionally been dominated by the claims of federal, state, and local interests, the new policy synthesis will develop around the "key elements of regional existence." Urban problems are now indisputably national problems; their claims for our attention and upon our governmental resources will increasingly override distinctions of sovereignty and the niceties of organization charts. The first order of metropolitan business, then, is the catalysis of this transformation of governmental arrangements for the planning and development of our metropolitan regions.

. . . . . .

These, then, are some of the main themes which this symposium evokes. There are others, perhaps more significant, but less dramatically argued in these papers. Urban space is a severe problem for this unfolding megalopolitan civilization, but essentially because it is a reflection of the almost unending array of problems which the historical forces of this age throw upon the beach of our social consciousness.

MELVIN M. WEBBER is associate professor of city planning at the University of California, Berkeley. He was recently the editor of the *Journal of the American Institute of Planners,* and before joining the University was senior metropolitan regional planner with Parsons, Brinckerhoff, Hall and Macdonald for the San Francisco Bay Area Rapid Transit Study. He has written on metropolitan transportation planning, on metropolitan spatial structure, and on planning theory. This essay is the sequel to "The Urban Place and the Nonplace Urban Realm," in *Explorations into Urban Structure* (1963). Mr. Webber was born in Hartford, Conn. in 1920. He holds degrees in economics and sociology from the University of Texas and in city planning from the University of California, Berkeley.

ORDER IN DIVERSITY: COMMUNITY WITHOUT PROPINQUITY

MELVIN M. WEBBER

THE SPATIAL PATTERNS OF AMERICAN URBAN SETTLEMENTS are going to be considerably more dispersed, varied, and space-consuming than they ever were in the past—whatever metropolitan planners or anyone else may try to do about it. It is quite likely that most of the professional commentators will look upon this development with considerable disfavor, since these patterns will differ so markedly from our ideological precepts. But disparate spatial dispersion seems to be a built-in feature of the future—the complement of the increasing diversity that is coming to mark the processes of the nation's economy, its politics, and its social life. In addition, it seems to be the counterpart of a chain of technological developments that permit spatial separation of closely related people.

At this stage in the development of our thinking, students of the city are still unable to agree even on the nature of the phenomena they are dealing with. But it should surprise no one. For the plain fact of the matter is that, now, when the last rural threads of American society are being woven into the national urban fabric, the idea of city is becoming indistinguishable from the idea of society. If we lack consensus on an organizing conceptual structure of the city, it is mainly because we lack such a

23

structure for society as a whole. The burden, then, rests upon all the arts, the humanities, and the sciences; and the task grows increasingly difficult as the complexity of contemporary society itself increases and as rapidly accumulating knowledge deprives us of what we had thought to be stable pillars of understanding.

In previous eras, when the goals, the beliefs, the behavior, and the roles of city folk were clearly distinguishable from those of their rural brethren, and when urban settlements were spatially discrete and physically bounded, schoolboy common sense was sufficient to identify the marks of "urbanness." Now all Americans are coming to share very similar cultural traits; the physical boundaries of settlements are disappearing; and the networks of interdependence among various groups are becoming functionally intricate and spatially widespread. With it all, the old symbols of order are giving way to the signs of newly emerging systems of organization that, in turn, are sapping the usefulness of our established concepts of order.

Especially during the last fifteen years, the rapid expansion of the large metropolitan settlements has been paralleled by a rising flood of commentary, reporting and evaluating this remarkable event; and we have developed a new language for dealing with it. Although the scholarly contributions to this new literature tend to be appropriately restrained and the journalistic and polemic contributions characteristically vituperative, the emerging patterns of settlement are typically greeted by both with disapproval if not frantic dismay. By now almost everyone knows that the low-density developments on the growing edge of the metropolis are a form of "cancerous growth," scornfully dubbed with the most denunciatory of our new lexicon's titles, "urban sprawl," "scatteration," "subtopia," and now "slurbs"—a pattern of development that "threatens our national heritage of open space" while "decaying blight rots out the city's heart" and a "demonic addiction to automobiles" threatens to "choke the life out of our cities." Clearly, "our most cherished values" are imperiled by what is synoptically termed "urban chaos." However, such analysis by cliché is likely to be helpful only as incitement to action; and action guided by obsolescent truths is likely to be effective only as reaffirmation of ideology.

We have often erred, I believe, in taking the visual symbols of urbanization to be marks of the important qualities of urban society; we have compared these symbols with our ideological precepts of order and found that they do not conform; and so we have mistaken for "urban chaos" what is more likely to be a newly emerging order whose signal qualities are complexity and diversity.

These changes now taking place in American society may well be compatible with—and perhaps call forth—metropolitan forms that are neither concentrated nor concentric nor contained. Sympathetic acceptance of this proposition might then lead us to new ways of seeing the metropolis, ways that are more sensitive to the environmental qualities that really matter. We might find new criteria for evaluating the changes in metropolitan spatial structure, suggesting that these changes are not as bad as we had thought. In turn, our approach to metropolitan spatial planning would be likely to shift from an ideological campaign to reconstruct the preconceived city forms that matched the social structures of past eras. Instead, we might see the emergence of a pragmatic, problem-solving approach in which the spatial aspects of the metropolis are viewed as continuous with and defined by the processes of urban society—in which space is distinguished from place, in which human interaction rather than land is seen as the fruitful focus of attention, and in which plans limited to the physical form of the urban settlement are no longer put forth as synoptic statements of our goals.

Metropolitan planning, then, would become the task of mutually accommodating changes in the spatial environment and changes in the social environment. And, because so much of the future is both unknowable and uncontrollable, the orientation of our efforts would shift from the inherently frustrating attempt to build the past in the future to the more realistic strategy of guiding change in desired directions—from a seeking after predesigned end-states to a continuing and much more complex struggle with processes of becoming.

So radical a revision of our thoughtways is not likely to come easily, for we are firmly devoted to the a priori values that we associate with land (especially with open land), with urban centers (especially with the more concentrated and culturally rich centers), and with certain visual attributes of the urban settlement (especially those features that result from the clean boundary line and the physical separation of different types of objects). And, above all, we are devoted to a unitary conception of order that finds expression in the separation of land uses, the classifiable hierarchy of centers, and the visual scene that conforms to classical canons.

So, let us briefly reconsider the idea of city and review some of the current and impending changes to see what their consequences are likely to be for future urbanization in the United States. We can then re-examine the idea of urban space to see how we might allocate it with some greater degree of rationality.

THE QUALITIES OF "CITYNESS"

In the literature and in the popular mind, the idea of city is imprecise: the terms "city," "urban," "metropolitan," and the various other synonyms are applied to a wide variety of phenomena. Sometimes we speak of the city as though it were simply an artifact—an agglomeration of buildings, roads, and interstitial spaces that marks the settlements of large numbers of people. On other occasions we refer not to physical buildings but to concentrations of physical bodies of humans, as they accumulate in nodal concentrations at higher densities than in "nonurban" places. At other times we refer to the spatial concentration of the places at which human activities are conducted. At still other times we mean a particular set of institutions that mark urban systems of human organization, where we mean to identify the organizational arrangements through which human activities are related to each other—the formal and the informal role allocating systems and the authority systems controlling human behavior. In turn, we sometimes refer to patterns of behavior, and sometimes we mean to distinguish the social value systems of those people and groups that are "urban" from those that are "nonurban."

The values, the ways of life, the institutional arrangements, and the kinds of activities that characterize people living in high-density clusters amidst large concentrations of buildings have been traditionally quite different from those of people living on farms or in small settlements. The large American city has been distinguished by a particular set of these characteristics, and yet, depending upon the specific purposes of our examination, not all these characteristics are necessary conditions of urbanness.

Large numbers of the people concentrated at the centers of New York, Chicago, and most other large metropolitan areas are recent migrants from "rural" areas. Their values, their life styles, their occupational skills, and their social institutions are certainly undergoing rapid change, but, nonetheless, these people are still rural villagers and are likely to retain many of their ways through at least another generation. After an intensive study of the residents of Boston's West End, Herbert Gans could best typify these second- and third-generation descendants of Italian immigrants as "urban villagers," whose way of life in the geographic center of a large metropolitan settlement has retained strong similarities to the patterns inherited from the villages of Italy.[1] The cultural diversity typified by the West Enders living adjacent to Beacon Hill residents—rather than any particular social pattern—is one of the distinctive marks of the city.

The city also is frequently equated with the greatest variety of economic activities; modern urbanization is often conceived as the counterpart of industrialization. Industrialization carries with it an increasingly fine division of labor and, hence, an in-

[1] Herbert J. Gans, *The Urban Villagers* (New York: The Free Press of Glencoe, Inc., 1962).

creasing interdependence among men having specialized skills, who exchange many types of goods and services with one another. As the industrial development process evolves, increasing varieties of goods and services are produced; purchasing power and hence consumer demands rise; and the economy moves ever further from the self-sufficiency of nonurban primitive societies.

Relatively few products and occupations are exclusively associated with urbanization. At an early date in history we might have been able to distinguish nonurban production from urban production by separating the extractive industries (agriculture, forestry, fishing, and mining) and their related occupations from all others. But this is no longer clear. When the skills of farmers and miners are so closely approximating those of men who work in factories and executive suites, the distinction is hard to retain. And when fishermen live on San Francisco's Telegraph Hill, when oilworkers are an industrial elite, and when farmers and foresters hold university degrees and maintain laboratories and research plots, it becomes very difficult indeed to avoid the conclusion that these men are more firmly integrated into the urban society than are Boston's West Enders.

To say this is not to extend the proposition that the amalgamation of the once-rural and once-urban societies is accompanying a movement to an "other-directed" "mass society." The opportunities for a diversity of choices are clearly much greater in the United States today than they were 150 years ago when industrialization and the opportunities for social mobility were just beginning to stir new ideas and new ways into a poorly educated and unskilled population. Despite some gloomy predictions of the impending impacts of the mass communications media and of the pressures for conformity, the American population is realizing expanding opportunities for learning new ways, participating in more diverse types of activities, cultivating a wider variety of interests and tastes, developing greater capacities for understanding, and savoring richer experiences.

In the next fifty years it is likely that the rate at which the opportunities for learning and for social mobility expand will be even greater than in the last sixty years, when millions of uneducated immigrants from all over the world were integrated into every stratum of American society. Urban life, the communications media, and the public education systems are not likely to reduce all to a lowest common mediocrity. They are more likely to open doors to new ideas, to increased opportunities for being different from one's parents and others in the subculture in which one was reared—as those who have enjoyed these benefits already know and as the American Negroes are coming to know. Rather than a "mass culture" in a "mass society" the long-term prospect is for a maze of subcultures within an amazingly diverse society organized upon a broadly shared cultural base. This is the important meaning that the American brand of urbanization holds for human welfare.

During the past half-century the benefits of urbanization have been extended to an ever-growing proportion of the population: differentials in income distribution have narrowed; formal and informal educational opportunities have spread; Americans have flooded into the middle class. Access to information and ideas has thereby been extended to larger and larger percentages of the population, and this has been greatly abetted by the increasing ease of communication and transportation, *across* space, bringing books, periodicals, lectures, music, and personal observation to more and more people. As the individual's interests develop, he is better able to find others who share these interests and with whom he can associate. The communities with which he associates and to which he "belongs" are no longer only the communities of place to which his ancestors were restricted; Americans are becoming more closely tied to various interest communities than to place communities, whether the interest be based on occupational activities, leisure pastimes, social relationships, or intellectual pursuits. Members of interest communities within a freely communicating society need not be spatially concentrated (except, perhaps, during the formative stages of the interest community's development), for they are increasingly able to interact with each other wherever they may be located. This striking feature of contemporary urbanization is making it increasingly possible for men of all occupations

to participate in the national urban life, and, thereby, it is destroying the once-valid dichotomies that distinguished the rural
from the urban, the small town from the metropolis, the city
from the suburb.

THE SPATIAL CITY

Nothing that I have just said depends upon any specific assumption about the spatial patterns in which urbanites distribute themselves. I am contending that the essential qualities
of urbanness are cultural in character, not territorial, that these
qualities are not necessarily tied to the conceptions that see the
city as a spatial phenomenon. But throughout all of human
history these nonspatial qualities have indeed been typically associated with populations concentrated in high-density urban
settlements.

Although, as some have suggested, there may be certain psychological propensities that induce people to occupy the same
place, there seems to be almost universal agreement among
urban theorists that population agglomeration is a direct reflection of the specialization of occupations and interests that is at
the crux of urbanism and that makes individuals so dependent
upon others. Dependency gets expressed as human interaction—
whether through direct tactile or visual contact, face-to-face
conversation, the transmission of information and ideas via
written or electrical means, the exchange of money, or through
the exchange of goods or services. In the nature of things, all
types of interaction must occur through space, the scale of which
depends upon the locations of the parties to the transaction. It
is also in the nature of things that there are energy and time
costs in moving messages or physical objects through space; and
people who interact frequently with certain others seek to
reduce the costs of overcoming space by reducing the spatial distances separating them. Population clusterings are the direct expression of this drive to reduce the costs of interaction among

people who depend upon, and therefore communicate with, each other.

As the large metropolitan areas in the United States have grown ever larger, they have simultaneously become the places at which the widest varieties of specialists offer the widest varieties of specialized services, thus further increasing their attractiveness to other specialists in self-propelling waves. Here a person is best able to afford the costs of maintaining the web of communications that he relies upon and that, in turn, lies at the heart of complex social systems. Here the individual has an opportunity to engage in diverse kinds of activities, to enjoy the affluence that comes with diversity of specialized offerings; here cultural richness is not withheld simply because it is too costly to get to the place where it can be had.

The spatial city, with its high-density concentrations of people and buildings and its clustering of activity places, appears, then, as the derivative of the communications patterns of the individuals and groups that inhabit it. They have come here to gain accessibility to others and at a cost that they are willing and can afford to pay. The larger the number of people who are accessible to each other, the larger is the likely number of contacts among pairs, and the greater is the opportunity for the individual to accumulate the economic and cultural wealth that he seeks.

Having come to the urban settlement in an effort to lower its costs of communication, the household or the business establishment must then find that location within the settlement which is suitable to it. The competition for space within the settlement results in high land rents near the center, where communication costs are low, and low land rents near the edge of the settlement, where communication costs are high. The individual locator must therefore allocate some portion of his location budget to communication costs and some portion to rents. By choosing an outlying location with its typically larger space he substitutes communication costs (expended in out-of-pocket transportation payments, time, inconvenience, and lost opportunities for communication with others) for rents. And, since rent levels decline slowly as one leaves the built-up portions of the urban settlement and enters the agricultural areas, while communication costs continue to rise as an almost direct function of distance, very few have been wont to move very far out from the center of the urban settlement. The effect has traditionally been a compact settlement pattern, having very high population and employment densities at the center where rents are also highest, and having a fairly sharp boundary at the settlement's margin.

It is this distinctive form of urban settlements throughout history that has led us to equate urbanness with agglomerations of population. Some architects, some city planners, and some geographers would carry it still further, insisting that the essential qualities of the city are population agglomerations and the accompanying building agglomerations themselves; and they argue that the configurations and qualities of spatial forms are themselves objects of value. The city, as artifact or as locational pattern of activity places, has thus become the city planner's specific object of professional attention throughout the world; and certain canons have evolved that are held as guides for designers of spatial cities.

Sensitive to the cultural and economic productivity of populations residing in large and highly centralized urban settlements, some city planners have deduced that the productivity is caused by the spatial form; and plans for future growth of the settlement have therefore been geared to perpetuating or accentuating large, high-density concentrations. Other city planners, alert to a different body of evidence, have viewed the large, high-density city as the locus of filth, depravity, and the range of social pathologies that many of its residents are heir to. With a similar hypothesis of spatial environmental determinism and looking back with envy upon an idealization of the small-town life that predominated in the eighteenth and early nineteenth centuries, this group of planners has proposed that the large settlements be dismantled, that their populations and industries be redistributed to new small towns, and that all future settlements be prevented from growing beyond some predetermined, limited size.

Others have offered still other ideal forms. The metropolitan plan for the San Francisco Bay Area and Washington's Year 2000 plan propose star-like configurations surrounding a dominant center, with major subcenters along each of the radials.[2] The Greater London Plan calls for a somewhat similar pattern of subcenters surrounding central London, but these are to be spatially free-standing towns at the outer edge of a permanent greenbelt. Alert to the external economies that accompany large agglomerations, while sensitive to the problems that accompany high density and large size, Catherine Bauer Wurster has eschewed both the British New Towns doctrine and the American metropolitan growth patterns. She urges instead that major new settlements be separated from one another and limited to some half-million inhabitants each.[3] Others have proposed slightly different modifications of the Bay Area–Washington, the Greater London, and the Wurster schemes in the official plans prepared for Detroit, Atlanta, and Denver.

Despite some important differences among these proposals, however, they all conform to two underlying conceptions from which they stem:

1. The settlement is conceived as a spatial *unit*, almost as though it were an independent artifact—an independent object separable from others of its kind. The unit is spatially delineated by a surrounding band of land which, in contrast to the unit, has foliage but few people or buildings. In some of the schemes subunits are similarly delineated by green-

[2] Parsons, Brinckerhoff, Hall, and Macdonald, *Regional Rapid Transit: Report to the San Francisco Bay Area Rapid Transit Commission* (San Francisco and New York: Parsons, Brinckerhoff, Hall, and Macdonald, 1956). National Capital Planning Commission and the National Capital Regional Planning Council, *Policies Plan for the Year 2000* (Washington: U.S. Government Printing Office, 1961).

[3] Catherine Bauer Wurster, "Framework for an Urban Society," in *Goals for Americans: The Report of the President's Commission on National Goals* (New York: Prentice-Hall, 1960).

belts; in others they are defined as subcenters, as subsidiary density peaks of resident and/or employed populations; but the unitary conception holds for all.

2. Whether the desired population size within the unit is to be large or small, whether subunits are to be fostered either as subsettlements within greenbelts or as subcenters within continuously built-up areas, the territorial extent of the "urbanized area" is to be deliberately contained, and a surrounding permanent greenbelt is to be maintained. The doctrine calls for distinct separation of land that is "urbanized" and land that is not. The editors of *Architectural Review* stated the contention with effective force, in "Outrage" and "Counter Attack," when they pleaded for sharply bounded separation of city, suburb, and country:

The crime of subtopia is that it blurs the distinction between places. It does so by smoothing down the differences between types of environment—town and country, country and suburb, suburb and wild—rather than directly between one town and another. It doesn't deliberately set out to make Glen Shiel look like Helvellyn; it does so in fact by introducing the same overpowering alien elements—in this case blanket afforestation and the wire that surrounds it—into both. The job of this issue [of the magazine] is to get straight the basic divisions between types of environment, and to suggest a framework for keeping each true to itself and distinct from its neighbors.[4]

Behind both ideas are the more fundamental beliefs that urban and rural comprise a dualism that should be clearly expressed in the physical and spatial form of the city, that orderliness depends upon boundedness, and that boundaries are in some way barriers. I have already indicated that the social and economic distinctions between urban and rural are weakening, and it is now appropriate that we examine the spatial counterparts of this blurring nonspatial boundary. I believe that the unitary conceptions of urban places are also fast becoming anachronistic, for the physical boundaries are rapidly collapsing;

[4] "Counter Attack," *Architectural Review*, 1955, pp. 355–56.

and, even where they are imposed by legal restraints, social intercourse, which has never respected physical boundaries anyway,
is increasingly able to ignore them.

EMERGING SETTLEMENT PATTERNS

It is a striking feature of current, physical urbanization patterns that rapid growth is still occurring at the sites of the largest
settlements and that these large settlements are to be found at
widely scattered places on the continent. The westward population movement from the Atlantic Seaboard has not been a
spatially homogeneous spread, but has leapfrogged over vast
spaces to coagulate at such separated spots as the sites of Denver,
Houston, Omaha, Los Angeles, San Francisco, and Seattle.

This is a very remarkable event. Los Angeles, San Francisco,
San Diego, and Seattle, as examples, have been able to grow to
their present proportions very largely as the result of a rapid expansion of industries that are located far from both their raw
materials and their customers. The most obvious of these, of
course, are the producers of aircraft, missiles, and electronic
equipment which use materials manufactured in the East, in
Canada, and throughout the world, and then sell most of their
product to firms and governments that are also spatially dispersed. They seem to have been attracted to the West by its
climate, its natural amenities, and by a regional style of life that
their employees seem to find attractive. Once there, they are
highly dependent upon good long-distance transportation. And,
since successful management of these industries depends upon
good access to information about technical processes, about
markets, and about finance, they are equally dependent upon
good long-distance communication.

It seems clear that the scale of growth there would not have
been possible without first the railroad, ocean freighters, and
the telegraph and then the telephone, the highways, and the airlines. All of these changes, we must remember, are very recent
occurrences in the history of urban man. (The centennial of the

Pony Express was celebrated in 1961, and the Panama Canal is scarcely two generations old.) These technological changes have made it possible for individual establishments to operate efficiently thousands of miles away from the national business center at New York, the government center at Washington, and the industrial belt between Boston and Chicago, to which they are very intimately linked. At least at this territorial scale, it is apparent that economic and social propinquity is not dependent upon spatial propinquity.

These distant metropolitan areas continue to attract a wide variety of specialized firms and individuals, and most of them still prefer to locate *inside* these metropolitan settlements. It is impressive that the television industry, which requires such intricate co-ordination and split-second timing, has chosen to operate primarily out of two metropolitan areas at opposite ends of a continent, yet its establishments are located within the midst of each. Similarly, the financial institutions and administrative offices of corporations which also rely upon quick access to accurate information are attracted to locations within the midst of these settlements. The reasons are apparent.

Just as certain businesses must maintain rapid communications with linked establishments in other metropolitan areas throughout the nation and throughout the world, so too must they maintain easy communication with the vast numbers of local establishments that serve them and that in turn are served by them. The web of communication lines among interdependent establishments within the large urban settlements is extremely strong. Today it is possible to break off large chunks of urban America and place them at considerable distances from the national urban center in the East, but it does not yet seem possible for these chunks to be broken into smaller pieces and distributed over the countryside.

Nevertheless, the events that have marked the growth of widely separated metropolitan settlements force us to ask whether the same kinds of processes that induced their spatial dispersion might not also come to influence the spatial patterns of individual metropolitan settlements as well. A business firm

can now move from Philadelphia to Los Angeles and retain close
contact with the business world in the East while enjoying the
natural amenities of the West; yet it has little choice but to locate within the Los Angeles Basin where it would be readily accessible to a large labor force, to suppliers, and to service establishments. It is attracted to the metropolitan settlement
rather than the more pleasant Sierra Nevada foothills because
here the costs of overcoming distance to linked establishments
are lower. *The unique commodity that the metropolitan settlement has to offer is lower communication cósts.* This is the
paramount attraction for establishments and, hence, the dominant reason for high-density agglomeration.

The validity of this proposition would be apparent if we were
to imagine a mythical world in which people or goods or messages could almost instantaneously be transported between any
two establishments—say, in one minute of time and without
other costs of any sort. One could then place his home on which-
ever mountaintop or lakeside he preferred and get to work,
school, or shops anywhere in the world. Goods could be distributed to factories or homes without concern for their distances from the point of shipment. Decision-makers in industry
and government could have immediate access to any available
information and could come into almost immediate face-to-face
contact with each other irrespective of where their offices were
located, just as friends and relatives could visit in each other's
livingrooms, wherever each might live. With transport costs between establishments reduced to nearly zero, few would be willing to suffer the costs of high density and high rent that are
associated with high accessibility to the center of the metropolitan settlements. And yet, accessibility to all other establishments would be almost maximized, subject only to the one-
minute travel time and to restraints of social distance. Under
these assumptions, urban agglomerations would nearly disappear. Were it not that the immobility of certain landscape and
climatic features would induce many household and business
establishments to seek locations at places of high natural amenity, that some people may have attitudinal preferences for spa-

tial propinquity to others, and that some industrial processes cannot tolerate even one-minute travel times between industrial establishments, we would expect a virtually homogeneous dispersion across the face of the globe.

Of course, zero communication costs are an impossibility, but the history of civilization has been marked by a continuous decline in the effective costs of communication. Time costs and the costs of inconvenience between any given pair of geographic points have declined consistently; and the financial capacity to bear high dollar-costs has tended to counterbalance the high expenses attached to high speed and high comfort. The concomitant effect of very high speeds between distant points and slower speeds between nearby points has been nearly to equate the travel times between pairs of points on the surface of the earth. Certain improvements in transportation equipment that are now becoming possible could gradually reduce differential time costs of travel to nearly zero. The effects of this potential change on the spatial patterns of settlements would be dramatic.

SOME POTENTIAL CHANGES IN TRANSPORTATION AND COMMUNICATION TECHNOLOGY

We are all aware of the fact that, within metropolitan areas in the United States, the widespread use of the automobile has freed the family's residence from the fixed transit lines that had induced the familiar star-like form of settlement. The pattern of residential scatteration at the growing edges of most metropolitan areas would clearly not have happened without the private car; indeed, this pattern was not apparent until the auto induced the suburban developments of the twenties. The telephone, the motor truck, and transportable water, fuels, and electricity have further abetted this lacy settlement boundary. And, of course, all these trends have been further nurtured by a rising level of average family income and by credit arrangements that have made it possible for the average family to choose—and get—one or more autos, telephones, and houses.

Similarly the new communication devices, higher corporate incomes, and federal financial encouragement have made it possible for some foot-loose manufacturers and certain types of commercial establishments to locate in relatively outlying portions of metropolitan settlements.

To date, however, very few of these families and business establishments have chosen to locate very far from the metropolitan center, because the costs of maintaining the web of communications that are essential to their cultural and their economic well-being would simply be too high. Even though they might like to locate in a mountain setting, the benefits that would accrue from so pleasant a habitat seem to be far outweighed by the difficulties of maintaining contact with the various specialists they rely upon.

But today a great many of them are much farther away from the metropolitan center, in mileage distance, than they were even fifteen years ago, not to mention the differences that have occurred since the beginning of the century. Even so, a great many have chosen outlying locations without increasing their time distances to the center. Increased mileage distance carries a necessary increase in dollar costs, but the more sensitive component of communications costs in the locator's calculus seems to be the time costs, as the recent traffic studies and the phenomenal rise in long-distance telephone usage indicate.

Increases in travel speeds within most of the metropolitan settlements have been relatively modest as compared to the changing speeds of intermetropolitan travel that the airlines have brought. In part because the potentials of the new freeway systems have been so severely restrained by the countereffects of congestion and in part because the improvements in transit systems have been rare indeed, peak-hour travel speeds have not increased appreciably. But off-peak increases have been great in some places, and some changes are imminent that are likely to cause an emphatic change.

Where the urban freeway systems are uncongested, they have induced at least a doubling in speed and in some places a quadrupling—and the freeways do run freely in off-peak hours.

As the urban freeway systems that are now under construction are extended farther out and connected to one another, an unprecedented degree of freedom and flexibility will be open to the traveler for moving among widely separated establishments in conducting his affairs. A network of freeways, such as that planned for the Los Angeles area, will make many points highly accessible, in direct contrast to the single high-access point that resulted from the traditional radial transit net. Even if new or improved high-speed fixed-route transit systems were to be superimposed on freeway networks, the freeway's leveling effect on accessibility would still be felt. And the positive advantages of automobiles over transit systems—affording, at their best, door-to-door, no-wait, no-transfer, private, and flexible-route service—make it inconceivable that they will be abandoned for a great part of intrametropolitan travel or that the expansion of the freeway systems on which they depend will taper off. We would do well, then, to accept the private vehicle as an indispensable medium of metropolitan interaction—more, as an important instrument of personal freedom.

There has been a great deal of speculation about characteristics of the evolutionary successor to the automobile, but it is probably too early to predict the exact form it will take. I would hazard some confident guesses, though, that it will not be a free-flight personal vehicle because the air-traffic control problems appear to be insoluble, that it will be automatically guided when on freeways and hence capable of traveling safely at much higher speeds, but that it will continue to be adaptable to use on local streets. If bumper-to-bumper movement at speeds of 150 miles per hour or more were to be attained, as current research-and-development work suggest is possible, greater per lane capacities and greater speeds would be realized than any rapid transit proposals now foresee for traditional train systems. When these on-route operating characteristics are coupled with the door-to-door, no-wait, no-transfer, privacy, and flexible route-end service of the personal vehicle, such a system would appear to be more than competitive with any type of rapid transit service now planned—with two important qualifications.

The costs would have to be reasonable, and the land use patterns would have to be compatible with the operating characteristics of the transportation system.

A system that would be capable of moving large numbers of cars into a small area within a short period of time would face the parking dilemma in compounded form. Although unpublished reports of the engineers at The RAND Corporation suggest that it would be mechanically possible and perhaps even economically feasible to build sufficient underground parking facilities on Manhattan to store private cars for all employees and shoppers who arrive there daily, the problem of moving large numbers of cars into and out of the garages during brief periods would call for so elaborate and costly a maze of access ramps as to discourage any serious effort to satisfy a parking demand of such magnitude. Before such an all-out effort is made to accommodate the traditional central business district to the private motor car, the summary effect of thousands of locational decisions by individual entrepreneurs would probably have been to evolve a land use pattern that more readily conforms to the auto's operating characteristics. With further increases in mass auto usage—especially if it could attain bumper-to-bumper, 150 mph movement—we are bound to experience a dispersion of many traditionally central activities to outlying but highly accessible locations. The dispersed developments accompanying the current freeways suggest the type of pattern that seems probable. Here, again, Los Angeles offers the best prototype available.

IN WHAT SENSE IS URBAN SPACE A RESOURCE?

I have been suggesting that the quintessence of urbanization is not population density or agglomeration but specialization, the concomitant interdependence, and the human interactions by which interdependencies are satisfied. Viewed from this orientation, the urban settlement is the spatial adaptation to demands of dependent activities and specialists for low com-

munication costs. It is helpful, therefore, to view the spatial city
as a communications system, as a vastly complex switchboard
through which messages and goods of various sorts are routed.

Information, ideas, and goods are the very stuff of civilization.
The degree to which they are distributed to all individuals
within a population stands as an important indicator of human
welfare levels—as a measure of cultural and economic income.
Of course, the distribution of this income is determined predominantly by institutional rather than spatial factors—only the
rare Utopian has even suggested that the way to "the good society" is through the redesign of the spatial city. And yet, space
intervenes as a friction against all types of communication.
Surely, salvation does not lie in the remodeled spatial city; but,
just as surely, levels of cultural and economic wealth could be
increased if the spatial frictions that now limit the freedom to
interact were reduced. This is the important justification for
city planning's traditional concern with space.

In the very nature of Euclidean geometry, the space immediately surrounding an urban settlement is limited. Given a
transportation-communication technology and its accompanying
cost structure, close-in space has greater value than distant
space, since nearby inhabitants have greater opportunities to
interact with others in the settlement.

But as the transportation-communication technologies change
to permit interaction over greater distances at constant or even
at falling costs, more and more outlying space is thereby brought
into the market, and the relative value of space adjacent to large
settlements falls. Urban space, as it has been associated with the
economies of localization and agglomeration, is thus a peculiar
resource, characterized by increasing supply and by ever-
declining value.

These cost-reducing and space-expanding effects of transportation-communication changes are being reinforced by most of
the technological and social changes we have recently seen. The
patterns of social stratification and of occupations, the organizational structures of businesses and of governments, the goods
and the ideas that are being produced, and the average indi-

vidual's ranges of interests and opportunities are steadily becoming more varied and less tradition-bound. In a similar way, the repercussions of these social changes and the direct impacts of some major technological changes have made for increasing diversity in the spatial structures of urban settlements.

Projections of future change, and especially changes in the technologies of transportation and communication, suggest that much greater variation will be possible in the next few decades. It is becoming difficult to avoid the parallel prediction that totally new spatial forms are in the offing.

To date, very few observers have gone so far as to predict that the nodally concentric form, that has marked every spatial city throughout history, could give way to nearly homogeneous dispersion of the nation's population across the continent; but the hesitancy may stem mainly from the fact that a non-nodal city of this sort would represent such a huge break with the past. Yet, never before in human history has it been so easy to communicate across long distances. Never before have men been able to maintain intimate and continuing contact with others across thousands of miles; never has intimacy been so independent of spatial propinquity. Never before has it seemed possible to build an array of specialized transportation equipment that would permit speed of travel to increase directly with mileage length of trip, thus having the capability of uniting all places within a continent with almost-equal time distance. And never before has it seemed economically feasible for the nodally cohesive spatial form that marks the contemporary large settlement to be replaced by drastically different forms, while the pattern of internal centering itself changes or, perhaps, dissolves.

A number of informed students have read the same evidence and have drawn different conclusions. Observing that the consequences of ongoing technological changes are spatially neutral, they suggest that increased ease of intercourse makes it all the more possible for households and business establishments to locate in the midst of high-density settlements. This was essentially the conclusion that Haig drew when he wrote, ". . . Instead of explaining why so large a portion of the population is found in urban areas, one must give reasons why that portion is not even greater. The question is changed from 'Why live in the city?' to 'Why not live in the city?' " [5]

I am quick to agree that many of the recent and the imminent developments are ambiguous with respect to space. They could push urban spatial structure toward greater concentricity, toward greater dispersion, or, what I believe to be most likely, toward a very heterogeneous pattern. Since administrative and executive activities are so sensitive to the availability and immediacy of accurate information—and hence of good communications—they may be the bellwether of future spatial adjustments of other activities as well, and they therefore warrant our special attention.

The new electronic data-processing equipment and the accompanying procedures permit much more intensive use of downtown space than was ever possible with nonautomated office processes; but they can operate quite as effectively from an outlying location, far removed from the executive offices they serve. The sites adjacent to the central telephone exchange may offer competitive advantages over all others, and establishments relying upon computers, that in turn are tied to the long-distance telephone lines, seem to be clustering about the hub of those radial lines in much the manner that they once clustered about the hub of the radial trolley lines. At the same time we can already observe that outlying computer centers are attracting establishments that use their services.

The recent history of office construction in midtown New York, northwest Washington, and in the centers of most large metropolitan areas is frequently cited as clear evidence of the role that face-to-face contacts play in decision-making and of the importance of spatial propinquity in facilitating face-to-face contact. And yet, simultaneously, large numbers of executive offices have followed their production units to suburban locations, and some have established themselves in outlying spots,

---

[5] Robert M. Haig, "Toward an Understanding of the Metropolis," *New York Regional Survey, Regional Survey of New York and Its Environs,* Vol. 1 (New York: Regional Plan Association, Inc., 1927).

spatially separated from their production units and from all other establishments. The predominant movement in the New York area has been to the business center, but the fact that many have been able to move outside the built-up area suggests that a new degree of locational freedom is being added.

The patterns in Washington, Detroit, and Los Angeles clearly suggest that the walking-precinct type of central business district (CBD), with its restricted radius, compactness, and fixed-route transit service, is not the only effective spatial pattern for face-to-face communication. Washington's governmental and private offices are dispersed over so wide an area that few are within easy walking distance of each other. Meetings typically call for a short auto trip, either by taxi or private car. In Detroit and especially in Los Angeles, establishment types that have traditionally been CBD-oriented are much more dispersed throughout the settled area. Relying heavily upon the automobile, Los Angelenos seem to be able to conduct their business face-to-face, perhaps as frequently as do New Yorkers. Highly specialized firms employing highly specialized personnel are located in all parts of the Los Angeles Basin—in some places within fairly compact subcenters, in other places in quite scattered patterns. But the significant feature is this: few linked establishments are within walking distances of each other, and an auto trip is thus an adjunct to a face-to-face meeting.

Even with a moderate speed of automotive travel, considerable mileage can be covered within a short time. At door-to-door average speeds of only 15 mph, it takes but four minutes to get to another's office a mile away; and, especially for long-distance trips, average travel speeds are considerably higher, probably exceeding 50 mph door-to-door off-peak in Los Angeles. Although I know of no measurements of this sort having been made, I would guess that (after adjusting for the total number of establishments within the metropolitan area) an establishment on Wilshire Boulevard in Los Angeles has as many linked establishments within a given time-distance as does a similar establishment at Rockefeller Center.

Comparable studies of traffic patterns in New York and Los

Angeles will be completed within a few years, and it will then be possible to compare travel-time costs to commuters and shoppers, as well as to men who need to transact business face-to-face. I think it is safe to predict, however, that large differences will not be found, that Los Angelenos are just about as accessible to their work places and to the various urban service establishments as are New Yorkers, and perhaps even more accessible. Moreover, I would expect to find that Los Angeles residents maintain as diverse a range of contacts, that they interact with others as frequently and as intensively, that they are participants in as broad and as rich a range of communications as the resident of any other metropolitan area. I believe the popular notion among outsiders that Los Angeles is a cultural desert, is a myth whose basis lies in the ideology of metropolitan form. We have equated cultural wealth and urbanity with high-density cities; since Los Angeles is not spatially structured in the image of the culturally rich cities we have known, some have therefore inferred that life there must be empty and deprived of opportunity. It is strikingly apparent, however, that nearly seven million people and their employers seem to find this an amiable habitat and that Easterners continue to arrive at a rapid rate. It is also apparent that a considerable part of its attractiveness has been the natural setting and the opportunities to engage in activities outside the urban settlement itself.

If most of the social and technological changes I have mentioned were in fact neutral in their spatial impacts, this itself would represent a powerful new factor at work on the spatial organization of cities. Prior dominant modes of transportation and communication, traditional forms of organization of business and government, the older and more rigid patterns of economic and social stratification, and prior educational and occupational levels and opportunities all exerted positive pressures to population agglomeration around dominant high-density business-industrial-residential centers. If these pressures for concentration and concentricity are ebbing, the effects of counter processes will be increasingly manifest.

THE ASCENT OF AMENITY
AS LOCATIONAL DETERMINANT

Throughout our history, the locations and the internal arrangements of our cities have been predominantly shaped by the efforts of individual establishments to lower the costs of transporting goods, information, and people. If our speculations concerning the secular declines in these costs should prove to be valid, we can expect that the nontransportable on-site amenities will come to predominate as locational determinants.

Population growth in California, Arizona, Florida, and other naturally favored places can be largely attributed to the favorable climate and landscape. At smaller scale, in turn, new residential accommodations and new industrial establishments are being developed at those sites whose natural conditions are most favored by groups of various types. This is a very remarkable development; the luxury of locational choice is now being extended to ever-increasing numbers within an increasingly diverse population.

During the past sixty years the work week of American manufacturing workers has fallen from about 59 hours to something under 40, while wages have risen from an average of about $450 per year to about $4,700 (in constant 1947–49 dollars from about $1,250 to about $4,000 per year). The prospects are for a continuing reduction in working hours and for a continuing rise in disposable income, perhaps accompanied by a narrowing of the extremes in income distribution. When compounded by the availability of credit, higher levels of education, lowering ages of retirement, and a further dispersion of middle-class ways to larger proportions of the population, the range of choice open to most people—including the range of locational choice—is certain to increase greatly.

Although it is undoubtedly true that the success of recent suburban developments to some extent reflects rather limited choices available within the contemporary metropolitan housing markets, it is also apparent that for most of their inhabitants these developments represent marked improvements in living standards. Most suburbanites in the upper-income brackets have made free locational choices, since they could afford more central sites. Even a recent disenchantment with suburban life has not refuted the compatibility of low-density housing developments with middle-class preferences for spaciousness, with middle-class attitudes about distance, with current status criteria, and with child-oriented family life.

Among certain professional groups that have recently been in high demand (most notably those specialists associated with research and development in the electronics, missiles, and petrochemical industries) the preferences for suburban-type residential environments within pleasant natural settings seem to have been so strong as to have affected the locations of these industries in California, Long Island, and the suburbs of Boston. To attract these skilled persons, whole industries have moved. Very few have chosen locations very far removed from the universities and the business complexes to which they are closely linked, but it is significant that they have tended to select outlying spots. With increasing leisure time, increasing mobility via automobiles, and increased spending power, we can expect the average family to take much greater advantage of outdoor recreational activities available in the countryside accessible to his home. As transportation facilities are improved and week-ends lengthen, families will be able to travel longer distances than before. Some will prefer to locate their homes near recreational facilities, and the recreation place might even replace the work place as the major determinant of residential locations.

The range of locational choice is broadening at the same time that changing characteristics of the national population are breeding increasing diversity in people's locational preferences. Simultaneously, all segments of the national population are being woven into an increasingly complex social, political, and economic web, such that no person and no group is entirely independent of all other persons and all other groups.

The growing pluralism in American society is more than a growing multiplicity of types of people and institutions. Each person, each group bound by a community of interests, is integrally related to each other person and group, such that each is defined by its relations to all others and that a change in one induces a change in all others.

The kinds of information that can be read from maps showing urbanized areas or land use patterns are therefore likely to be misleading. Suggesting that settlements of one size or another are in some way independent units, in some way separated from each other and from the spatial field in which they lie, maps of this sort miss the essential meaning of urbanization. Whether the maps represent existing patterns or plans for future patterns, they present static snapshots of locational patterns of people or buildings or activity places and say nothing (except as the reader may interpolate) about the human interaction patterns that are at the heart of complex social processes. When people can interact with others across great distances and when they can readily move themselves into face-to-face positions as the need to do so arises, it scarcely matters whether a greenbelt intervenes or whether the space between them and their associates is used for houses and factories. Surely Los Angeles is an integral part of the national urban system, despite the 2,500-mile-wide greenbelt that separates it from New York. Surely Bakersfield is as integral a part of the southern California urban system as is Pasadena, despite the intervention of the Tehachapi Mountains and some 90 miles. Surely the researchers in Los Alamos are as much a part of the world-wide community of atomic physicists, as if they happened to be at Brookhaven or Berkeley or Argonne.

Spatial separation or propinquity is no longer an accurate indicator of functional relations; and, hence, mere locational pattern is no longer an adequate symbol of order. The task of the spatial planner is therefore considerably more difficult than we have traditionally thought. The normative guides that we have used have been oriented primarily to the form aspects that can be represented on maps and have applied static and simplistic concepts of order that are not consonant with the processes of growing and complex urban systems.

It is a fairly simple matter to prepare a land use plan for a territory, if its spatial organization is to follow any one of the simple universal models that city planners have promulgated. Sites for "self-contained and balanced" new towns are readily found, and site plans are readily made. It is quite another matter to get the townspeople to behave as though they comprised a "self-contained and balanced community"—nor would many of us really want them to be deprived of the enriched lives that come with free communication with the "outside world." Plans for increased centrality and higher density can also be portrayed readily within the traditional idiom of land use planning; but, again, it is hard to believe that the advocates would be willing to deprive the residents of the opportunities to choose outlying locations. Nevertheless, whether small town or large concentration, the rules are clear and simple; the variables to be accounted are limited in number and in complexity; and the solution is determined before the problem is attacked.

It is considerably more difficult, however, to plan for diversity in settlement and land use patterns, for here the formal rules of urban form are not very helpful. No single scheme can be taken as a rule to be applied to all establishments and to all places. Rather, the locational requirements of the many diverse groups of establishments must establish the rules, and the optimum pattern would then resemble none of the doctrinal models.

The optimum land use pattern of the future metropolis is likely to be highly diversified. Since transportation costs will never fall to zero, the external economies associated with clusterings of similar and dissimilar establishments will continue to induce certain types of establishments to seek centers and subcenters of many types. Some of these will be of the familiar employment and shopping-center types, whether in the CBD or in the unitary "regional center" molds. Other establishments, mutually linked to a third type of establishment, will undoubtedly continue to cluster about it wherever it may be, whether it be a stock exchange, a major university, an airport, or a large manufacturer or retailer. Other establishments will form sub-centers, largely as a result of their mutual desire to occupy a particularly pleasant site, although such growth inducements are self-limiting, of course. Those establishments that depend upon good access to information will undoubtedly continue to seek locations that best facilitate easy communication. For some, formal meeting places that accommodate scheduled encounters will suffice, and for many of these the airports and the convention halls are already serving a large part of their requirements. Others, such as the ladies' garment industry and the securities exchanges, may be so sensitive to changes in styles and/or market conditions as to induce even more intensive business concentrations of the sort that Manhattan typifies.

Simultaneously, the optimum patterns would include scattered developments for a great variety of establishments in a great variety of land use mixes and density patterns. For those manufacturers who prefer to locate factories and workers' housing near mountain skiing and hiking areas, for those lone wolves who prefer solitude and possibly a part-time farm, and for all those for whom a high-speed auto drive is no commuting deterrent, we can expect (and should encourage) scattered developments of the type now becoming common east of Boston and north of New York.

The future land use pattern will certainly not be one of homogeneous dispersion. Transportation and communication costs will never permit that, and the very uneven distribution of favored climates and landscapes would strongly discourage it. But a much greater degree of dispersion is both likely and desirable, while centers and subcenters of various compositions and densities persist and grow in a range of sizes spanning the whole spectrum from "center" to "sprawl."

If we are willing to accept the idea that the optimum urban settlement and land use patterns are likely to be as pluralistic as society itself, then the conceptions of spatial order will follow from our conceptions of social order. Our spatial plans, then, will be plans for diversity, designed to accommodate the disparate demands upon land and space made by disparate individuals and groups that are bound up in the organized complexity of urban society.

PLANNED ALLOCATION OF URBAN SPACE

One of the planner's major tasks is to delineate the probable range of real future choice—the envelope within which goal-directed actions are likely to pay off. I read the evidence concerning the qualities and magnitudes of some uncontrollable aspects of future change to say that many of the spatial forms to which we have aspired are no longer within that envelope.

Moreover, I contend that we have been searching for the wrong grail, that the values associated with the desired urban structure do not reside in the spatial structure per se. One pattern of settlement and its internal land use form is superior to another only as it better serves to accommodate ongoing social processes and to further the nonspatial ends of the political community. I am flatly rejecting the contention that there is an overriding universal spatial or physical aesthetic of urban form.

Throughout this essay I have laid heavy emphasis upon the communication patterns that bring people into contact with others and that have created our traditional settlement patterns. I have done so because communication is a very powerful influence that has scarcely been studied. But it is not my view that this is the only important factor affecting urban spatial structure, or that the criteria for planning the spatial structure for complex urban communities stem from this relationship alone. No simple cause-and-effect relationships are likely to be uncovered in this field, for the maze of relationships within such complex open systems as urban societies are such that a change in one part of the web will reverberate to induce changes throughout all parts of the web. The problem of planning for the optimum utilization of urban space is far more complex than our present understanding permits us to even realize.

No attempt will be made here to catalogue the kinds of criteria that a rigorously conducted planning effort would need to weigh. I leave this omission not from modesty—only ignorance. But a few considerations can be mentioned, if only to suggest that my ignorance may not be complete.

I have chosen to deal with space, not with land, because, for the paramount purposes of men who engage in nonextractive industries, the surface of the earth has meaning as representation of communication distance rather than as inherent characteristics of the soil. I have contended that all space is urban space, since interaction among urbanites takes place through, or is inhibited by, all space. Space has significance for the urban planner primarily because of the implications that locational patterns have for fruitful interaction, hence for social welfare.

For some purposes, however, the surface of the earth does have meaning as soil or as minerals or as water storage; and in this context planners are indeed concerned with allocating *land* judiciously. With the prospect of increasing space utilization by urban activities, a growing conflict is inevitable between land users and space users. Fortunately the rate of increase in agricultural productivity continues to outpace the rate of population increase in the United States; and, in the face of embarrassing agricultural surpluses, the conflict is likely to thrive only in ideological disputes rather than in market competition.

Largely, I suspect, as vestige of our agrarian ancestry, many city planners and others hold to a rather fundamentalist belief in land. Land is seen as a scarce and sacred resource to be saved against those who would "encroach" upon and "desecrate" its natural features. To use good soils for housing is frequently decried as wasteful of a valuable natural resource, all the more objectionable because these changes are effectively irreversible. But the answer is surely not that simple. There may indeed be areas that would most profitably be retained in crops rather than in houses and factories, but in the places where the question arises the balance is probably more often in favor of the houses and factories. The values inherent in accessibility, that make those places attractive to the house buyer, are quite likely to weigh more heavily than the values to be derived from crops. But no answers can be found a priori. Each site must be evaluated for the relative costs and benefits implicit in the alternative purposes for which it might be used.

Similarly, lands that might provide the recreational opportunities that are increasingly in demand might also be used for other purposes. But, again, no doctrinaire answers are likely to be found supportable. Again, each site must be subjected to an analysis of the welfare implications implicit in the substitutable uses. The benefits from recreational use are quite as real as those deriving from farms and houses. Within the total spatial field, places for recreational activity need to be developed. But no ready solutions are in hand; certainly the greenbelt doctrine in itself is insufficient basis for the investments that are required.

. . . . . .

Within any given territory at any given time, space is finite. Present and future demands for it are highly diverse in their requirements, but we can surely learn enough about the characteristics of each type of user to equip ourselves to make more rational allocations than would occur under unguided market conditions. The task is not to "protect our natural heritage of open space" just because it is natural, or a heritage, or open, or because we see ourselves as Galahads defending the good form against the evils of urban sprawl. This is a mission of evangelists, not planners.

Rather, and as the barest minimum, the task is to seek that spatial distribution of urban populations and urban activities that will permit greater freedom for human interaction while, simultaneously, providing freer access to natural amenities and effective management of the landscape and of mineral resources.

This is no mean task. And probably the meanest part of the task will be to disabuse ourselves of some deep-seated doctrine that seeks order in simple mappable patterns, when it is really hiding in extremely complex social organization, instead.

The late STANLEY B. TANKEL, at the time he wrote his contribution to this book, was planning director of the Regional Plan Association, New York City, where he had worked since 1955. For two years he served as project manager of the Association's Recreation and Open Space Project. Mr. Tankel also was lecturer at Columbia University's School of Architecture, where he conducted a seminar in urban planning. He was a member of the Board of Governors of the American Institute of Planners and a member of the Landmarks Preservation Commission, City of New York. Previous associations include the Ministry of Town and Country Planning, London (on British New Towns), the Westchester County (New York) Planning Department; Knappen, Tippetts, Abbott Engineers, and Passaic Valley Citizens Planning Association. He had also been a designer and builder of houses. Mr. Tankel was born in New York City in 1922. He received his education in architecture at Yale University and in city planning at Harvard University (B.C.P., M.C.P. '49). In 1952 he studied city planning in France as a Fulbright scholar.

THE IMPORTANCE OF OPEN
SPACE IN THE URBAN PATTERN

STANLEY B. TANKEL

OPEN SPACE HAS BECOME THE SUBJECT of a remarkable, new interest. The words are echoing even in the halls of Congress and state legislatures. And the voices behind the words are those of *urban* senators, *urban* congressmen, and *urban* legislators. This is no faddist, back-to-nature movement; it is a direct expression of concern about the present and future use of urban space.

This paper will attempt to put the interest in open space into its only systematically relevant context—the needs and activities of urban man as they are expressed in the physical design of his environment. For this purpose I define open space broadly to include not only all land and water in and around urban areas which is not covered by buildings, but the space and light above as well. Under this definition, open space happens to take up far more room than all the other elements in the urban pattern put together. But the emphasis will be not on amount but on location. Indeed, it will be shown that the amount of open space is relatively fixed, and its disposition is what really matters.

I propose to go a step beyond the recent emphasis on open space per se to suggest a comprehensive framework into which to fit the pressing issues of urban open space. I contend that a framework based on scale of development gives the best perspective on the role of open space.

The paper has three parts: first, a brief discussion of the *function* of urban open space; then a longer one on the *scale* of open space; finally some observations on the *future* of urban open space.

THE FUNCTIONS OF URBAN OPEN SPACE

Few attempts have been made to classify the functions of open space in urban terms. Two concise but comprehensive classifications have been set out in Charles Eliot's distinction between open space for *service* and open space for *structure* and in the Tunnard-Pushkarev identification [1] of four functions served by open space—*productive, protective, ornamental,* and *recreational.* My own approach is close to both of these, but especially to Eliot's. I distinguish between the kind of open space of which people are personally aware and the open space of which they may be unaware but which nevertheless affects their daily lives.

The open space of which people are aware has three functions: it is *used*—for the wide range of active and passive recreation activities, for circulation; it is *viewed*—from the home, the road, or other vantage points; and it is *felt*—it gives privacy, insulation, a sense of spaciousness and scale.

Urban open space of which people are not necessarily aware is of two kinds: open space which *does urban work*—protects water supply and prevents floods by soaking up runoff, acts as a safety zone in the path of aircraft takeoffs and landings; and open space which *helps shape the development pattern*—as space between buildings or communities, as space which channels development, as a land reserve for the future.

The problem of the function of open space—why we have open space—is complicated by the fact that individual physical

[1] Christopher Tunnard and Boris Pushkarev, *Man-made America* (New Haven: Yale University Press, 1963).

open spaces do not sort themselves out according to function. It is a rare bit of open space which does not perform many of these roles. And each category encompasses a wide variation in scale (open space for water supply can be a small man-made recharge basin in a subdivision or a vast mountain catchment area) and a wide range of uses with quite different implications (recreation areas can be as much for resting as for playing, as much for solitude as camaraderie). To further confuse the issue, functions can change: in Perugia and some other Italian towns, a daily change in the main piazza occurs after the evening rush hour when automobiles are prohibited and the pedestrian takes over. In a Manhattan public housing project, Albert Mayer has just converted a typical bleak space between buildings into an American piazza, a real center of activity because it is based on an understanding of the needs of the residents.

In the midst of all this complexity of function, the physical shape of any open space sits there aloof and unchanging, a setting for a wide variety of functions. Not only is the physical configuration of open space less elusive than its function, it has intrinsic qualities which, I believe, make it the main basis for a policy and program for open space.

THE SCALE AND DISTRIBUTION OF OPEN SPACE

The definition of open space in this paper—all land and water not covered by buildings—makes open space a question not of "how much," but of "where," and particularly "where" in relation to buildings and the people in them. To illustrate, if a sheet of paper represents the total coverage of buildings to be built in a given area, and the area itself is a table, one can distribute the paper on the table in any number of pieces and in any variety of shapes. But the amount of paper (buildings) and the amount of table which is not covered (open space) remains the same (see Figure 1).

Putting this in terms of urban development, any variation in the incidence of multi-story structures is likely to be minimal. For example, residential development, whose floor space far exceeds that of all other structures put together, is not likely to vary greatly in the proportion and land coverage of apartment houses and one-family houses; the critical question is how these structures are distributed. The same applies to the way clusters of buildings are distributed at such larger scales as the neighborhood, the group of communities, or the region.

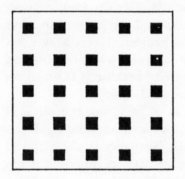 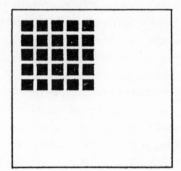

Figure 1.

Table 1 identifies a hierarchy of scales of urban development and suggests the role of open space at each scale. At each scale of open space extensive variation in design is possible which can greatly affect the quality of urban living. What is more, the pattern of open space at any one scale has an impact on the pattern at other scales, although the potential impact is not equal at each scale. For example, the permanent reservation of open space at the scale of the region theoretically may have the effect of reducing lot sizes, depending on its amount, its accessibility, and suitability for development; but the reverse phenomenon is of far greater importance: large average lot sizes may be associated with inferior regional and county-level open space. At each scale urban open space has critical policy implications, in terms of its effects on other open space and its relation with its adjacent development, which warrant some exploration.

Table 1. Classification of Urban Open Space

Scale or level	Present examples of open space (Land)	(Water)	Quantitative importance of open space in developed portion of New York region suburbs 1960
I. STREET			(acres/1,000 pop.)
a. Building site	Yards, courts (i.e., sites less bldgs.)		60
b. Group of bldgs.	Rights-of-way, streets, piazzas, plazas, residential commons, tot lots		
II. COMMUNITY			
a. Neighborhood	School grounds, playgrounds, small parks to 10 a.		2 0
b. Municipality	Parks to 100 a., playfields	Ponds, streams	3
III. COUNTY			
(group of municipalities)	Parks 100–1,000 a. golf courses, minor conservation areas (flood plains, watersheds, wildlife)	Lakes, rivers	4
IV. REGION			
a. Metropolitan region	Parks over 1,000 a., large conservation areas, major water bodies, private farms, woodland and other land on the urban fringe		
b. Megalopolis	Coastlines, mountain ranges, milksheds	Oceans, great rivers	

Open Space at the Scale of the Street

The open space immediately associated with homes and workplaces is experienced more than all other open space. This is open space in microcosm. It literally "hits us where we live," day in and day out; it is more a part of us than we are of it. There is much more of it than of the other types of open space in the developed parts of urban areas—mainly public recreation areas and private golf courses. This dominance amplifies its impact on the role of the other levels of open space. Open space at the street scale also is unique because it is the most man-made both in its quantity and design. Nature can be of some help, a few trees in a subdivision may save it from barrenness, but for the most part street-scale urban open space is a creation of man.

Relationship with other scales of open space. Street-scale open space has a critical impact on regional open space. The effect of the total amount of street-scale open space, that is the composite of individual lots and streets, on the accessibility of regional open space is determined by the total number of lots (number of households) and size of lots.

The New York Region provides me with the most striking example of the impact of lot size on the regional scale of open space, perhaps because I know it best. The development of this metropolitan region, in gross terms, has spread outward in concentric rings. Important physical interruptions were dictated by the blessing of an interesting topography, especially of water, which comprises over a third of the region's area—principally the Atlantic Ocean, Long Island Sound, New York Harbor, and the Hudson River—and which so interlards the New York area that it is, at a larger scale, a sort of Venice! Since no significant wedges of regional open space except water have been preserved as the region has grown, access to real open country has depended on the *extent* of the urban pattern.

The changing extent of urbanized land in the New York Re-

gion and its impact on accessibility of regional open space has
been dramatic. The circle of urbanization has grown steadily at
a much faster rate than has the population. The radius of this
circle was five miles in 1900, twenty-five miles in 1960 and may
become fifty miles by 1985 unless present trends change and
new policies are introduced. Recent studies by the Regional
Plan Association show that two-thirds of all the vacant land in
the region is zoned for half-acre lots or larger. Should the zoning
hold, twice the amount of land will be developed in the next
twenty-five years as in the region's entire history.

Table 2 demonstrates how lot size contributes to the growing
remoteness of open space on a regional scale, that is to say, undisturbed countryside. The columns on typical housing and its
density are included because residential lots with their associated streets take up about two-thirds of the region's developed
land. By my definition of open space, the balance is shifting

Table 2. Residential Density and Extent of Urbanization,
New York Region [1]

Year	Total pop. (000's)	Type	Dwelling units per acre of land in residential use	No. of sq. mi.	Pop. per sq. mi.	Extent in mi. from center
					All urbanized land	
1900	5,514	Tenement	250	150	37,000	5
1940	12,518	One- and two-family houses	25	1,000	12,500	15
1960	16,139	One-family house	4	2,000	8,000	25
1985 [2]	22,200	One-family house	2	5,000	4,500	50

Dominant housing type in growth areas

[1] While this table presents rather gross figures, the relationships in each column are
sufficiently accurate for the purposes of this paper.
[2] 1985 figures assume development according to the 1960 zoned density of vacant
land. There is, of course, the question whether the region will actually develop in this
fashion.

toward the house lot. The squirrel is replacing the deer in the region's effective open space.

The intrinsic qualities of street-scale open space. Street-scale open space is completely bound up with urban activity and buildings. The architect who creates the buildings automatically, but not often deliberately, creates this open space. Except perhaps at extremely high densities, the arrangement of street-scale open space is more significant in determining its social usefulness than how much of it there is.

Here we look to urban design only to be greatly disappointed. The paucity of attempts to relate buildings by design is a serious failure across the nation. The world abounds in examples where buildings and their related open space were planned together, but in our country a few well-designed urban spaces and subdivisions—including, among others, Radburn, Chatham Village, Chase Manhattan Plaza, some aspects of Penn Center—stand out as stark exceptions. This stems in part from outmoded legal and economic concepts which demand a publicly owned street bordered by rows of individually owned lots, and which ignore the more basic consideration of what kind of open space people like to use with their *neighbors* and what kind with their *families*. This is one of the factors which has discouraged any interest in urban design and public architecture.

The tradition of what is public and what is private has largely denied us the open space benefits possible in "clustering" or "density zoning." Clustering, as you know, consists merely in taking the number of dwelling units permitted by the zoned minimum lot size and distributing them on smaller lots, so that while the over-all density is unchanged, some larger, more natural chunks of land are left open for common use. It has appealed to builders because it lowers site improvement costs and many local officials have recognized the community advantages of clustering (although they have still not weathered the shock that something that benefits the developer might also benefit the community). But the fly in the ointment is the question of who *owns* the open space. The builder usually doesn't have

enough incentive to keep it or to organize a sharing of ownership among the new residents (an important exception is Eichler
Homes in California who are producing well-designed and useful common areas and facilities and inducing home owners to
participate jointly in their ownership and operation). The community won't assume the "maintenance" and other responsibilities it entails, although it cheerfully accepts streets. It is not a
simple problem, but the solution clearly lies in our ability to
find ways to combine shared *use* of open space with shared
ownership of it. In this sense, the ownership of open space is an
important consideration, along with function and scale.

Open Space at the Scale of the Community and the County

Community and county open space, separately or together,
do not consume much land. In further contrast to street-scale
and regional open space these levels of open space have not appreciably influenced other levels nor shaped the urban development pattern in any significant way. Their function has been
limited largely to recreation. However, the growing importance
of outdoor recreation at the county level, a prospect amply
documented by Marion Clawson and others, suggests that a
change is in the offing.

The Regional Plan Association [2] has estimated that there will
be a greatly increased demand for swimming, golf, boating and
a whole range of natural area activities within fifteen or twenty
minutes of the home, in part because of the increased half-day
use on weekdays which we foresee. This, to a large extent, will
be a county responsibility, and we have estimated requirements
at 12 acres per 1,000 population which works out to more than
5 per cent of a county's land area for the counties in the New
York Region. Other county open space needs such as conservation, and opportunities for integrating with some community
and regional open space will present the county with quite a
challenge. County-level open space can become an effective part

[2] *The Race for Open Space* (New York: Regional Plan Association, 1960).

of the development pattern at that scale: some of the old park-ways, which were as much parks as ways, have influenced county structure in the past. The stream valley seems uniquely suited to serve as a basis for a system of county open space and in fact is being so used in several counties in the East.

Open Space at the Scale of the Region

Urban open space at the scale of the region is continuous countryside or wilderness which is accessible. No physical dis-tinction exists between urban regional open space and the Great Outdoors; rather, they are separated by an imaginary line which is, say, two hours away from most people in an urban area. Earlier, I pointed out how such regional open space and open space on house lots are interdependent and how enough large house lots can put the countryside out of reach. Is the opposite possible? Can a regional open space pattern affect lot size or, if not, at least influence the shape of development?

Regional open space and the regional development pattern. William H. Whyte, Jr. sees the preservation of open space as a weapon against urban sprawl; Washington's Year 2000 Plan sees the protection of its green wedges as one of the levers in shaping development. The first view emphasizes more accessible regional open space; the second stresses more compact development for its own sake. I happen to concur in both of these objectives, arguing that they must, in fact, be considered together, that a particular development pattern is accompanied automatically by a particular open space pattern.

Three broad alternatives in the relationship of development to open space are possible: First, uninterrupted, concentric, low-density development, today's typical pattern, which progres-sively reduces usable regional open space; second, channeled low-density development, which could result in a desirable pat-tern of regional open space; third, channeled higher-density development, which should produce the optimum pattern of regional open space, as well as offer the economic and social advantages of a compact pattern. The three patterns are illustrated in Figure 2.

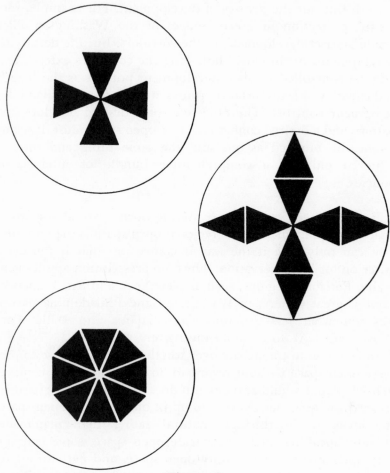

Figure 2.

If you sense that I reject the greenbelt principle, you are correct. A greenbelt is about as useful as a leather belt in containing development. For flexibility in the regional development pattern and for general access to regional open space, the green wedge makes more sense.

Returning to our earlier question—whether an open space policy can influence regional growth, I would answer that an effective open space preservation program could influence the *pattern* but not the *density* of development. For example, successful protection of green wedges of the Washington Plan would restrict development to the corridors. But the density of development, or, in effect, how long the corridors extend, can only be controlled by such development policies as the length and capacity of transportation routes and the nature of land development controls. The objectives of a desired development pattern and a desired configuration of open space must, it seems to me, be pursued as one and the same thing and can be achieved only by a comprehensive bundle of interrelated policies.

Regional open space per se. While open space at the street scale is uniquely man-made, regional open space is the opposite. You can only take it the way it comes and that is the chief criterion for its preservation. Thus, no prescription applies generally. For some regions, such as New York and San Francisco, there is great variety; in Washington and Philadelphia nature was somewhat less generous; Indianapolis and Dallas–Fort Worth will have to be more inventive.

In response to the debate over whether it makes sense to preserve open space without regard to how it relates to a comprehensive plan, I would argue that it does to the extent merited by its intrinsic qualities. As you go up in our scales of open space, the areas are increasingly natural rather than man-made. Broadly speaking, little street-scale open space, some community open space, much county open space, and perhaps all regional open space boast natural features worth preserving. These features are identifiable without a plan, and it is not only appropriate but essential that more of such areas be captured quickly.

THE FUTURE OF URBAN OPEN SPACE

The significance of open space is not its quantity but how it is arranged in relation to development. The most significant open space is that at the scale of the street because its design affects our lives from day to day and because its quantity is likely to bear directly on access to the countryside, on the amount of usable regional open space.

The critical open space decisions will in fact be development decisions—decisions about building density and site design. It is therefore not surprising that when two distinguished scholars recently sought new means of preserving open land, they came up with techniques for achieving comprehensive development, of which open space was merely a part. I refer to Shirley Adelson Siegel's *land agencies on the urban renewal principle* [3] and Marion Clawson's *suburban development districts.* [4] These provocative ideas really confront the issue of a political mechanism for realizing an over-all plan.

But what of the plan itself? Its nature will depend on the answers to some baffling questions which are raised with real insight by Catherine Bauer Wurster elsewhere in this volume. Let me just mention some of them.

Where will we come to rest between an advancing technology which has the capacity to spread us farther and wider over the landscape, and the persistent need that people have to be close to other people? Will the American family with children continue to dream of its own house on its own lot? If so, how big a lot will it dream of? Will the economy, the housing, transportation and other public policies make the dream come true? Will our old cities be revitalized, and if so, in what form? Will we develop the means of making a "social calculus" of alternative patterns? And if we know the costs, will we care? That is, are

[3] Shirley Adelson Siegel, *The Law of Open Space* (New York: Regional Plan Association, 1960).
[4] Marion Clawson, "Suburban Development Districts," *Journal of the American Institute of Planners,* May 1960.

we likely to be swayed more by psychic costs than social costs?

The choice of an urban pattern with its open space dimensions involves the weighing of numerous complex factors, which makes it difficult to say with any degree of certainty what will emerge. But I will risk a prediction that the future use of urban space will tend toward a more dense, more nucleated, more clustered pattern than we are now building in our suburban areas. Accompanying the tighter development and stronger centers, there will be less private open space (that is, we will have smaller lots) and, at every scale of development, substantial continuous open space, commonly enjoyed and publicly or commonly owned.

Why this in the face of a technology that will make it increasingly possible for people to separate themselves physically from their neighbors? The answer: human nature is what it is. Propinquity is not passé, as has been suggested elsewhere; it is the essence of urban life. The spatial community is not a product of mere ideology or an aesthetic; it is the physical expression of basic social needs.

I predict that more traditional urban values will reassert themselves after a lapse during the past generation and that we will increasingly appreciate the difference between city and country, knowing that you simply can't have both in the same location. We will renew our vital contact with Nature, and there may even be pedestrians again!

There are signs that this change has already begun. I believe that the current open space boom reflects a growing popular concern that the way we urbanize today is wasteful of land, has no focus, drives up the cost of interaction and development. We are less willing to pay this cost: the spectre of Spread City is beginning to disturb many leadership groups.

Whether this view is right or wrong, we need to get into much more discussion of alternatives for the urban pattern with the confidence that it *is* within our power to guide our destiny and plan for satisfying and efficient urban areas. We are developing highly sophisticated techniques for discerning the nature and the implications of alternative patterns of development for our cities. But here I would like to make a closing plea that we not become so preoccupied by the process of decision-making that we default our obligation to inspire, to experiment, to be visionary. Decision-makers and people in general want more than scientific method. They also want, and the problem of the future use of urban space demands, appealing alternatives in the form and organization of our cities which are fortified not just with facts but with imagination and with sensitivity to the attributes of a rich and rewarding metropolitan environment.

The late CATHERINE BAUER WURSTER, professor of city and regional planning at the University of California, Berkeley, who died in November, 1964, had been a critic and writer in the fields of architecture, housing, and planning for many years, and a consultant to numerous public and private agencies. She was an honorary member of the American Institute of Planners and during the past few years was primarily concerned with problems of metropolitan expansion and urban structure. Her recent publications include: "Framework for an Urban Society" in *Goals for Americans* (1960), "Urban Living Conditions, Overhead Costs and the Development Pattern" in *India's Urban Future* (1962), and (as a co-author) "Housing Trends and Related Problems in California," for the Governor's Advisory Commission on Housing Problems. Mrs. Wurster was born in Elizabeth, N.J. in 1905. She received her A.B. degree from Vassar in 1926.

THE FORM AND STRUCTURE OF THE FUTURE URBAN COMPLEX

CATHERINE BAUER WURSTER

TRADITIONALLY, AN URBAN COMMUNITY WAS A CITY, and the nature of a city was obvious. In a limited space it brought together a wide variety of people; it made them accessible to one another, provided them with communication with the outside world, and stimulated them to engage in many kinds of specialized but interdependent activity. The city had a government whose essential functions were to resolve the people's differences in the common interest and to provide their necessary services. The city was a little world and its tight-knit, articulated form reflected its structural unity.

Modern metropolitan trends have destroyed the traditional concept of urban structure, and there is no new image to take its place. Blind forces push in various directions, while urban environments are being shaped by decisions which are neither based on any real understanding of cause-and-effect nor geared to consistent purposes. But the problems are steadily mounting, and all levels of government are called in to solve them. Public actions and expenditures of many kinds play an ever-increasing role in shaping the urban and regional environment. But the problems cannot be solved piecemeal by *ad hoc* decisions unrelated to any clear consensus about public purposes. Costly conflicts must be resolved, alternative directions identified, and the nature of the big choices, which tend to come in packages, thoroughly understood.

Efforts to develop effective concepts and criteria for modern urban organization, and to create new public images of the desirable metropolitan community, have come from various sources. Utopian ideas have had considerable influence, from the old Garden City movement which produced the British New Towns program to the reaction against all forms of decentralization reflected in the current zeal to "save the central cities" by local renewal programs, a kind of inverted or anti-Utopian Utopia. But the much less romantic push for effective metropolitan planning is finally focusing attention on the basic questions of urban form and structure in the United States, in various ways. The practical requirements of transportation planning have brought scientific methods of systems analysis and computer techniques into the development of alternative models for metropolitan growth and change, most advanced in the Penn-Jersey project. The equally practical requirements of public communication have stimulated such schemes as the Year 2000 Plan for the National Capital Region which dramatizes the problems and possibilities of future growth by presenting clear-cut alternative patterns. Finally, in the academic retreats, there is a fresh if belated wave of interest in theoretical explorations of the metropolitan wilderness, exemplified in the pioneering contributions of Walter Isard, Jean Gottmann, Lloyd Rodwin, Kevin Lynch, Stuart Chapin, and Melvin Webber.

This essay falls into none of these categories. It espouses no specific goals, Utopian or otherwise, nor does it promote any particular program of public action. It tries to be reasonably objective and more or less systematic in suggesting a range of alternatives for the spatial organization of the future urban complex, with some of their possible implications. But neither the arguments nor the evidence pretend to be "scientific"; they are simply an array of ideas, opinions, facts, and hunches.

THE PRESENT APPROACH

Even accepting these limitations, it proved to be a difficult task to suggest viable choices for future urban organization, briefly yet with some degree of logic and comparative interpretation. The following approach is no more than a brave experiment, but it does hang on a fairly clear-cut set of premises which should at least provide some basis for argument. Since my concern throughout is with urban form and urban structure, essentially as a pair of dimensions, my use of the terms should be defined. "Form" means the physical pattern of land use, population distribution, and service networks, while "structure" signifies the spatial organization of human activities and interrelationships.

Underlying assumptions: a pair of key variables. In a discussion of "practical" alternatives, it is necessary to begin with the trends and forces that seem to be shaping present patterns. Then one can try to diagnose the major issues and the potential for change: problems, conflicts, shifting goals and values, new tools, which together might alter the course of environment-shaping decisions in various ways, leading toward different types of form and structure. Alternatives can then be suggested, with some of their possible implications. In other words, the test of viability must rest on judgments about the dynamic drives behind the development process, however difficult they may be to assess.

The trends and issues in metropolitan patterns of land use and communication seem to relate primarily to a pair of variables which can be loosely considered co-ordinates, one a rough key to "form," the other to "structure." The first falls along a scale which ranges from extreme dispersion to extreme concentration in space of urban activities and artifacts. This is the obvious metropolitan dichotomy: the tendency of certain functions to spread out horizontally over huge areas, while other functions pile up together. I have assumed that the major force behind dispersion is the propensity to seek "private" space values, a push which has been amplified by automobility and the increase in long-distance communication. Concentration, on the other hand, indicates close-knit physical linkages at the expense of private space. This may reflect purposeful choice, for example in office skyscrapers, or simply the lack of any other choice, as is often the case for low-income and minority residence.

The other variable is more difficult to characterize in simple terms, because the issue is seldom clearly posed although it is fundamental for all metropolitan planning. Indeed, the continuing controversy between the "decentrists" and the Big City defenders comes down to this question: at what physical scale can (or should) a significant degree of integration take place among the various specialized activities and functions of a regional complex? Specialization implies interdependence, with more or less coherent organization at one or more levels, for urban areas as well as for industrial production. The questions are: where, at what scale, and for what purposes?

These are obviously very complex questions, since the realms for various types and degrees of interaction and interdependence extend all the way from the house and the neighborhood with their limited domestic functions, to the nation, the world, and the universe. Let us agree, however, that the city was traditionally an important and relatively balanced realm for a certain set of functions in that it provided a varied population with housing, employment, and other frequently used and essential services. Most of these functions are still performed within a metropolitan area, but individual cities tend to be more and more specialized, serving a limited range of populations and activities. So the questions are: Do the pieces fit together only at the metropolitan level no matter what its size, or are there limitations of scale for certain everyday urban functions? Is the implicit assumption of most metropolitan transportation plans substantiated—that the metropolis is essentially a single diversified market for housing, jobs, and leisure-time facilities? Or is relatively balanced and integrated development feasible or desirable within metropolitan subareas? This is the premise behind proposals for New Towns or relatively self-sufficient satellite communities, and for more housing in the central city suited to the tastes and resources of middle- and upper-income people who work there.

This variable ranges from the metropolitan Super-City—a single system with highly differentiated and interdependent parts, through various transmutations to a group of smaller urban communities, each providing for most of the ordinary economic and social needs of an approximate cross-section of the urban population. This factor has obvious implications for governmental structure and social relations as well as for functional organization.

Selected alternatives and some qualifications. This pair of variables, viewed as co-ordinates, suggests a wide range of hypothetical choices for future form and structure. In practical terms, however, an assessment of current trends, countertrends, and the forces behind them leads to the selection of four possibilities. They would not all be equally possible everywhere, and certain limitations should be noted at the outset. The stage of growth is a constraint: the form and scale of past development in a large old community, and the strengths of vested interests, are likely to impede any radical change in spatial organization, as compared with a relatively new metropolis most of whose growth is yet to come. The choices open to New York will be different from those for Los Angeles, Denver, or Sacramento, owing to the differences in what is there already and in the probable rates of future expansion.

The dominant functions of the region will limit choice, as will its particular endowment of resources: wealth, knowledge, energy, and ability, existing natural or man-made attractions; the area and character of land available for new development and redevelopment; the capacity for effective action toward common ends, via market and political processes.

Finally, whatever the local variables, the alternatives are more a matter of pursuing a fairly consistent course toward a certain set of goals than of achieving any particular kind of community in neat, pure form. The development of an entirely new urban agglomeration of major proportions is unlikely, though not impossible. Thus, conflicts between the old pattern and new directions have to be resolved gradually along the way, with considerable flexibility.

With these qualifications the accompanying diagram indicates roughly how several alternatives might relate to the two coordinates:

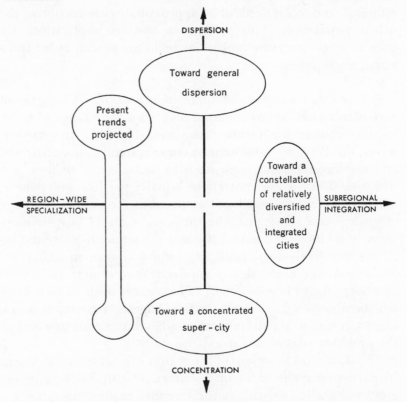

1. *Present trends projected.* Region-wide specialization with most functions dispersed but with a push toward greater concentration of certain functions in the central cities. Per-

haps unstable, likely to shift toward one of the other alternatives.

2. *General dispersion.* Probably toward region-wide specialization of certain functions but a considerable degree of subregional integration might be induced.

3. *Concentrated super-city.* Probably with a strong tendency toward specialized sectors for different functions.

4. *Constellation of relatively diversified and integrated cities.* With cities of differing size and character a range from moderate dispersion to moderate concentration would be feasible.

Terms for comparison: ends and means. Differences in urban form and structure must be evaluated in terms of the set of human ends (or benefits) they will serve, the other ends foregone, and the differing means (or costs) required to achieve these benefits. Each of our alternatives is a package of goods favoring a particular set of values and life-styles and having a particular price tag attached. But it is a hypothetical package, and in the present primitive state of urban cost-benefit analysis it is impossible to know exactly what the goods are, or what we would have to pay for them.

The ends can be compared in relatively simple, concrete terms, such as housing choice, job accessibility, class and race patterns. But the deeper social and economic effects will be harder to assess: productive efficiency and individual opportunity; family welfare, privacy, security, and cosmopolitan stimulation; quality of communications, adaptability to further change, social relations, and responsible citizenship. In a period when social science is mainly telling us how little we really know about needs and tastes, perhaps the range of environmental choice afforded by a particular urban pattern may be a factor of major importance. And this may be especially true of the residential environment, which offers very limited choices to most households today.

But the desirability of a particular package also depends on the means required to achieve it. Appropriate cost comparisons include the private and public expenditures for major items such as housing, transportation, redevelopment, and open space; the forms and degrees of public power that must be exercised at various levels of government; and broad social costs such as enforced dislocation, destruction of existing values, and waste of resources. In an extremely rough and general way, some of these differentials may be fairly obvious, while others are impossible to evaluate.

These are complex questions in a pioneering field, and all I can provide are some tentative and undoubtedly biased judgments. If they provoke debate and more systematic analysis, they will have fully served their purpose.

TRENDS, COUNTERTRENDS, AND THE POTENTIAL FOR CHANGE

Planning, in Perloff's and Wingo's words, must be related to "the things that matter: the major social movements." I have tried to identify some of "the things that matter" which have a direct influence on urban form and structure because they are the forces behind certain key trends and variables. Two dimensions have been selected: from extreme dispersion (low density and scatteration) to extreme concentration (high density, contiguity, and strong centering); and from large-scale integration (a single metropolitan system with specialized parts) to small-scale subintegration (diversified communities within the region with relatively balanced facilities for most ordinary functions). In these terms, what are the significant current trends and the forces behind them? What are the resulting problems and conflicts which could change the present picture?

Centrifugal forces: the selective push for private space. The dominant trend toward low densities and scatteration in outlying development reflects the demand for private space for certain functions: large areas to permit greater freedom on the site for industrial production and building operations, for shops and schools, and above all for middle- and upper-class family life. Closely related to the latter is the desire for natural amenity at home in private gardens and attractive vistas (and also increasingly in vacation cabins which produce a much wider ring of scattered development). Land speculation enhances the trend but is not the prime cause. In addition to these outward pulls, there is also the push to escape from city conditions—obsolete housing or inadequate schools, racial and cultural diversity, conflict, discomfort, high taxes, and helplessness—into small, safe, homogeneous, self-run communities with middle-class standards and status.

These varied "private" purposes which are related to the qualities of a particular site or small neighborhood area have been brought within reach by the achievement of another kind of private value, *automobility,* which permits individual freedom of circulation in a piece of personal property. Because private autos perform badly in the traditional type of multipurpose urban center, automobility has also contributed to the dispersal of business, cultural, and service facilities. Technology is serving these ends in other ways too: new equipment makes both houses and factories more self-sufficient; large-scale building operations provide most of their own utilities for standardized one-price homes; and rising opportunities for long-distance communications—mail, phone, radio, TV, and travel—make the individual or firm less dependent on immediate physical contacts within the metropolitan area.

These choices are open today, however, only to limited groups and functions: relatively foot-loose industries and businesses; the services that follow resident populations; families able to acquire suburban homes despite high prices, restrictive zoning practices, race discrimination, and rising taxes.

Of course, there is a great deal of medium- and high-density development, old and new. But dispersal has been the dominant trend for several decades, reflecting the conscious choice of multitudes of consumers and entrepreneurs. It has produced unanticipated problems and generated some counterforces, but unless these actually weaken the basic drives for private space they will probably not have much effect. In these terms, is the push for dispersal likely to increase or decline in the future?

The desired life-style of most American families with children still seems to call for the private home with a yard. High marriage and birth rates, and upward mobility with rising incomes and education, will only increase this demand, as will any abate- ment in race discrimination, or policies to provide cheaper housing in outlying areas.

There are, however, some qualifying factors in the trend toward endless suburban sprawl. Rising land prices and the demand for a wider range of dwelling types to suit varied household types and tastes are producing a greater admixture of multifamily rental units in some localities. Large-scale operations tend to result in patches of contiguous development, sometimes at "city" scale and including rental housing, community facilities, and industry. Public awareness of the costs of scatteration is likewise mounting, due to high taxes for inadequate services on the one hand, and the rising demand to preserve public open space and natural amenity within metropolitan areas, on the other. But measures to insure more compact development, or open space reservation, are not yet generally effective.

The force of purely "escape" motivations can become either stronger or weaker, depending largely on the increase or decline of race and class prejudice for whatever reasons, and the degree to which older cities become more or less ghettoized, or suburbia more mixed.

Accessibility to work is also an ambivalent factor. The business and professional people who continue to work in central cities have been willing to pay a high price for their home environment, in transportation time, trouble, and expense. But as their journey to work increases, or requires both a private car and one or more public conveyances, other solutions may be sought. If the offices move out to accommodate them, this can mean more dispersal. But if they settle for higher density housing, whether in the city or near a mass transit stop, it would have the opposite effect. Similarly, the factories and services which depend on relatively low-paid labor cannot move very far away from the old central districts, so long as the supply of cheap housing is predominantly located there. But if the suburban housing market were broadened, these jobs might become more dispersed.

The number of second homes for leisure-time use will probably increase enormously. This will broaden the extent of scatteration throughout a vast region, but at the same time it might conceivably mean greater acceptance of compact development, with greater convenience to work and other urban facilities, for weekday use.

In any case, centrifugal forces and private values, however dominant in new development, are still countered by some opposing influences, actual or potential.

Centripetal forces: by choice and by compulsion. The revival of skyscraper office development in many downtown districts reflects the continued demand among certain types of business enterprise for face-to-face contacts and adjacent services within "walking precincts," or merely for the prestige value of a particular location. This is clearly a conscious choice, despite the increased ease of long-distance communication and the increased burden of commuting; and it is therefore a centralizing factor which is likely to endure in some form. However, routine or mechanical office operations are beginning to move out, along with industry and consumer services. Over-all employment is unlikely to increase in most central cities, and business districts may tend to become specialized enclaves, whether they stay downtown or move outside.

In most cities, the old consumer uses of the center for shopping, amusement, and cultural pursuits have either remained static or declined, despite metropolitan growth. Where entertainment does thrive, it seems to owe its existence primarily to "visiting firemen," business travelers, vacationers, and convention-goers rather than the local suburbanites who, as a matter of fact, may be more likely to patronize a central theatre or restaurant when visiting in some other city.

In general the choice of central locations for business and leisure use still appears to be strongest in cities with traditionally strong centers, like New York and San Francisco, and weakest in cities which have always been more or less dispersed, such as Detroit and Los Angeles.

The other major use of central cities is both more universal and much more involuntary: lower-income and minority households are forced to concentrate there, by and large, because old districts provide the only major source of cheap or unrestricted housing—whether in obsolete structures or new subsidized projects, and regardless of locational trends in their particular job opportunities. If the rate of upward mobility increases, or if the flow of disadvantaged in-migrants finally begins to dry up, or if the suburban housing market is expanded, this part of the picture might change quite rapidly. The degree to which they would choose suburban living, if they could, is sometimes questioned. The crowded slum enclave offers a semblance of security to the recent arrival and the disadvantaged, as Leonard Duhl points out elsewhere in this volume, and as redevelopers have belatedly discovered. But all our urban history suggests that their aspirations are probably not very different from those of the millions who have moved upward and outward before them.

Some middle- and upper-income white people have stayed in the cities by choice, of course, but increasingly these have been single workers, adult households, Bohemians, and—if the attractions are great enough—wealthy families who put their children in private schools and have second homes in the country.

Those who voluntarily select a tight city environment for homes or business have something in common. They all value private space and the freedom of automobility far less than the attractions of convenience to work, the opportunity for specialized contacts and facilities within a small area, the stimulation of diversity, or the sense of being part of a cosmopolitan community in direct touch with world affairs. These are traditional urban values, and it is quite possible that more would choose them if they could be had without a heavy sacrifice in private living conditions. Yet, the half-worlds of City-and-Suburb rarely offer such a choice.

This is the background situation, but there is a rising push to "save" the central cities which is taking two positive forms: urban renewal programs with federal aid, and efforts to create or improve mass transit systems for commuting. These movements stem primarily from the increasingly desperate desire of economic and political interests in the central cities to protect property values and the tax base, with a variable intermingling of other forces, such as the need to provide better housing for slum-dwellers and the new wave of intellectual concern for urban historical and cultural values, which also tends to be anti-suburbia and anti-automobile.

Redevelopment brings new private and public structures of various types—office buildings and apartments, civic and cultural facilities—usually at increased densities and all subsidized to varying degrees. Expensive apartments predominate, but there are also middle-income ventures and low-rent public housing projects. In addition (often in opposition) conservationist programs are active here and there.

Central city traffic conditions have been worsened by the tremendous expenditures in freeway construction since the war, and it is now widely recognized that large-scale concentration is incompatible with universal dependence on private automobility. Despite the declining use of public transportation, the improvement or creation of metropolitan transit systems is a lively issue with several entirely new schemes either built, approved, or under discussion.

To the extent that these movements fulfill their present aims they will tend to maintain or promote concentration, at least for certain types of residence, work, and leisure-time activity. But these programs are very expensive, in terms of both financial subsidy and such disruptive social costs as forcible dislocation, and the degree to which they can actually offset the predominant trend toward dispersal depends on many imponderables. Will the restrictions of the housing market continue to force most low-income and minority households to live in the old cities, whether in successive blighted areas or in heavily subsidized public housing projects? Will the Negroes use their rising political power for greater integration throughout the metropolitan area or for separatist strength within the central cities? To what extent will middle-class white families and business enterprise favor convenience and city attractions if it means political domination by lower-income and minority voters? Will mass transit mainly facilitate more two-way commuting, instead of more jobs in the city?

The movement to save old cities has been narrowly focused on central problems thus far, with little concern for the pattern of outlying development or the desirable form and structure of the region as a whole. This may change. It is already recognized that transportation is a region-wide problem in its political as well as in its functional aspects. Regional population distribution is likely to become a mounting issue, in terms of housing choice, suburban race and class discrimination, the increasing disparity between residence and job opportunities, and, above all, the tendency of central cities to become ghettoized with all the related implications for tax-base problems and renewal hopes.

These issues are just beginning to be posed, however. Effective measures to deal with the shape and structure of regional development have not yet been devised, and no public image of the appropriate goals has developed. Housing, land use, transportation and renewal policies could be used not only to promote either dispersion or concentration, but also to encourage a wider range of residential choice in both outlying and central areas. This leads into the whole question of "balance" and the level of functional and political integration, which is the second dimension I wish to discuss.

Toward region-wide specialization: a single super-city? The widespread dispersal of certain functions, while others remain highly concentrated, generates a pattern which poses some basic structural issues. In a way it is still the classic form of the modern city, with business in the center, industry on the fringe, and the outward neighborhood succession from poor to rich, only greatly expanded in all its dimensions and administered by hundreds of independent local governments. At the moderate scale of a single municipality, the urban community had problems of slums and services, but the pattern itself posed no great difficulties. For the metropolitan complex, however, communications and integration are critical issues which raise questions about social, economic, and political structure.

Above the neighborhood level with its domestic functions, is the metropolis necessarily a single organic system with highly differentiated parts? Is it essentially one labor and job market, one housing market, one set of leisure-time and service facilities? Is it made up of so many specialized but interdependent activity orbits of varying scale that they can only be integrated at the metropolitan level? If this is true, then the basic problems are likely to be intercommunications and unified regional government.

Or can it be too big to operate sensibly or efficiently as a single system? Could the ordinary activities of the vast majority of people be better cared for within subregional sectors or smaller diversified communities? If so, then basic changes in housing and land use policy are required within a structure of stronger local governments co-operating through some kind of regional federation. There are influences in both directions, and the picture presented here is inevitably over-simplified, but the strongest current trends seem to lean toward specialized sectors and communities rather than subregional integration, with central cities and outlying areas serving quite different but highly interdependent functions. Consider the distribution of resident population, jobs, and leisure-time facilities with some of the resulting disparities.

The social divisions among residents of old cities and newer suburbs are increasingly sharp, by income level, by age group, and, above all, by race. These divisions are largely created by the housing pattern, and strengthened by the limitations of the current housing market, which by and large serves only upper and upper-middle income white families in areas of recent growth. If present trends continue, low-income and minority households will soon predominate in many central cities.

Meanwhile, the locational specialization of employment and business enterprise is following a different pattern, with most new industrial and service jobs outside the cities, and certain types of office and professional work still downtown. As for outdoor recreation, any major open spaces that may yet be saved are likely to be out beyond the fringe, near people who already have private land but far away from the families who live in crowded slums or high-rise projects and who frequently do not have automobiles. For urban leisure-time activities, the old multipurpose centers provide cheap attractions for the poor, and also, to varying degrees, Bohemia for the beatniks and intellectuals, and very expensive entertainment for the rich and the visiting firemen. Equivalent middle-class facilities are likely to be scattered around outside or in specialized suburban "centers" for shopping, culture, or amusement (Disneyland, for example).

This pattern poses obvious problems of extended cross-commuting, of limited housing choice, of accessibility to an adequate choice of leisure-time facilities, and of critical tax-base discrepancies. It is a serious threat to the future of current renewal efforts. These problems may be the inevitable price of the increasing specialization which produced great urban agglomerations in the first place, and their solution may require a strong metropolitan government to insure over-all productive efficiency, equity, and effectiveness of intercommunication. The inherent trends, however, confront us with a paradox: the sharpening class and race divisions along with the tax-base disparities lead to deepening political conflict between central cities and suburbia which makes metropolitan unification ever more difficult, if not impossible, unless it is imposed by direct state or federal intervention.

The potential for subregional integration. The American metropolis has in certain ways been moving toward a vast unitary "city"-type structure with highly specialized interde-

pendent parts, and it cannot be claimed that there is any conscious countermovement to encourage a greater degree of functional balance and self-containment within subregional sectors.
Proposals for "satellite communities" keep coming up in metropolitan plans, however, doubtless stimulated by the evidence
from Britain and elsewhere that relatively independent new
towns can be developed successfully, while renewal programs
reflect efforts to create in central areas a better balanced population related to downtown employment opportunities. But the
relation of the functional structure of metropolitan areas to the
development pattern has received inadequate research attention; we have little practical understanding of how it works now
or how its workings might be improved. Obviously it is an overlay of numerous interlocking activity patterns, large and small,
including many that extend far beyond the region, and many
that are normally circumscribed within a neighborhood. But we
do not really know to what degree and for what specific purposes
the entire region is necessarily a single system. In question particularly are certain functions which used to be integrated at
the city-wide level, such as the special consumer demands which
brought people to central districts, and above all the trip between home and work. It is frequently assumed that these activities, with their implied range of choices, can only be encom-
passed to any significant degree today at the metropolitan-wide
scale. But there are trends and pressures which tend to favor
some form of subregional integration.

Human activity systems range all the way from the bedroom-
bathroom trek to the astronaut's orbit around the moon. Within
the metropolitan complex, a great many functions have catchment areas which are normally quite limited: schools, playgrounds, meeting-halls, churches, ordinary shops, services and
amusements, even junior colleges, general hospitals, super shopping centers, and little theatres.

The pattern varies tremendously with personal means and
tastes. Some people go to any lengths to visit a race track, a sym-
phony concert, an exotic restaurant, or a wilderness park, which
others would ignore if they were next door. In between, a grow-

ing number of people would enjoy such specialties if they were fairly accessible. By the same token, many of the special "goods" can and should be more numerous and more accessible—in theory at least—because it would take a smaller over-all population to provide the selective demand. Mumford's principle of the cultural "grid," based on the British Museum's decentralized library service, is important for some of the highly refined but mobile resources. And if a tight multipurpose center has the stimulating and universal advantages claimed for it by central city saviors, then a large metropolitan region should probably have several such centers to serve the potential demand.

The critical questions seem to stem from the relations between the spatial systems of residence and employment. We have been acquiring some information about commuting patterns, and there will be more from the 1960 Census, but intensive analysis is also needed: case histories for a sampling of different occupations in different areas, including employment changes, residential changes, and how both jobs and homes were found. From preliminary Census data on commuting patterns as well as from more intensive recent studies it appears that the number of employed people who somehow manage to live and work in the same subregional sector may be surprisingly high, considering the limitations of choice in the housing market. Both home-moves and job-moves within a metropolitan area appear to be frequently influenced by a desire to reduce the journey-to-work, even at the cost of breaking family ties or living in a less desirable home on the one hand, or subordinating economic opportunity to home values on the other. People who make such choices do not see or use the whole region as a single urban community: many of its opportunities might as well be in another area entirely. The lack of convenient jobs may therefore promote residential mobility, neighborhood instability and long-distance commuting, while the restrictions on housing choice can tend to limit economic opportunity, particularly for low-income and minority households. Of course, accessibility is more important than mapped distances, and my rather conservative judgments must be balanced against Webber's revolutionary concepts of metropolitan communications potentials (outlined herein in his essay). But it seems fairly clear that technology has not yet overcome the friction of space for the metropolitan commuter.

Although the residential pattern is greatly influenced by public actions, these broad locational issues have not yet been seriously posed in American planning or policy. The suburban market for new housing is limited more than ever to upper-income white families, while federal aids for low-cost housing are confined to city renewal and rehousing programs. Most European countries, however, have long assumed that new housing development must accommodate a more or less cross-section population. In the United States strong pressures are building up against suburban racial barriers and for a wider range of housing choice for middle- and lower-income families of all races and household types. The central cities may come to support these pressures, although their political motivations will be mixed. But both state and federal governments will be increasingly involved in the rising metropolitan issues of class and race, of city and suburbs, of tax inequities, transportation costs, and general inefficiency.

Present trends might shift, therefore, toward a somewhat wider balance of population in both outlying areas and the central city, posing the possibility of greater functional integration below the metropolitan level. Strong resistance from existing suburban communities will affect the resulting pattern, however. Will there be a scattering of additional types of one-class enclave, for middle-class Negroes, for the aged, for cheaper homes? Can the present suburban communities, many of which already have industries, be induced to become socially diversified? Will entirely new cities be developed on the remote fringe where a wide range of housing and job choices may be particularly desirable? Can a reasonably healthy social balance be maintained in the central cities?

ALTERNATIVE DIRECTIONS FOR FORM AND STRUCTURE: SOME ROUGH COMPARISONS

The wide range of hypothetical possibility seems to come down to four reasonably practicable alternatives. The dominance of one or the other in a particular situation would depend on the dominant public, private, and individual purposes behind the environment-shaping decisions, the acceptibility of the means required to achieve certain purposes, and differing local conditions which might enhance or impede the feasibility of moving in certain directions.

Before considering these alternatives and their implications in more concrete terms, let us try to summarize the conceivable public attitudes that would lead in one direction or another— the various common images of the future metropolis that might be influential. At the same time, certain precedents and prototypes which relate to these different sets of attitudes will be suggested, including Utopian images and practical experience.

Common Images and Their Prototypes

1. "There's nothing serious that can't be solved by better transportation and central improvements."
Seen from this viewpoint, quite prevalent among business and political leaders, it seems that some of the experts are making too much fuss. There's nothing abnormal or seriously wrong about the present metropolitan pattern, they feel. A lot of people like suburban living, and it's fine if they can afford it. The others must naturally live in older districts, but they will gradually move outward into better dwellings as we tear down the worst to make way for new apartments and office buildings. If necessary we can build some public housing. Of course, the metropolitan area is essentially a single community, and there

should really be some kind of over-all government and planning, but local vested interests may be too strong. However, the state and federal governments can help to equalize the tax burdens a bit, to save some open space, and above all to solve the transportation problem. As long as we can get around, whether by automobile or mass transit or both, we'll be all right.

Since this simply assumes the projection of present trends which are visible in most American metropolitan areas, no additional illustrations or prototypes are necessary.

2. *"Let people have what they want: space and mobility."*
This attitude, very unfashionable in intellectual and downtown business or government circles today, reflects such powerful popular forces, however inarticulate, that it might win out. The rationale behind it might be put into words as follows:

It is stupid and reactionary to put huge public investments into central redevelopment and mass transit. People don't want to live or travel that way any more, and they won't unless they're forced to. Open up plenty of new land and build plenty of homes on it for all kinds and classes. Even if some of it were subsidized it would be a lot cheaper than current redevelopment and public housing projects. And it would offer the slum dwellers a real choice which many of them would be glad to accept, instead of merely forcing them out of their present homes into something no better. More and more jobs will follow the people, and perhaps commuting could get easier. When the old city is thinned out, it will be simpler and cheaper to fix it up for the few things that really need to be there, which people can then reach by car. Most of the old-time city attractions are better outside where they have more space.

These are the forces that shaped Los Angeles and stimulate its fantastic growth despite the smog and other problems. At the Utopian level, the same values are reflected in Frank Lloyd Wright's "Broadacre City," and in Buckminster Fuller's lifelong effort to develop a completely mobile and self-contained house, free of the utility network. In some ways Melvin Webber's theoretical emphasis on the spatial freedom resulting from communications technology leads to a similar viewpoint.

3. *"The Metropolis is a single Great City: pull it together and urbanize it."*

This is the fashionable sophisticated view among the new urbanists, including many critical writers, social scientists, modern architects, central renewal promoters, and certain economic interests. The number of conscious adherents is probably quite small, but the intellectuals have often turned out to be the vanguard of much larger movements, and the potential strength of this view should not be discounted. It has various facets which are oversimplified and perhaps exaggerated in this brief interpretation:

Great concentrated cosmopolitan cities, with their close contacts and stimulating diversity, have always been the source of civilization. The metropolitan community is still essentially a city, no matter how many people there are in it, but it is being disintegrated by the boring sprawl and stupid escapism of suburbia and the automobile. City and country are two entirely different things, while the suburban hybrid has the virtues of neither one nor the other and is rapidly destroying both. We should put a stop to all scattered fringe development, fill in suburbia with apartment houses, greatly densify and diversify the old center (although some would like to save its historic flavor), develop the best possible mass transit system, forbid private cars in cities wherever possible, and in general promote an exciting and civilized life. Week-ends, if we want a change, we can go to real country or the wilderness. Nearby open spaces for everyday recreational use can also be saved, if we stop suburban scatteration in time.

Utopias related to this view range from the technocratic models of Le Corbusier and the Bauhaus leaders to the nostalgic humanism of Jane Jacobs. It is also reflected in official planning practices, inevitably somewhat modified, in many central city renewal programs (with no suburban jurisdiction however), and in metropolitan planning for Philadelphia, Copenhagen, and (mixed with the fourth alternative) Stockholm.

4. *"The behemoth is too big to be a single city: guide growth, at least, into relatively self-contained communities."*

This is an old reform movement which has had many followers and widespread international influence in various guises. Rather scorned by the current *avant-garde,* it is quite as much an urbanist, anti-sprawl philosophy as it is anti-Big-City, and still has considerable appeal to a large and varied group of people, roughly in the following terms:

Instead of scattering houses, factories, shops, offices and services all over the landscape, we should pull them together into compact cities, with adjacent open space saved for recreation, agriculture and general amenity. There would be disagreement as to ideal city size, but suitable housing for a cross-section population should be provided, with more emphasis on row houses and garden apartments. A variety of employment opportunities should be encouraged, as well as a bona fide urban center. The cities would be readily accessible to each other and to the central city; indeed, such a pattern would favor a mass transit system if it is needed. The central city would normally provide certain region-wide services, and its population should also become better balanced. Some kind of regional federation and effective regional planning would be necessary. But local government would in many ways be strengthened, and democratic citizenship made more meaningful. A balanced choice of city and nature, privacy and opportunity, would be available to everyone.

These principles were originally stimulated by the Garden City movement, which led directly to the postwar British program of New Towns and expanded old towns. But they also have much broader manifestations: the current reorganization of Greater London into moderate-sized districts with considerable powers of self-government; Israel with its carefully developed state-wide system of cities and towns; the great metropolitan circle of old and new cities in Holland with the center reserved for agriculture and recreation; Stockholm's arc of satellites within the city limits; and various planning efforts in the United States, including the Year 2000 scheme for the National Capital Region and some California proposals.

Four Alternatives

How would these variant directions tend to work out? Would they fulfill the claims made by their proponents? What local conditions would favor one or the other? Following are some brief personal judgments:

1. Present trends projected. The wider dispersal of certain special classes and functions into outlying areas, with greater concentration of others in central districts, would probably tend to magnify the present problems of accessibility, inadequate choice, social and political schisms, and rising costs, particularly for transportation and housing. This might therefore be an unstable pattern, likely to push eventually toward one of the other alternatives, and there would in any case be an increasing degree of intervention by state and federal governments. The ultimate direction taken in a particular locality would depend in part on present limitations and opportunities in the area, in part on locally determined goals and actions, and in part on federal and state inducements.

2. Toward general dispersion. The underlying popular forces which favor low-density scattered development, particularly the desire for private space and automobility, are still very strong. If they become increasingly dominant, more housing for lower-income and minority households will be made available in outlying areas, with federal and state assistance in new forms. This will hasten the decentralization of industry and even the most specialized consumer services. Some office functions may try to remain downtown where they are now highly centralized, and it would be easier to provide acceptable housing for middle-income and upper-income families in the old centers as they are thinned out and become less dominated by lower-class population. But the expanse of the region would be so enormous in the larger metropolitan areas that even the region-wide functions might tend to be scattered around, in some cases in close but highly specialized groups.

There could be a tendency for homes and work opportunities to be somewhat closer than they would be if present trends were projected. But subregional integration in any clear-cut form is highly unlikely. Instead there would be a complex chain-like system of overlapping catchment areas for daily activities, extending outward indefinitely, as is already more or less visible in southern California. Residential development would probably continue to take the form of socially specialized enclaves, and class and race conflicts would make the creation of large suburban cities even more difficult than it is today. Service costs would be high, due to scatteration. Because there would be no strong reason for new development to be close to existing development, public open spaces and agriculture could be preserved, but this would call for direct state action. Indeed, all the unified powers required to maintain service and communications networks, and equalize tax burdens, would probably have to be exercised by state and federal agencies, either directly or through the creation of a regional government by their initiative.

Some will argue, with Webber, that increasing accessibility plus aspatial communication overcomes distance, with the result that people living at exurban densities can participate effectively in numerous realms, including a strong local community, and enjoy urban values along with their private space and mobility. This is a real issue, worthy of the most intensive study, but I am yet to be convinced. In my perhaps conservative and rather anti-technocratic view, the argument holds up for most of the personally selective and specialized realms of communication and interaction, and of course for one-way mass communication by TV and such, but not for the kind of community which provides contacts and responsibilities that cut across special interests creating common ground and stimulating mutual adjustment and integration. And I suspect that specialization, without an effective framework for integration, may be the basic curse and threat of our times, whether at the local, national, or international level. In our social, civic, and political life we have not learned how to apply the real lesson of the scientific and industrial revolution: the cross-communication and inter-dependence that make specialization effective in the common interest.

This pattern is hardly possible in regions with highly concentrated populations where metropolitan areas are already beginning to overlap, such as the central section of the Atlantic Coast. To accommodate future growth they will be forced to choose one of the other alternatives. To the extent that these values have universal force, however, the rate of westward migration is likely to be stimulated. On the other hand, the people who have moved to the West are already somewhat self-selected to favor a dispersed pattern of living.

3. Toward a concentrated super-city. This is probably the least likely alternative, except under very special conditions. But if we are at the start of a general swing toward a Manhattan life-style, with supporting policies at all levels of government, programs for high-density redevelopment in central cities will be greatly accelerated for all income groups and for a variety of functions. State and federal action would prevent further sprawl in outlying areas, and a powerful metropolitan government would fill in the scattered spaces between present suburbs (often with industrial development) and rezone them for multiple dwellings. The most advanced technology would be applied to mass transit and high-rise structures, perhaps with co-ordinated three-dimensional circulation in central districts. Private automobiles would be banned wherever possible, and pedestrian enclaves encouraged.

This pattern would tend, I think, toward a high degree of functional and social specialization in its various sectors. Structures and subareas would have to be carefully designed to fit particular activities, and social conflicts among heterogeneous populations could be aggravated if they were mixed up together in such close quarters.

One problem will be difficult to solve: the enormous demand for week-end homes in secluded locations, with attractive natural surroundings. Perhaps this could be managed by providing air or rail service to many distant centers where family station-wagons would be kept.

Costs would be very high for central reconstruction and transportation, and would be increased by the demand for second homes with automobiles for recreational purposes.

The New York region particularly might tend in this direction because it has limited space, a highly centralized power structure, and a population that is probably more or less self-selected to favor these values.

4. Toward a constellation of relatively diversified and integrated cities. If the desire for private space and natural amenity is modified by greater concern for accessibility, diversity, and other traditional urban values, a tendency toward subregional integration could take various forms. Housing for all classes, races, and age-groups would, in any case, be provided in new outlying development, at mixed densities, and related to varied employment opportunities in the same general area. Since these cities would be fairly self-contained, they could be located quite far out on cheap land. This would require strong public and private initiative combined in some new form of agency. It could also be done by stimulating more balanced development in suburban communities already started, but this would encounter considerable resistance and require very ingenious inducements not yet devised. A system of greenbelts or wedges could be preserved, but this would require state or federal initiative at the start, when it would be most needed, pending the formation of a regional federation of cities with the necessary powers.

The transportation system would be subject to the same conditions. It could either be predominantly by rail (if larger, denser cities are favored) or by automobile for relatively small, low-density communities. Mass transit would not be as necessary for commuting as it is now, and distant intercity communications could conceivably be handled by air.

The old central city might remain quite strong, for region-wide functions and highly specialized facilities, but it would have less employment and a relatively balanced population with mixed densities and dwelling types. There would be far less disruption and dislocation than in the Super-City alternative with a much greater chance to preserve the diversity and historic qualities which make for real "urbanity." Where dominant central cities do not now exist, there might be a tendency for the specialized regional functions to settle in various cities (Clarence Stein's model), strengthening their centers and differentiating their region-wide attractions. In general, the cities might vary greatly in size and character, and they could either become a fairly close-knit regional network with minimal space between or spread quite far out into a larger region, depending on variable purposes and conditions. For those who prefer them, there could be homogeneous, but only partly self-governing, enclaves. Except for the extremes of scatteration, concentration, and specialization, this pattern would probably offer the greatest choice in life-styles.

Costs would be relatively low, compared with any of the other alternatives, due to less scatteration on the one hand, and less high-density construction on the other. If rail mass transit is provided in addition to automobile circulation, this would add to costs but strengthen centers. Property values in the old central cities would have to be written down to some degree, but on the other hand, land for new development and big parks could be quite cheap if it were acquired in time.

In one form or another, this alternative would be feasible in almost any metropolitan area. It calls for no greater exercise of public power than is now applied to redevelopment, but basic innovations in policy and purpose would be required.

.   .   .   .   .   .

These are very sketchy and personal judgments as to the nature of the alternatives, the forces behind them, and their comparative significance. I would only argue that this *kind* of approach is needed to make both the science and art of environmental planning effective. Within a framework which poses a range of hypotheses as to the future form and structure of the urban complex, our pioneering efforts toward systematic understanding of the development process should be applied to the analysis of ends and means, and the weighing of costs and benefits, in particular situations. The same framework can, I think, enhance the art of public communication, which is a major responsibility of both planner and researcher. With creative imagination based on scientific analysis, the big choices open to public decision can be clearly presented.

FREDERICK GUTHEIM is president of the Washington Center for Metropolitan Studies and is well known as a writer on planning and urban design. His books *Frank Lloyd Wright on Architecture* and *Alvar Aalto* are the authoritative presentations of these architects, and in translations and paperback form they have achieved a wide international recognition. Mr. Gutheim has served as a planning officer, consultant, and member of federal, local, and metropolitan planning agencies. He was appointed by President Kennedy to the Advisory Board of the National Capital Transportation Agency, and also serves as a member of the Administration's Advisory Council on Pennsylvania Avenue. Mr. Gutheim was born in Cambridge, Mass., in 1908. He studied regional planning at the University of Wisconsin, where he received the B.A. degree in 1931, and later studied public administration at the University of Chicago.

URBAN SPACE AND URBAN DESIGN

FREDERICK GUTHEIM

I BELONG TO A GENERATION which, in the late 1920's, was encouraged by Lewis Mumford and others to re-establish a critical line that puts more emphasis upon the purposes of buildings, and thus interprets their architectural design largely in terms of function.

Accordingly, my first writing on this subject was an appreciation of the organic functionalism of the Gothic town and a resounding and moralistic rejection of the Renaissance city of illusion. But the intervening thirty years have taught me that the doctrine could not be eaten as hot as I had cooked it. Rather early, indeed, I came upon a sort of *reductio ad absurdum* in the form of a book by an enthusiast who found himself obliged to reject everything from the pyramids to Rockefeller Center that had not been built by a card-carrying Gothic craftsman. Later on, the widening division between Frank Lloyd Wright and the European exponents of *Die Neue Sachlichkeit,* and the followers of Le Corbusier and *l'Esprit Nouveau,* showed that the modern movement in architecture was destined to develop its own opposing wings, as had earlier periods, and indeed, the tendency suggested that this was not only the expression of enduring personal stylistic characteristics but an essential pendulum in the dynamics of architectural progress.[1]

My own aesthetic orientation has tended to remain rather close to Wright, but with increasingly heavy additions from the social side of architecture where the psychology of environment, the social uses of architectural and urban space, and a generally humanistic orientation have augmented an earlier functionalism whose recommendation has become almost wholly structural and economic.

Perhaps the legacy of functionalism is the question: What does the city do? That is the starting point of its design.

ART, ARCHITECTURE, AND URBAN DESIGN

As the modern movement sought to broaden the definition of architecture, substantial contributions to urban aesthetics were made by the architects. Perhaps the decisive effect was to make us think of the city today as an architectural affair, to the point where it comes as a surprise to discover that the Greek city was probably more influenced by sculpture, and the Renaissance city was largely a matter of the painter's perspective. Even the Italian view of cities today is much more apt to reflect how De Chirico and later modern painters think about form problems. (Figure 2 of illustrated insert following page 122.)

It is not a digression to note the extensive influence which painting has exercised even upon modern urban design. Not only has the painter's vision held up the mirror to the visual chaos of the modern city; the painter's organization of such impressions has yielded valuable clues to architects and designers, often (as in the work of Antonio Sant'Elia) of startling relevance. (Figures 1 and 3.) If you think of cities as having texture as well as form, color as well as line, a night-shape as well as day-shape, it is not a little due to Jackson Pollock, his predecessors, and successors in abstract painting.

[1] As I proposed in some detail in a review of Talbot Hamlin's "Forms and Functions of Twentieth-Century Architecture," in *Architectural Forum*, vol. 96, no. 6, June 1952, pp. 152–54.

Sculpture, too, has responded to modern times with space-creating inventions, strong and original silhouettes, the recovery of tactile values. (Figure 10.) While this is by no means a development unique to abstract art, as such civic sculptures of Maillol as the *Air Memorial* or the *Monument to Cézanne* illustrate, it is to Giacometti, Lipchitz, David Smith, Lipton, Calder, Moore, Noguchi and others of their kind that we look for the sources in sculpture of urban design. Sometimes, as in Noguchi's lunar landscapes, which are directly reflected in his designs for New York City playgrounds, the connection is close and obvious. Often, as in Giacometti, the source is deeply spiritual and plastically suggestive of environmental moods. In the case of Henri-Georges Adam, the sculptor has actually turned sculpture into architecture, as in the projects for monuments realized experimentally in the 1961 Paris Biennial. To modern abstract sculptors like Mary Callery, Jean Arp, and José de Rivera, in addition to those earlier mentioned, we are indebted for the lighter and more spacious forms which, like Henry Moore's splendidly sited reclining figure in the garden of the Chermayeff house, or Lipchitz' *Joie de Vivre* in the garden of Vicomte de Noailles at Hyères, have given new possibilities to outdoor sculpture. Sculpture is also the eternal source of the monument, the symbol, and hence the highest civic art.

The three leading architectural exponents of our time— Frank Lloyd Wright with his Broadacre City, Le Corbusier with his Ville Radieuse, and the German school led by Walter Gropius—have all developed comprehensive and characteristic doctrines of urban form. They are the modern utopias. The work of other architects concerned mainly with housing produced the neo-romanticism of Camillo Sitte, the theory of the lineal city voiced by Soria y Mata, and the garden city or new town especially as developed by Sir Raymond Unwin and Clarence S. Stein. This rich urban design inheritance of the last five or six decades has still to be assessed, despite much study of the subject. It is more than a speculative effort, the practical significance being found in the large areas of recent urban development that have explicitly reflected these theories.

The interest of architects in urban design is limited as well as recent. In a national survey of the profession made in 1948, less than one per cent of all architects acknowledged any interest, much less activity, in community planning and urban design of any sort. Today, however, characteristic design problems are suburban housing developments and new towns, new city centers and redevelopment projects, medical and cultural centers, university campus planning and airport master plans, not to mention shopping centers of all kinds. At the scale of individual skyscrapers, even buildings that were monuments to soap or whiskey found their way into planning by their recognition and development of urban spatial values.

While architectural work was thus increasing in scale, broad-brush planning was being broken down and made more detailed in specific designs for city centers, residential neighborhoods, special-purpose precincts and other districts. Helped by a strong infusion of architects to its ranks (one consequence of the postwar shortage of otherwise-trained planners), city planning began responding to legitimate earlier criticism that plans had been too much conceived in two dimensions, stated merely as land use arrangements. Its work began to develop three-dimensionally, and not merely perspective sketches but renderings and models began to appear in planning presentations. Between the professions of architecture and city planning a bridge was built by such early teachers as Walter Gropius at Harvard and Eliel Saarinen at Cranbrook. Their teaching was translated into impressive demonstrations by such leaders as Edmund N. Bacon of Philadelphia and Charles A. Blessing of Chicago and Detroit.

THE ELEMENTS OF URBAN DESIGN

What is urban design? It is that part of city planning which deals with aesthetics, and which determines the order and form of the city. If such determination seems arrogant, the urban designer might well ponder this quotation from Jean Giraudoux: "Faced with the apparent incoherence and injustice of the world around us, we may react by anger, resignation, or the resolve to introduce order by the physical or moral means into a universe whose first principles escape us. The introduction or discovery of such an order has ever been the task of statesmen, moralists, metaphysicians and poets. Each creates the order he can for himself and, it may be, for his fellows."

Urban design must meet certain engineering and economic tests, but these projections must acquire popular sanction. Any apprehension about the implied dictatorial power of the urban designer is countered by the public consent required for the realization of his proposals; the instrument of criticism is an essential part of this process.

The urban designer has not succeeded to the autocratic position of earlier planners. Today the urban designer is regarded as a member of the planning team, and his contribution is made both in the design of a specific project plan intended to be executed like a building design, a bridge, or a garden and in a design activity unique to planning, the organization of a process by which cities or parts of cities are brought into being. The scope of urban design as such seldom embraces the planning of the whole of large cities or metropolitan regions, nor does it ordinarily extend to the architectural design of particular buildings. Residential areas, essentially vernacular in character, also elude urban design.

What the designer contributes to the process of city building, then, is not only the final form of a concept of the city largely given him by others. He also contributes valuable hypotheses, perhaps to be tested by research before execution, but in any event leading to the creation of new and alternative modes of urban life as well as urban forms which, once realized, research may be able to confirm. This is not simply to contend that art is experiment, but to argue that design is the only creative element in the city building process. The rest is measurement, analysis, projection, effectuation.

The elements of design, furthermore, comprehend all the substance of the physical city, not simply those factors of strategic importance to its expression or appreciation, for the aim of the designer is to structure life and not merely to shape its external appearance. The processional approach to the Acropolis, a winding route in which glimpses of the culminating structures are provided at intervals and a sequence of introductory architectural experiences is offered, well illustrates the importance of controlling human movement. It is a story repeated in many pilgrimages and shrines. Contrast this slow unfolding process, with its gradually developed meaning, to the alternative of a direct approach as in a baroque perspective exercise, or the swift arrival by auto in front of a building, which is then entered with scarcely a glance. It is the difference between painting and printing.

Consider the fragility of urban space. When Bernini erected his famous colonnade, providing a theatrical forecourt to St. Peter's, he destroyed the earlier and more intimate space the Cathedral's original designer had in mind; but he created something else. But when the Fascist architect Piacentini cut through a direct approach to St. Peter's from the Castello San Angelo, he effectively destroyed the architectural and urbanistic values of all that had gone before, allowing them, as it were, to escape via Mussolini's new route.

Such illustrations—drawn from the world's great and familiar monumental buildings, the set pieces of urban design—may be accepted even today as the designer's legitimate impositions on the plastic behavior of human beings. In a religious or even a civic setting, we are willing to sacrifice some convenience, such as driving our cars directly to the Tomb of the Unknown Soldier, and to accept that the creation of architectural values obliges such choices. We are saying, in effect, that if we elect the domination of the route, the destination itself may disappear.

At the destination we are not dealing with ephemeral architectural atmospheres and meanings but with human activities. In contemporary terms, one might observe that unlimited and unheeding access to the central area of many cities, as is proposed in most current city plans, will result in coreless cities offering little or nothing in the way of a central city destination. The activities once found there will have leaked away to specialized locations elsewhere in the metropolitan region, and the great radial expressways will have lost their function. The suburbs, having struggled for maximum efficiency in connecting themselves to the center by a transportation mode that is intrinsically diffusing in its effect, will have shattered the once efficient because congested central city, and find themselves facing the task of travelling to the periphery instead of the center to reach those destinations where jobs, bargains, pleasures, and opportunities exist.

THE AESTHETICS OF PERCEPTION

If there is to be such a thing as urban design, it must be related to some perception of the city as a whole. It cannot deal simply with parts of the city at architectural scale. The unity of the city as an absolute fact, however, need not be thought of exclusively in terms of a single *coup d'oeil,* encompassing the entire urban area to the horizon, but as a unified experience that may take place over many miles and many days. The essential factor is that all parts of the city, so experienced, must be recognizable as parts of the whole city.

Of the many parts of the city, the most important certainly is the core. And in the tradition of western urbanism no urban center is more fully expressive of the core than the Piazza San Marco. If you are lost in the byways of Venice and wish to return to the great piazza, even the guidebooks tell you simply to "follow the crowds." Here the religious, civic, ceremonial and social life of the city is concentrated, and neighborhoods repeat in their own campi the more universal life of the great piazza. So minor Venice conveys its own lesson, relating the core of the city to its principal subdivisions. The core of the city is not its geographical center, or its business district. It is the place to which the public repairs spontaneously on occasions of the greatest urgency, as Washington flocks to its rudimentary civic square, the space between the Willard Hotel and the District Building, when war ends in armistice, or Roosevelt dies; as New Yorkers throng Times Square. This relationship of the part to the whole, of a single center to the greater organic complex, is a major key by which we can understand the whole of a city as an urban design without ever being able to experience all of it at once.

Perception of the city today is more than rude contact with its physical solids and voids. It requires a new kind of insight. I speak not of maps and abstractions but of unifying personal experiences. When we leave a central city hotel early in the morning and drive to an outlying airport, we can see the entire city—a twenty-mile cross section of it—come to life. Time and space are equated in experience. We see whole quarters of the city simultaneously, both in their physical appearance and as we know them from statistical tables and social facts. Today we can see by a perceptive technique that Leonardo Ricci has called "X-raying cities," an intellectual device in which "the city presents itself to your sight somewhat like certain architectural structures painted on medieval tablets, with the walls removed so as to reveal the life inside." [2]

The aesthetics of the city thus involves a new conception of realism. When in a design we see consistency with the urban forces at work, harmony with social, political and economic facts, the design acquires a quality of naturalness, inevitability, acceptance. To be thus in the grain of the city does not mean that there can be no innovation, that design merely projects what has been. On the contrary, the best design is frequently a reaction to historic trends rather than a continuation of them. A skillful and experienced urban designer has called attention to the importance of having "the seeds of fulfillment" in a design.[3] That is a splendid and not altogether pragmatic criterion of success in urban design.

The most important design characteristic of a city is coherence. This means more than order. Indeed, order alone leads but to monotony and deadness. It provides no role for the imag-

[2] Leonardo Ricci, *Anonymous (20th Century)* (New York: G. Braziller, 1962), p. 169.

[3] Morton Hoppenfeld, "An Approach to Urban Design," *Potomac Valley Architect*, vol. 6, no. 5, January 1962, p. 4.

ination. Cities are alive, and their living quality must come through in the articulation of the various parts of the city, in its adaptations, in its growth. A city tells us things, and our body responds to the perception of whether they are places of good or bad air, hot or cold, comfortable or uncomfortable, or provide other bodily sensations.[4] But these responses must be supplemented by an understanding rooted in knowledge as well as in experience. The organic relations of the city—the interaction of its transportation and its land use, no less than of its people and their recreation areas—is an important theme of design. Such recognition also mirrors understanding of the city and our individual relationship to it, and this meaning is also a kind of coherence. While symbols are not unimportant in urban design, the city speaks to us more directly as a place where opportunity is extended or denied, where life is valued or suppressed, where the common good is recognized or ignored. The city is also directly apprehended as a place of exaltation or of seclusion, of restlessness or repose, of boring monotony or exciting variety. The city, in short, declares whether it is true or false to life. Thus, in aesthetic terms, it provides what Bernard Berenson has called "ideated satisfactions." We realize its entity and live its life.

THE INTERPLAY OF URBAN DESIGN AND SOCIAL FORCES

Insofar as urban design is accomplished by buildings, we may accept it as a matter of architecture. Architecture is a transparent art. It betrays insincerity and compromise. It may ex-

---

[4] Before St. Paul's Cathedral, "All the weights in his body seemed to shift. He had a curious sense of something moving in his body, in harmony with the building; it righted itself: it came to a full stop. It was exciting—this change of proportion." Virginia Woolf, *The Years* (New York: Harcourt, Brace, 1937), p. 227. Perhaps the evidence of the cosmic response to the urban scene is best found in painting. Oskar Kokoschka's views of Lyon and Prague, in the Phillips Gallery, show what many of us can only feel. (This is one aspect of "The City and the Arts," as Eduard F. Sekler has discussed it briefly in *Daedalus*, Journal of the American Academy of Arts and Sciences, vol. 89, no. 1, Winter 1960, pp. 74–78.)

press religious convictions or centralized political power. When Paul Valéry (in *Eupalinos ou l'Architecte*) spoke of buildings that sang, spoke or were mute, he could easily have amplified the catalog to include those that lisped, stammered, spoke double talk or out of the corner of their mouths.

Even such an insubstantial art as stage design must convince us, and contribute to the total theatrical effect. The aim of the artist has been vividly suggested by Tennessee Williams. In the introduction to *Camino Real,* he explains, "My desire was to give these audiences my own sense of something wild and unrestricted that ran like water in the mountains." What kind of a theatre will do that? The realism may be of many kinds. It is equally real in the theatre to be convinced we are in the Forest of Arden or on the steps of the Campidoglio, or more abstractly to be convinced that we are really in an atmosphere of horror or sun-bathed romance.

But in urban design we must allow, in addition, for intellectual perceptions and satisfactions. To our insight into such aspects of urban design as historical continuity, the vitality of urban centers, functional coherence, urbane forms, and planning as a mirror of civilization must be added our understanding of the social city. We know whether the city is true or false to life. The requirements of individual, family, and community life are recognized in urban design—or they are ignored. Either will tell us something about the city and the people who built it. Every physical planning decision has its social impact and implications. These human and social factors have been etched into our consciousness by formal education, personal experience, popular discussion, and even by political campaigns. The low-income slum, the racial ghetto, the billboard-ravaged highway, the denial of youth's social problems—to mention but a few—are as real and immediate to most of us as the law of gravity or a post-and-lintel structural system. Increasingly they are seen as inseparable from the physical environment. We are repelled by a planning proposal just as readily when it violates our perceptions of social reality as when it goes against engineering principles.

If the beauty of cities is what we perceive, we are responding to a quality which has been projected by the urban designer. As well as perceptive witnesses, we must consider the talented projector. This interrelationship is different from the familiar doctrine that "we shape our buildings, and our buildings shape us," which Sir Winston Churchill once applied with precision to the interior design of the House of Commons. It specifies that the pencil in the urban designer's hand is held by social forces, and cities are thereby stamped not only by functional but by formal conceptions of society's world view. Such cities are perceived not only as religious or commercial or university centers but as formed cities in which such dimensions as image, symbol, perspective, structure, and such emotional values as grandeur and exaltation, intimacy and privacy, are to be found.

In freeing urban aesthetics from architecture, we must make sure that in addition to emancipating ourselves from Ruskin we do not remain shackled to Geoffrey Scott. Scott voiced an aesthetic, shorn of Victorian taste, that is as appealing to modern ears as it is relevant to urban design problems. Scott's theory, stated concisely in his own words, is that "The tendency to project the image of our functions into concrete forms is the basis, for architecture, of creative design. The tendency to recognise, in concrete forms, the image of those functions is the true basis, in its turn, of critical appreciation." [5]

The forms of urban design, however, extend from the functions of the individual to social functions. What does a city do? That will determine its form. But experience with functionalism in architecture has long since demonstrated that it is by no means the sole determinant of design, and in the more complex realm of urban design I should expect that to be still more the case. We are living in a time when imagination is required to see the truth, and the limited ability of function to shape a tool fails before a building or a city in whose form greater demands must be reflected. Purely functional design reflects an attitude adopted rather than a creed confessed. While there may

[5] Geoffrey Scott, *The Architecture of Humanism* (2d ed., rev.; New York: Scribner's, 1924), p. 213.

still be widespread differences of opinion about what should be added to the functional statement of the problem, there is very little question that the limited answer, even when given by such talented exponents as Mies van der Rohe, falls short of providing full satisfaction.

THE RESIDUE OF THE PAST
IN THE PERCEPTION OF THE CITY

The impression made by a city is often more culturally valid than its reality. The shimmering light of Venice, the pastel colors, the delicate tracery of its architecture are remembered long after the stench of its open sewers, the poverty of its inhabitants, and the dilapidation of its ruined grandeur have been forgotten. Much of urban design is, indeed, the remembrance of things past, not simply in those overwrought romantic imaginations that have been described by Rose Macaulay [6] but in the experience of every perceptive traveller.

These echoes of cities known and remembered, a kind of cultural time clock, must be given their weight. They suffuse more formal descriptions with an atmosphere, a mood, even a music that cannot be given those whose lives do not embrace this experience. As John Keats observed, "Nothing ever becomes real till it is experienced." These values are strongest in such capitals as London, Paris, Rome, Vienna, and Peking. They are generated not from climate as in Naples, or geography as in Sidney or Vancouver; not from time as in Isfahán, or season as in Charleston; not even from buildings as in Leningrad, or parks as in Mexico City; but from the totality of the city. Our experience unites myriad fragments into a single whole, and persuades us that in this reality much is embraced that is excluded from the shrewdest analysis. In the end we desperately fall back upon exclamations or futile attempts to describe an elusive charm. Lin Yutang has recently written such an ultimate accolade: "Great old cities are like tolerant grandmothers. They represent

[6] Rose Macaulay, *Pleasure of Ruins* (London: Weidenfeld and Nicolson, 1953).

to their children a world vaster than one can explore or ex-
haust, and one is happy merely to grow up under their all-
embracing protection." [7]

One of the features that distinguishes urban design from
painting, sculpture, or even architecture is that it seldom offers
a carte blanche. The designer of cities—despite the occasional
Brasília, Canberra, or Washington—has to start with a city. For
him it is not simply so much raw material to be remolded, as
the sculptor regards wood or plaster, but a complex set of political, economic, and aesthetic factors that are not only "given"
but must be manipulated by the designer if anything viable is
to result. Even in the scrape-clean period of urban redevelopment, to which the great project for Southwest Washington belongs, the factor of historical continuity asserted itself. The an-
cestor of I. M. Pei's plan, the one drawn by Elbert Peets for
the National Capital Park and Planning Commission in 1950,
was based less upon wholesale clearance than upon a doctrine
of urban continuity. Features of this plan survived successive
bureaucratic transactions to dominate much later proposals that
pretended to deny these values, and thus in turn became as important as the facts of geography, underground utilities, or the
land use restrictions imposed upon the redevelopers by the Planning Commission. But we have still not pressed matters back to
their origin. Back of the Peets plan, as there lie back of every
complex social resolve, are formative historical factors of fundamental and continuing significance to be untangled. But this is
a task of urban and architectural history rather than of urban
design.

The form of cities, as we perceive it and as it affects the decisions of urbanization, must be given a setting in time and place.
An intense localism has marked urban life during most of history. In western civilization it reached a formal peak in such
medieval cities as Nuremberg. But the regional theme is found
equally in sixteenth century Amsterdam, eighteenth century
Edinburgh or twentieth century San Francisco—to cite a few
examples where physical form reflects a strong local attitude

[7] Lin Yutang, *Imperial Peking* (London: Elek Books, 1961), p. 11.

no less than inherent limitations. Much of this localism was based on a limited range of local building materials, a vernacular technique, and consequently a homogeneous building form. You can see it today in Assisi, or at Taxco where the whole colonial town is hung out on the hillside, like washing on a line. Design was not made. It appeared. Its qualities were inherent and inevitable. If you didn't like the city, you didn't like its life.

The departure from the traditional urban vernacular, once industrialism had conquered both the physical and cultural limitations of building and urban design, led to a kind of demoralized uncertainty. Not only was a bewildering variety of urban design now possible, but the deterioration of the universally held concept of what a city was, the end of its earlier determination by a handful of educated men, and its abstraction into modern engineering and technology, left open the question of responsibility for the appearance of the city. The city of the industrial age took its form from the market; private transactions in land, the needs of manufacturing, the freedom of enterprisers, and the raucous voices of sellers pursued men wherever they lived or went.

UGLIFICATION AND DERISION

To the visually trained or sensitive person today, the assault of urban anarchy on the senses is remorseless and unremitting. It is an outstanding fact of modern life, an expression of brutalism as harsh and as significant as slave labor, atomic warfare or genocide—and it reveals the same disregard for life.[8] Our cities are neither an expression of civilization nor a creator of civilized men. We see this anarchy in the crumbling hearts of older cities

[8] We are criticizing, as we should, from potential. It is worth remembering, as G. Holmes Perkins has, that whatever their visual anarchy or horrendous desecration of nature, "our cities today are probably the best cities we have ever had in the history of man." (*Journal of the American Institute of Architects*, vol. xxxvi, no. 6, December 1961, p. 92). But the accomplishments of public health and engineering have not been equalled in urban design and architecture.

—the wasteland of Chicago's west side, the industrial ruins of northern New Jersey's older cities, the splintering, festering square miles of wooden houses in Detroit's grey belt, the smoke and odors of East St. Louis. But equally fearsome are many of the most modern urban areas—the tangle of urban superhighways in Los Angeles, Daly City, that checkerboard suburb of San Francisco, the subtopias (as they call suburbs in England), or the slurbs (as they are known in California) that project the image of standardized, anonymous, dehumanized industrial man. Nor have we escaped this gloomy catalog in the cream-of-wheatish cities like Santa Barbara, that have erected "good taste" into a bland, inoffensive but equally repugnant because false, urban "style," or the institutionalized design of "housing projects" and most urban renewal areas. Urban uglification is a world-wide phenomenon. In ecumenopolis it is writ large. Historic Great Britain compounded it with grinding poverty, alcohol, domestic tyranny; romantic Mexico City with smog, filth, and bad smells; sunny Italy with the world's most blatant outdoor advertising, unsanitary streets, and rapacious speculation in land and buildings.

Those who do not flee them are conditioned not to see, hear, feel, smell or sense modern cities as they are. The greatest obstacle to seemly cities has become the low standard of demand and expectation of their present inhabitants, a direct expression of their having become habituated to the present environment and their incapacity to conceive of any better alternative. Those who have made this adjustment are aesthetic cripples, permanently handicapped in the use of their senses, brutalized victims of urban anarchy. Urban design cannot accept this "demand" in a Madison Avenue spirit of "giving the public what it wants."

This does not seem the place to examine in detail the shortcomings of what has been called "The Ugly American City," [9]

[9] Karl L. Falk, president of the National Association of Housing and Redevelopment Officials, has contended, "It is not enough to live in a beautiful home—even though that should have a high priority in our desires—if we have to go to work, possibly even to an attractive office, store, or factory, through congested traffic, past unsightly junkyards, screaming billboards, unattractive and unnecessary telephone and electric poles and wires, dilapidated and unimaginative housing, rundown hamburger stands, and indiscriminately zoned com-

or to explore an otherwise productive topic: the economic value of a beautiful city as distinguished from a merely workable city. We live in a time of great changes in our conception of the city. But this is not the occasion to discuss in aesthetic terms the great alternatives of urban form—the metropolitan satellite system with its new towns, the radial corridor city plan, the new doctrines of organic extension of unified cities, the theory of the coreless city—or to describe recent experiments in two-level city centers and similar innovations in more detailed urban design.

But we do need to mention, if only in passing, the popular view. The traveler's perceptions are essentially popular in character. An Italian visitor to Washington once seriously asked, "Where can you take a walk?" He didn't mean a hike in Rock Creek Park, but a walk along a city street where you can see the people, admire the buildings, inspect the goods, and learn about life in the process. An even more cutting observation was given me by John McAndrew, "In Washington you often feel that you are on a street parallel to the main street, and just a block away, around a corner or two, you will come to it. But you are on the main street all the while." As for the future, Tracy Augur has asked slyly whether the resident of one of the communities in the radial corridor plan for Washington in the year 2000 will ever declare, "I am a citizen of no mean nodule." Perhaps we need a simple litmus-paper test of the good city. Who lives there? Sing one song written about it? Who wrote its immortal movie? Find five post cards to send to a discriminating friend? Where is the center? What do you do when you get there? Popular urban design also involves urbanity, the quality the garden city forgot. It is found in plazas and squares, in corsos and boulevards, in the alameda and the promenade. It can be found in a railroad station, like "the street between two buildings" in Rome; in the *gallerias* in Milan or Naples; or in a main street like the Kurfürstendamm. When you find it, never let it go. It is the hardest thing to create anew.

---

mercial properties." (Karl L. Falk, "The Ugly American City," *Journal of Housing*, vol. 18, no. 11, December 1961, p. 495.)

Even to the man on the street—or on the bus—today's city is visually dominated by engineering forms. Bridges and highway structures, television masts and radar domes, electricity pylons, and tanks are part of an increasingly dehumanized environment.[10] Such basic needs as housing and community institutions are trying to escape the new realities. Only seldom do they attempt to adjust. Almost never is there a popular demand or an effort to insist that the new forms themselves take on the civilized character they have been made to assume in some other times and lands. While by no means the only problem, the ubiquitous automobile and the highway have become the focus of the struggle between what may broadly be characterized as the forces of society and those of technology.

THE AESTHETICS OF "AUTOPIA"

The automobile, and all that it requires and implies, offers a further innovation in community design. Barely a half century old, we have still to learn how to use it, store it, provide for it, and incorporate it into our lives. Even such a distinguished monument to the automobile as the General Motors Technical Center fails to achieve a workable scale, and those who think the problem an easy one might look at that contemporary Versailles, the new University of Mexico, where 60,000 students are united, if at all, by a circular bus line. To achieve a design that we can recognize as appropriate, that does not do violence to life, requires the satisfaction of more factors than have been recognized as present in problems such as these. The computer can embrace these factors—but it cannot yet design cities.

The outstanding importance of the automobile in urban design has recently received more attention than any other single factor. The characteristic urban utopias, the modern ideal cities, all seem based on the automobile as the primary element, to be embraced or repelled as the case may be. There are the advo-

[10] Harold F. Searles, *The Nonhuman Environment* (New York: International Universities Press, 1960).

cates of the lineal city, like Soria y Mata, who proposed as early as 1882 a continuous lineal residential zone as a way of developing suburban Madrid. (Figures 4a and 4b.) Later the road and its connection with airports and other forms of transportation became the principal theme of Richard Neutra's Rush City Reformed. Radburn, the chief American residential design, is an auto-scaled superblock. Frank Lloyd Wright's Broadacre City is essentially a prairie strewn with factories and other centers, linked by a web of superhighways. (Figure 13.) Le Corbusier's regional city was composed of characteristic urban concentrations, distributed and united by great transportation corridors served by many different forms of transportation. (Figure 12a, 12b, 12c and 12d.) These fantasies have been projected into reality in city plans, urban redevelopment programs, and the schemes of private promoters like the Great Southwest Corporation's new city between Dallas and Fort Worth.[11]

The use of the automobile, the commuting routine, the view from the road, the experience of arrival in the city, the design of parking facilities as civic art—these have been continuing themes in Philadelphia planning design for more than a dozen years and have produced a great series of interesting suggestions. (Figure 11.) In their article in the 1957 issue of *The Annals* devoted to the metropolis, the Philadelphia designers concentrated their search for a new urban aesthetic around the automobile. Their sketches show a clear distinction between urban scale as experienced by the man on foot and the man on wheels, in a car or a train. They concentrate upon the formulation of new types of urban institutions, buildings, and monuments to heighten the clarity and meaning of the city. They say, "The threshold will announce the nature of the city—hospitable, sensitive to the arts, formal. The transition from wheels to feet will be pleasantly accomplished. The reception will be fitting

[11] These and related projects were reviewed in an exhibition prepared for the symposium, "The New Highways: Challenge to the Metropolitan Region," organized by the Connecticut General Life Insurance Company in September 1957; and in the exhibition, "Roads," shown at the Museum of Modern Art in New York City in August 1961.

and gracious, indicative of what is ahead." [12] But the main idea is unmistakably in the end to get the man out of the car. Another Philadelphia designer, Louis Kahn, has given still more vivid sketches showing how great parking structures (really roads curled up like a spring) announce the arrival of the city and serve as monuments bounding its central area, much of which, including upper levels, is pedestrian islands.[13]

In more rudimentary form these ideas have already found application. Their principal formulation is still Victor Gruen's plan for Fort Worth, which called for surrounding a compact business district with a tight belt of expressways and separating this route from the inner core by five enormous parking structures. (Figures 5a, 5b, 5c, and 5d.) Although the Gruen plan proposed heavy reliance upon bus transportation, its principal disqualification appears to have been a demand for so much parking for individual cars that any plan would have been spread out to impracticable dimensions. (Figure 6.) (It is yet to be seen if a similar later plan for Dallas, prepared by Charles R. Colbert, overcomes these objections.) Many central city plans—and twenty examples could be given—have failed to grasp this point. (Figure 7.) Cities have either rejected them, or have embraced them without fully realizing their incompatibility with the universal use of the private automobile. Great Britain, whose struggle with the automobile in city design has just commenced, has produced three pedestrian islands in the new town of Stevenage (Figure 14), the redeveloped area of Coventry (Figure 15a and 15b), and proposals for the Barbican area lying immediately north of the City of London (Figure 9).[14] None will survive the full impact of automobilization. Neither will the Conservative Political Centre's program for acceptance of urban motorways as a prime element in Britain's

[12] Willo von Moltke and Edmund N. Bacon, "In Pursuit of Urbanity," *The Annals of the American Academy of Political and Social Science,* vol. 314, November 1957, p. 105.

[13] Louis I. Kahn, "Toward a Plan for Midtown Philadelphia," *Perspecta,* no. 2, 1953, pp. 10–27.

[14] C. D. Buchanan, *Mixed Blessing: The Motor in Britain* (London: L. Hill, 1958).

future "regional cities." Even such extravagantly admired urban designs as Vällingby, oriented to excellent rail commuter service to central Stockholm, failed to provide enough shopping center parking and are now menaced by the rise of the car pool and other familiar difficulties. Until a new future mass transportation is assured, it must be acknowledged that we have today no solution to the design of central areas or even to their preservation.

As cities are now formed, only the dominant functional interests are usually expressed. The city as a commerical center is not much more than a decorated warehouse, empty except during shopping hours, where the main thing to see is goods and the main thing to do is buy them. Downtown is a sometime thing, plodding a treadmill of obsolescence as inevitable as the FHA Handbook version of residential neighborhood decline. This is the city that urban design must save from the city planners.

WHAT URBAN DESIGN REQUIRES

Teachers of architectural history are frequently desperate in their efforts to make their students see and feel the beauty of buildings after years of protecting themselves from the assaults of ugliness. It takes the exceptional enthusiasm of a great teacher like Vincent Scully to break the protective shell. A few years ago, in an exhibition at the National Gallery of Art describing a century of American architecture, I had occasion to experience the inadequacy of the conventional photograph as a way of communicating architectural values to those who had not experienced them. In the end it was necessary to resort to dramatic photographic tricks: to such devices as Ernst Haas employs when he calls the fire department and wets down an entire street in Venice to photograph colored reflections, or those invented by W. Eugene Smith when he captured one moment of sunset light turning the Connecticut General Life Insurance Company building into a glowing pearl set in a snow-covered field, or

1. Antonio Sant'Elia, *La Città Nuova*, 1914. Courtesy *L'architettura* archives.

2. Victor Servranckx, *The Town No. XLVI*, 1922. Courtesy Yale University Art Gallery.

3. Antonio Sant'Elia, *Stazione Aeroplani*,
   1912. Courtesy *L'architettura* archives.

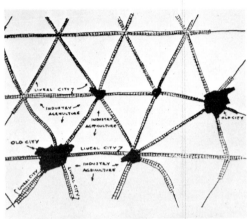

4. a) Arturo Soria y Mata, *La Ciudad
   Lineal*, 1929. b) *Journal of the
   Society of Architectural Historians*,
   May, 1959.

a

b

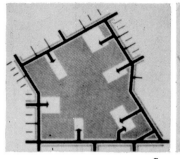

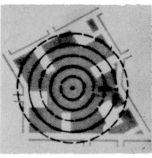

a   b   c

5. Victor Gruen Associates, proposal for Fort Worth's central district: a) Pedestrian island, belt-line access roads, perimeter parking lots; b) taxi and public transportation along loop roads; c) walking distances; d) slow-moving, electric shuttle cars.

6. Cars surrounding American shopping center. Courtesy London County Council, *The Planning of a New Town,* 1961

d

7. Detroit's Cobo Hall and Convention Arena. Courtesy Department Report and Information Committee, City of Detroit.

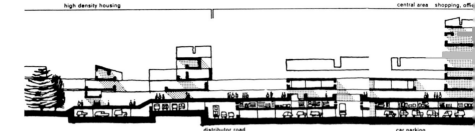

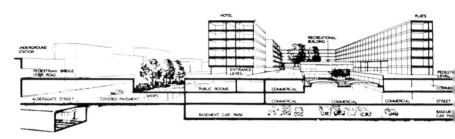

9. Barbican redevelopment, principle of multi-level circulation. Source: *The Architects' Journal*, June

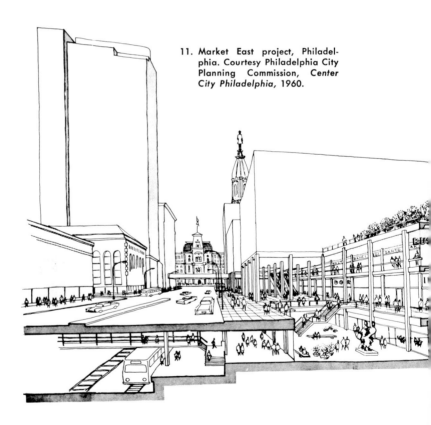

11. Market East project, Philadelphia. Courtesy Philadelphia City Planning Commission, *Center City Philadelphia*, 1960.

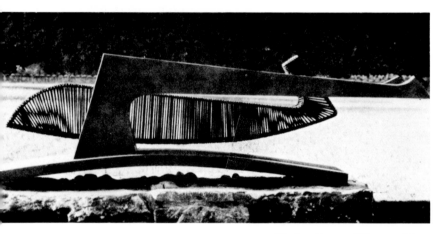

estrian deck

kanine storage   spine road

8. Central area of Hook, Hampshire, organization of traffic levels—design for a new town of 100,000. Courtesy London County Council, *The Planning of a New Town*, 1961.

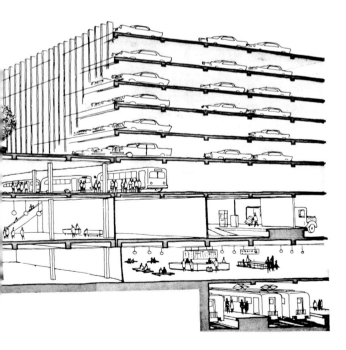

10. Jean-Georges Gisiger, sculpture.

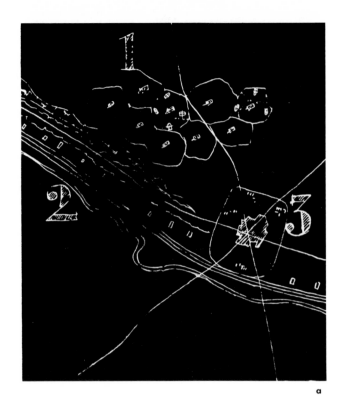

a

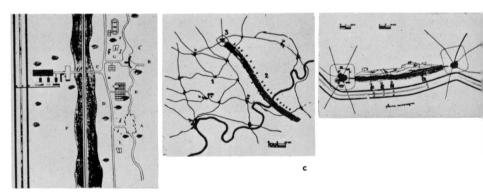

b

c

12. Le Corbusier, *The Regional City:* a), b), c), and d) Natural corridors between major cities lend themselves to rationalized linear development; transportation, industrial plants, residential communities. Entire scheme is envisioned as superimposed upon and insulated from countryside of village agriculture. Source: *Les Trois Établissements Humains*—Urbanisme des CIAM, Collection ASCORAL—Paris, Éditions Denoël, 1945.

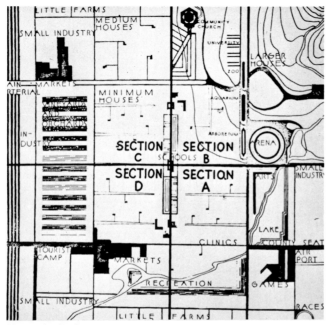

13. Frank Lloyd Wright, *Broadacre City*. Source: *When Democracy Builds,* by Frank Lloyd Wright, Copyright 1945 by University of Chicago Press.

14. Town Square, Stevenage, Hertfordshire. Courtesy Stevenage Development Corporation, Copyright.

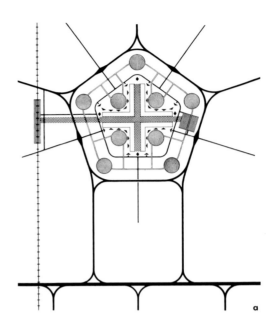

a

15. Coventry: a) Diagram of "city center"; b) upper shopping precinct. Courtesy Department of Architecture and Planning, City of Coventry.

b

photographed the Price Tower as a bronze spike driven into the Oklahoma sands at dawn, and the Northland shopping center as a glowing night-time fairyland at the end of a bloody flood marked by automobile tail lights. These are split-second impressions, relaxed moments in the great continuum of time— but they are the moment of revelation, the instants of recognition, when we learn what to seek in the experience of architecture and urban space.

Perhaps the best self-therapy for those who in self-defense have become city-blind is association with writers for whom the city is a passionate experience. Mary McCarthy's books on Florence and Venice offer such antidote. Eleanor Clark's *Rome and a Villa* is a work of the same genre but with even greater literary distinction. Coming still closer to grips with their subject, much the same enthusiasm is conveyed by Steen Eiler Rasmussen in his youthful love affair, *London: the Unique City.* The same city has also received in the artist James Bone's *London Perambulator* one of its few descriptions drawn from life unmarred by antiquarianism and nostalgia. One might enlarge the category to include guidebooks to the physical city, such as Ada Louise Huxtable's walking tours of New York City. Shoe leather is the cheapest teacher. It is no accident that powerfully motivated planners (like Haussmann) have been great walkers. But the urban vision, recalled and reshaped by the imagination, as well as the *aperçu,* has an important place in urban description, and some cities are almost incomplete without it. Lin Yutang's recent splendidly descriptive account, *Imperial Peking,* rightly contends that cities like London, Paris, Rome, and Vienna inspire affection, and his own book is almost a model of the art of recollection.

If we are to overcome the handicap of weak demand from aesthetic cripples, the indifference of fugitives from the city, and the lack of effective leadership in qualitative issues of urban form, a massive educational effort is required. The classroom is certainly a beginning. Exhibitions and books must be supplemented by films and other educational tools. But the best tool is experience, and the greatest need therefore is not only travel but the creation by every appropriate means of good examples. It has been well said that the city is a teacher. (Marc Chagall wrote of Paris, "At every step the city itself was my teacher in everything. The tradesmen in the market, the waiters, the porters, the peasants, the workmen—all were surrounded by something of that astonishing atmosphere of light and freedom (*lumière-liberté*) I have not found anywhere else." [15]) But we have not sufficiently realized that in addition to what Eduard Sekler has said about the tensions generated between extremes of choice, and the ensuing challenge of commitment that gives art reality, urbanity also educates in formal appearance.

One may be encouraged by the increasing recognition of these factors in urban design, but much remains to be done before the making of new cities and the refashioning of old ones can be viewed with satisfaction.

TOWARD A NEW URBAN DESIGN

Despite exceptions such as the great communal civic works of the Middle Ages, or the vast baroque monuments to autocracy, cities have been built in units of the individual lot and the individual building. Often these have been united by vernacular design principles. Continuity has ordinarily been achieved through tradition (as in Peking) or adherence to a continuing design principle (as in the arcades of Turin). Modern urban design is in the larger scale of contemporary building operations and more unified spans of design control. Today we build entire sections of a city or its suburbs according to a single master plan. The British or Swedish new towns with their social ideals, our own large-scale communities that are more often expressions of mass production efficiency and economy, the redevelopment of obsolescent urban areas that range up to 350 acres each, the building of universities, industrial complexes, or shopping centers according to a single plan—these enclaves constitute a unique contemporary urban design problem. There is neither

[15] Sekler, *op. cit.*, p. 75.

historical precedent for such scale, nor present means to control its design; nor can we find in the more organic cities of the past much help for the disjointed present.

The form of cities is set in part by such factors as the scale of development, which determines whether we shall have large office buildings or small shops; by transportation technology, which fills the city with elevated superhighways or the skies with jet planes; by an economic system of weak civic activities and aggressive private initiative, which leaves the appearance, location, and timing of principal buildings to the individual developer; or by a democratic form of local government in which a city council and mayor will decide on behalf of the local power structure what, for example, the proper form of recreation will be.

Much uncertainty among those concerned with urban design originates from the embarrassing wealth of new possibilities that have poured out of the industrial cornucopia, and the fertility of the modern architectural imagination. Ours is a period when new concepts of the city abound. A review of these visions and ideals is in progress, but it should be noted here that cities in the hands of their designers grow toward such concepts as well as out of existing conditions. Future cities may be a rationalized pioneer society of relatively self-sufficient families, each living on its own subsistence plot, interconnected by expressways, as Frank Lloyd Wright envisioned in Broadacre City. Or it may be the human swarm projected by Le Corbusier in urban concepts he has advanced since 1925 and realized more recently in his Marseilles apartments. It can be an almost wholly technical contrivance, as in the very beautiful conceptions of Paolo Soleri; or the social city of Vernon DeMars that is almost a theatre— perhaps a kind of Balinese theatre, in which the people are both actors and audience. Like the theatre, urban design can focus, concentrate, and enhance human experience.

From this situation we have come to face new and characteristic problems, the very statement of which would have sounded bizarre to the pre-industrial designer. One of these is the problem of urban vitality, how it can be assured, and how planning can contribute to the continued existence of the city. How, for that matter, can design contribute to urban life itself? It is at this point that reference should be made to the hoped-for vernacular city, the inescapable outgrowth of Jane Jacobs' recent writings and activities. Another problem is continuity, both of one building with another in the same sequence along a street, and historical continuity of later buildings with earlier ones. Wrapped up in this question is another: that of the preservation of historic areas, as in Annapolis, Maryland, not simply as museums (like Williamsburg) but as effectively functioning components of the city.[16]

One other characteristic of design deserves mention. Among the greatest satisfactions is to approach a design with the question "Where but here?" and to perceive how its innovation responds to a new potentiality in modern society or technology. Contemporaneity is an awful word but a useful concept. And it is a bracing experience. It is here, perhaps more than anywhere else, that urban designers reflect their debt to modern art and show that both are part of the same culture. Decisions about color, lighting, typography and signs, and other telltale details convey immediately and indelibly whether an urban design is old or new, whether it belongs to us. Contemporary urban design also expresses a concept of space, of buildings creating space and standing in space, that is distinctly of our time. It is a concept that breaks sharply with Alberti's Renaissance perspective, or with baroque spatial ideas as we see them at Versailles or in Washington.

Since urban design is commonly regarded as concerned with the "how" of city building rather than the "why" of it, may I again warn that this distinction seems to me futile in the face of the wellsprings of human need, the nature of design and designers, and the feedback or interrelationships that may readily be perceived in the urban design process. Based on the usual practice in architecture, where it is equally false, it is commonly assumed that the urban designer commences with a "program"

[16] Stephen W. Jacobs and Barclay G. Jones, "City Design through Conservation" (Berkeley: University of California, 1960) preliminary draft (mimeo.), 2 vols.

in which the utilitarian conditions of the city are set forth, and which it is his business to reflect and resolve in the design. So notorious has this lack of relationship become that the commonest criticism of urban designers is that they have "ignored the program." The fallacy of this approach is that design deals with potentialities, and no program is based on more than the sum of current experience. To design too close to such a program, therefore, is to condemn the new urban design to repeat the mistakes and limitations of the existing city. Unless we are to foreclose all prospect of forward development in our ideas of the city, and in the design of future cities, we must expect a larger contribution by designers; indeed, demand it of them, not simply at the end but at all stages of the urban design process. Fresh possibilities, offered by urban designers in the earliest sketches, should be received as inputs to survey and research efforts. If this is not done, the designer commences with a largely sterile analysis and sets of data that are scarcely related to the problems of design. Instead, we need dynamic design to which society can respond, and through which it can develop.

The existence of cities today is threatened by the disappearance of their traditional reasons for being, which largely determined their historical forms. Far from offering a means of defense against enemies, cities are particularly vulnerable to attack. Cities have no monopoly on trade as they had when the medieval markets flourished. People are not obliged to live in cities because the only jobs are there, or because transportation is lacking to allow them to live elsewhere. No city has a cultural monopoly; these are the days of mass media. The search for original art, music, theatre, dance takes one not merely to the central city but to many cities, suburbs, and summer festival centers, and ubiquitous transportation has led to the city that, like Wright's Broadacre City, "is everywhere and nowhere." Our cities are formed not by necessity and tradition like the design of a Navajo blanket, but by discipline, desire, and design.

If we are to have cities, I suggest, it must be because they make men. To do this our cities must be more attractive, more socially agreeable, offer higher standards of comfort and convenience, better opportunities for exchanging ideas and experiences as well as goods, and hold more beauty, than other possible ways of life. In ever-new ways, they must be strong magnets, vital centers. The reason for living in a city, or going there at all, as many since Aristotle have observed, is that it offers a better way to live.

CONCLUSION

Let me note with satisfaction the inclusion of the topic of urban design in a series such as this concerned mainly, as it should be, with the sober economic and political realities of urban development. Increasingly there is recognition of the failure of the wholly quantitative solution to urban problems. In its final report, the Outdoor Recreation Resources Review Commission has specifically noted the deficiencies in design of suburban communities built since the war as a major factor in the lack of common, everyday, outdoor recreations such as walking and cycling, and in the failure to provide public recreational areas over many square miles of recently developed residential suburbs. This is not a quantitative determination of open space. Population densities are low enough. But the place for much open space is not a superfluously large back yard but a suburban park. The problem is therefore one of suburban design. Cities are such compound structures of social activity as well as bricks and mortar, political loyalties as well as transportation movement, civic art as well as water supply and sewage disposal, that our contemplation of the motives of change, and any balanced proposals for new direction of growth, must reflect all the relevant factors. Otherwise, as Alan Jarvis has feared, we are in danger of becoming "a nation of Gross National People, chained by thoughtlessness and greed to that progress measured so well and so often by the Gross National Product." John Kenneth Galbraith's bitter "picnic by a polluted stream" has its urban equivalents in other environmental defilements of an affluent society whose cost is not measured in dollars alone. Nor is it the negative aspect that should concern us. The failure to develop more positive ideals toward which we can move is far more important, and the consequence of such failure will be far more profound.

As a plastic creation the city must speak to us of humanistic values. The dehumanized city that is hardly more than an artifact, a nonhuman world of technology and machine-made sterility, must give way to a city that has new meaning to the individual and the community as a social environment. In its form the individual should find the satisfactions of human scale, order, and coherence, and perceive in both function and symbol those qualities of the city which command his loyalty. In its form the community more broadly should find those perceptions and social values which support strong family and community activities and are fundamental to a workable urban society and a strong urban economy. The planning of such a city is dictated by the highest ideals of our civilization. It is not inconsistent with other parts of that civilization, or with city planning activities, but is rather its fulfillment. Its realization is the key to urban vitality and the continuity of historic urban social and aesthetic values into our own time.

A NOTE ON RESEARCH

Research in the aesthetics of urban form remains in a very undeveloped state. The principal effort thus far is exploratory, that made by Kevin Lynch in his initial work.[17] Lynch has inquired into such distinctively urban phenomena as pedestrian movement in city streets, and perceptions of the relationship of buildings of different uses as well as different sizes and shapes. In later investigations still to be published he has studied the city as perceived from the high-speed expressway. His approach is experimental, and it cannot yet be said to have gone far enough to be definitive. What Lynch has done, however, is important. He has formulated for the first time

[17] Kevin Lynch, *The Image of the City* (Cambridge, Mass.: Technology Press, 1960).

certain distinctive form problems of the city and outlined experimental methods and studies likely to resolve these problems. While there may well be a continuity between architectural aesthetics and the problems of urban form, Lynch has taken a fundamental step in establishing the latter as posing their own questions.

The rejection of the obsolescent, nonhuman urban creations of the nineteenth century, especially the flight from certain slum areas, may be a truer index of the value of a sound aesthetic environment than the deficiencies of the new suburban environments we have been creating since the war. Too little effort has been expended in the search for the economic value of the aesthetic environment. In housing economics we have been able to attribute specific values to apartments with balconies, houses with fireplaces, and other design features having little to do with the raw facts of space and structure but much to do with amenity. We know that certain tenants will pay more for these features, and we know how much more they will pay. We also know that location has a specific value, one not always attributable to economic factors, but frequently linked to design. Here we tread more uncertainly; but it should be possible, for example, to compare a house in Georgetown with an identical house in the adjoining community of Foggy Bottom, and to disentangle what parts of the extra value of the Georgetown house are due to its location in a community with definite boundaries, quiet streets, shade trees, ample gardens, historical associations and architectural homogeneity, and what parts are due to its location in a community of high-income families, high property values and accessibility. We can also determine just which families will pay these premiums. Studies of aesthetic value can be usefully pursued at the point of decision when families move in or out, when they buy or sell. They should have a priority second only to experiments and demonstrations in the design of the urban environment itself.

The search for more seemly cities has received the highest legal endorsement (if, indeed, it were needed) from the Supreme Court in *Berman* v. *Parker*. But if the goal of the future city is thus established, and the social and economic rationale for it is being developed, the methods by which it can be realized are still to be formulated and accepted. These questions have been posed most sharply in the efforts to create new sections of cities through urban renewal, and it is there that design competitions have both clarified the issues of urban aesthetics and surmounted the sternly economic admonition that the job should be awarded to the lowest cash bidder. In Philadelphia, San Francisco, and Washington, outstanding designs for new urban areas have been selected from among those submitted by teams of architects and developers. These now deserve critical appraisal and will receive it in Grady Clay's forthcoming work, *The Competitors.* Perhaps the most notable result of this experience is the rapid evolution of design concepts under the stimulus of competitive conditions that reward such development. The pursuit of new urban aesthetics can also be seen in Philadelphia, Detroit, Washington, and other cities where the two-dimensional analytic planning techniques have been balanced recently by a new emphasis on design, where the model has begun to supplement the plan, and the image of a city has begun to appear that more nearly fits our more numerous, affluent, mobile, leisured and better educated urban society.

. . . . . .

For editorial assistance and the preparation of the accompanying illustrations I am indebted to Miss Gail Raywid and Mrs. Gudrun Huden.—F.G.

LEONARD J. DUHL, M.D., is a psychiatrist at the National Institute of Mental Health who has long been concerned with social problems and the urban community. As part of his work in long-range planning and development he has worked closely with city planners, economists, educators, and others, trying to understand the relationship between these factors and mental health, and has written extensively in professional journals on aspects of this subject. Dr. Duhl was born in New York in 1926. He received his training at Columbia University, Albany Medical College, and the Menninger Foundation School of Psychiatry.

THE HUMAN MEASURE: MAN AND FAMILY IN MEGALOPOLIS

LEONARD J. DUHL

GLENN WAS A SEVEN-YEAR-OLD BOY living in an urban village of 5,000 persons on the West Coast of the United States. I remember Glenn as a smiling, toothless urchin, dark as pitch, dressed in long pants. He was shoeless, standing in the middle of a mud puddle on a main street in the community.

Glenn lived in a slum. The surrounding communities called it a slum, as did the health officials, welfare people, and the police. The city planners in their evaluation of the area made it official: anyone could see that Glenn lived in a slum. It covered an area of thirty blocks; a railroad bounded it on one side, heavy industry on two others, and a swampy, grass-filled bay on the last. Rain made the wooden dwellings look like the stilt houses of the tropics as it filled the streets and yards around them. Glenn and his friends splashed in the puddles of rain water mixed with sewage which came from a better part of town through 10-inch sewer pipes emptying into an open ditch close to Glenn's house.

Of the many churches in this small community, most were odd sects with poorly trained ministers. The stores scattered throughout the community were typically small, and they boasted high prices for the people who shopped for one or two items many times each day.

"No co-operation" was the verdict of the Health Department. It reported a lack of interest in the free, mass X-ray program; inadequate diet was frequent. Desertions, common-law and impermanent marriages, and a dearth of males supporting families caused welfare agencies much concern. The police could point to a street of bars, joints, prostitutes, and narcotic dens. The planners pronounced that the site utilization was all wrong: the slum could better be used for industry. The site, the buildings, the human problems, and the official reactions led to an almost unanimous conclusion to "wipe it out!"

Each of these specialized community viewpoints saw the area as an inescapable problem; a piece of land that must be dealt with. The ground rules by which planners plan the use of space validated the decision. Indeed, the current hierarchy of values in our urban communities may not have permitted other kinds of alternatives, but ground rules are subject to challenge, especially when they find human life and needs to be less important than the other factors which go into this kind of decision-making. Two kinds of values conflict here; to resolve the conflict not unfavorably to the human factor will require a deeper and more sympathetic perception of the life patterns and needs of the many little societies of which the city is compounded.

The case of Glenn is instructive. His mother was a "widder woman" with five other children, some younger and some older. Most of the women around were "widders," some of whom had even been married in church, but not Glenn's mother, Bessie.

Most of Glenn's neighbors, tempted by the high wages that would bring them a few of their desires—a radio, a car, clothes, and other material things—had migrated from the rural Deep South during the war to answer the need for labor in the big city not far from Glenn's swampy street. Unlike many others, they did not take to the nearby city's war housing, the crowding, dirt, or noise. These people had a long history of women-run households dating from the period of slavery, and the women wanted homes. Economics and segregation dictated their settling in this unlikely spot almost as squatters. The men came, built homes, produced children, and went; the women stayed and raised families. For them the community offered some security and stability.

The women loved their young children. Shamelessly, they breast-fed them at home or in public. They took chicken bones out of soup for them to suck as their first foods. Glenn was raised on scrapings from adult foods; he had hot food before he went to school, and most of the time he found limeade in the house when he came home. The maternal factors in Glenn's life were many and positive.

Glenn went to school until he was 15. Then the world closed in on him and his family, and he had to work. His sisters started work even earlier because the family needed money, and it was easy for the girls to find unskilled jobs.

The street with the bars causing the police so much concern was shunned and condemned by the local Negro community. Not only did Glenn's neighbors avoid it, they often found ways to by-pass the whole street. The pleasure-seekers and the pleasure-givers came from elsewhere, and the worthless land allowed them a place to operate undisturbed. Delinquency was high on this street, in contrast to the surrounding lower class Negro community. The members of the Negro community were shackled by their previous lack of opportunity. They were lost in the political and economic jungle around them, a jungle that others know well and have techniques to handle. They did not understand that doctors, social workers, and police were there to help. *All* agencies were equated with the police—part of a hostile, threatening world compelling them to conform to values they didn't understand. "If they'd only change their ways," was the plaintive hope of the outside community. "If we could seduce them to change" was the sophisticated way to say the same thing. No one accepted them with their different values. No opportunity was allowed them to change themselves or define their futures . . . and this is the way it usually works out.

Glenn's case makes a powerful perspective for the curious fact that man is conquering outer space before he is master of his earth space, an historical heirloom of haphazard development by human beings with needs for space in which to work, live, play, and procreate.

Planning for the use of space is a complex process of design and choice which involves innumerable variables. Social and technical advances have reduced this complexity through the dimensions of economics, transportation, design, and engineering; but human, psychological, and social values still follow as afterthoughts, like icing on the planning cake. Glenn and the nameless multitude like him make a powerful case for psychosocial values transcending all other considerations in the planning of urban space and its physical environment.

THE ECOLOGY OF URBAN SPACE

The apparently haphazard development of our urban communities has a historic logic. From the beginning of time, communities have grown to meet the functional and psychological needs of individuals, families, and social groups. The physical form of each community reflected the psychological needs and the hierarchy of values of its citizens. A social emphasis on self-preservation produced a community surrounded by a protective wall or moat. A scarcity of usable land led to a concentrated pattern of development. Trading centers exploited the intersections of water and land routes and centered around great open market squares. The form of the urban community evolved from the social needs and opportunities for meeting them.

The modern American world has many patterns. The upper-income groups who desire space can afford to move from the center of the city to choice land farther out. Room is left in the center, or in undesirable swamplike areas such as Glenn's home, for the continually needed new migrants. The increasing productivity of the labor force, the growth of the service industries, and welfare services provide opportunities for members of the working class to move up and out of the slums. However, the fact that lower-income groups want greatly to increase their income and live more comfortably does not necessarily imply any great desire to change their patterns of living. There is security in crowding and closeness to people with similar religious views, values, recreations, family patterns. Ghettos are made by both the oppressors and the minorities themselves.

The employment slots for unskilled or semi-skilled workers are filled by workers from the rural South, the Appalachian Highlands, or Puerto Rico. Since comfort and security come from people they know, they create in the slums urban versions of rural villages which become tightly knit communities with more social value than the sterile new housing which wouldn't meet their needs even if they were acceptable as tenants. The few who can move may find themselves unable to adapt to their new environment. This may result in a lashing out at the environment leading to destruction of property and their ultimate removal.

Many critics of the Megalopolis point to the current disorganized state of our urban areas, claiming that its pattern does not meet basic human needs. Some have asked for the development of garden cities, restricted in size and providing for all the needs of people. But not all will find a garden city a welcome relief from the chaos of a modern city. For some people the design of a clean new city may mean not peace and serenity but boredom, a lack of the color and vitality that old cities have provided in chaos. Color and vitality need not be lost in new communities if we consciously tried to build it into our planning.

The ecological world of some human beings cannot be contained within a physically or geographically defined community: they use the physical environment as a resource in contrast with the lower socio-economic groups who incorporate the environment into the self. The ecological community for this upper stratum of society is, in fact, the world. When we design any one community, plans for utilizing its space are dependent both upon the internal needs of this group and its relationship to the total world. Communication and transportation have become very important for this group whose ecological world has become so broad. For others the world is still quite small, and most often it is a world of slums—even Brasília sprouts its slums. And within these chaotic slums the total life of the poor is led. The current concept of garden cities leaves the needs of these people unmet.

I will leave to the economists and others the responsibility for coping with the economic interdependence of the world of the upper socio-economic classes, and to the communication experts to point out the mass interdependence of our information needs. My concern is with needs of the individual, the family, and various significant groups and institutions within this large ecological system. The lower socio-economic strata appear to some to be not so fortunate as the upper classes. They lack mobility. Though they often work in the better areas, manual workers tend to live closer to their relatives than clerical and professional people. Their ties of kinship mean more to them, and with less money available, distance is more of a handicap.

Geography has more meaning. The importance of a house close to other houses, gregariousness, an apparent absence of privacy, and the presence of noise are but some of the needs of these people. The physical environment is part of the individual's identity. Being squeezed into the sterilized sardine-can-existence of the housing project, being forced to move to a fearful world away from their own kind is too much for them to take. They are more likely to choose another slum over our new communities, housing projects, or garden cities. And this is all we have to offer.

These slum communities have attractions for many groups that cannot be surpassed by anything we now have on our planning boards. This does not mean slums must be preserved, but rather that new cities must find ways of responding to the needs of all segments of our population. Social welfare services which offer the possibility of a changed way of life have their attractions, but involuntarily changed behavior can be costly to the individual concerned. A variety of apparently unrelated pathologies may develop which on careful evaluation can be traced to the impact of a forced change in life style. The impact of the planners' manipulations of our physical space falls most heavily on the lower socio-economic groups. Their rights to their aspirations and the satisfaction of their needs require a new dimension of physical planning.

HUMAN BEHAVIOR AND COMMUNICATIONS

In the past an individual was born, lived, and died within one small community. His home was a place within which almost all the important functions of life were performed—birth, child-rearing, education, marriage, and death. The home was the prime meeting-place; colleagues working on the same problem met there, discussed their work, and laid plans. Furthermore, the home was often one of the most important centers for religious activity. Such communities still exist. Many of the communities of the lower socio-economic class still have this pattern. Change is imminent or already here for many of these persons. Raising the standard of living, changes in land policy and public ownership, and an increase in welfare, health services, and education have in many places caused marked changes in life patterns. Housing and new buildings without concern with these issues offer no solution.

As the amount of communication and the possibility of mobility increases, the home, and thus the family, begins to play a slightly different role. Aspirations change, but basic patterns remain. The place where people must get together for some combined activity, such as drawing water from the pump for washing or drinking, becomes a center of socialization. As men become involved in trade, their places of business become centers for communication between themselves and those to whom they sell their wares. The inn, the tavern, the coffee house replace some of the functions of the earliest home. There are fascinating documentations of the English tavern being used for business transactions; a coffee house was the birthplace of Lloyds of London, and a pub was the site of the beginning of the Royal Society. Modern equivalents of these institutions are credit restaurants for Madison Avenue, and groceries for the slum.

As the social and economic dimensions of our world have grown and changed, more and more functions of the home and community have been taken over by specialized institutions. Discussions of business and science take place in convention cities in hotels and meeting halls that specialize in these services. A large variety of specialized professional, lobbyist, business, or special interest organizations develop which, through their central headquarters, provide meeting space, opportunity for communication and for effecting decision-making. Not all parts of the population have this opportunity.

When Glenn's family and neighbors had community and personal problems, they gathered in stores and homes to talk them over but rarely had any opportunity to be effective. They did not know how to deal with the planning body, the welfare board, or the health department. To cope with a middle-class officialdom they needed a kind of help which required not so much changing their values as developing relationships to allow them to participate in decisions affecting them. Co-operation was attained only when they learned that they too had political power and, accordingly, the ability to influence planning decisions. In this fashion, land planning *is* related to social welfare planning. It is related to community development, as well. Such a behavior-changing process depends on the effectiveness of arrangements to facilitate social communications. Thus, to plan today for this exceedingly complex world, we must develop a *comprehensive* system of communication at a relatively low cost in money and time. Community development is one of the means of communication offering high return for the dollar. In the past, community development had been applied to rural, non-urban, and underdeveloped areas; now ways must be developed to apply community development approaches in the complex urban world. Urban development requires data collection, planning, co-ordination, service, and evaluation. At present, we have the technology but not the social machinery to cope with this problem.

THE FAMILY IN THE URBAN CULTURE

Even if we assume that society wishes and is willing to allocate its funds, and that we have the ability to take care of the basic nutritional, biological, medical, and economic needs of individuals not answered by a technologically perfect society, there are still the questions of meeting the psychological and social needs of individuals. We know that a child, soon after birth, requires a close and intimate relationship with a mothering figure. In our society we have made the decision that in all possible cases this will be the real mother; arrangements such as "widder women" may be acceptable to the child and family, but not to society at large.

Other countries have found a variety of ways to care for children so that the mother could work outside the home. To meet the needs of the very young infant and the working mother there must be space for communal nurseries in which substitute parents provide the attention, welfare, and warmth that the child needs. In Israel, the *kibbutz*—a reflection of a social philosophy of a large segment of the population—has pioneered in the development of such programs. The child *can* develop into a psychologically secure individual, but his long-range social development is affected so that he can not effectively fill other roles of which the country has need. There are reports that, for this reason, in some quarters these programs are losing popularity and support.

In the U.S.S.R., children are placed in communal nurseries as early as possible. The Soviet Union feeling that it is more important for the child to become identified with the state than with the family is reflected in decisions about the utilization of space. Housing does not provide space for the many activities we associate with the American family and home, but space is usually available for communal clubs and for worker and group activities. Despite the scarcity of home space, the family has survived. Reports indicating that Soviet family life is similar to American patterns suggest that basic psychological needs can neither be legislated away nor crowded out. Family life can take place in a coal mine if necessary; but why subject people to this?

In America, we feel it is extremely important to maintain the integrity of the family. In large portions of our population some of the traditional roles of the family are now taken over by the community, but the individual family is left with the basic responsibility for the early nurturance and beginning socialization of the child. Living situations must, therefore, provide for families to raise their children in as close and as intimate a manner as they wish. Where we do not ensure that families can do this, or where society does not provide or communicate a clear model for behavior, other sanctioning groups take over the responsibility; the delinquent gang, for example, while sanctioning asocial behavior, demonstrates again in its concerns with "turf" how important place and space are to one's identity.

The mother's needs must be recognized, too. They can be met by a variety of means. She needs to share her experience and concerns with others. Wherever several generations still live together—as in the lower socio-economic classes—she obtains support and knowledge from this extended family or from neighbors. In the United States these extended families have begun to break up with inadequate replacement.

Mobility within the United States, however, is making a marked impact on the extended family so that the new mother has to turn to other resources. Many of our suburban communities are composed of young families, all at about the same stage of family development, who become very dependent upon each other for support. This is a need to be considered when we plan urban communities. This kind of suburban community, which provides support services either officially or unofficially, is capable of meeting some of the needs of even the lowest socio-economic groups in ways that could avoid the large drain on the official agencies which take over the role of the extended family.

Middle-class suburbs that have become maternal communities may seem no different from the manless Negro community previously mentioned. However, the meaning of father is as different in the two groups as is the physical environment. Ideally, fathers are vital to the upbringing of all families. In the Negro community father has never been there, and thus in some ways is not missed. Only outsiders see the need for the missing father. In middle-class suburbia a missing father is of concern to almost everyone.

Increasing mobility and the decreasing role of the extended family and intimate friends generate a rising demand for public health, education, and welfare services. Community after community is reacting to newly apparent needs of children. Where heretofore we were satisfied with modest education, recreation, health, and welfare services, the demand for comprehensive services is increasing markedly. Although this is more vocal in upper-middle-class communities, nevertheless they foretell the values of other parts of our American society.

THE CHILD IS FATHER OF THE MAN

As a child grows he learns how to behave and what to expect from those around him. In earlier times the child learned these things primarily from the parents; now the school has replaced the parents both in time spent with the child and in this socializing process. However, learning does not come exclusively from school. It is an inconceivably complex process which is fed by one's peers, mass communication media, and the total community. It feeds upon vital experiences—the exploration of new environments, the sensing of open space, perception of nature, and the stimulation of a city.

Glenn learned his lessons well from his peers. His attitude towards marriage was set by his mother's experience. The role of the man and his relationship to women became clear. The value of education, the reasons for work, the type of play, the relationship to the "outside world" and the meaning of authority were taught him overtly and subtly. The information he received from television and other outside communication reinforced his separateness. No school, no social worker, no new housing project could teach him differently, unless *he* was motivated to learn. The learning of new ways is a slow process and cannot be spoon-fed. The desire to change can be encouraged and supported, but when the supports and silent arguments from one's own social environment are against change, little can be done.

A child reared in a community in which there is a homogeneity of city values and opportunities has little chance to develop his abilities and skills. In our more rural communities the consolidated school district can counteract its isolation, if it is aware and economically able, by offering a multiplicity of subjects and experiences. The child coming from a larger community, paradoxically, is faced with a relatively specialized education that reflects the dominant values of the surrounding community; the limited choice offered by both the school and the community reduces his opportunities to utilize his potentials. In major cities, such as New York, where the population and resources are very large, specialized schools offer some chance for matching the child and the school. In most urban communities this opportunity is not available.

James Conant points out that the children of the suburban schools lack the opportunity to go into non-academic training even if their abilities point in this direction. The child in the slum school is confronted with a school which has become a controlled disciplinary institution, or with a value system that directs him toward white-collar work for which he is ill prepared and to which it is not likely that society will admit him. The motivations of the disadvantaged child and his community in all of their social and economic facts of life, plus the positive conviction that change is possible offer the only feasible starting point. To go beyond this will require a new kind of planner with the potential, skill, and motivation to work with these people.

URBAN RENEWAL AND SOCIAL CONSERVATION: THE CONFLICT

It has been argued that the availability of cheap transportation and communication will make it possible for people to come in contact with an increased number of opportunities. However, no matter how complex and advanced our world is, propinquity still plays an important role in the development of values, careers, and patterns of behavior. Various studies point to the importance of groupings in the development of friendship and socialization patterns. Like attracts like; even within heterogeneous communities, similar people most often attract their counterparts; color segregation is replaced by economically and socially determined segregations.

There are critical moments in the lives of individuals when they cast about for new ways of behaving which will be determined in large degree by the opportunities around them. Under certain kinds of stress, people are willing and able to learn skills of which they never thought themselves capable. The armed forces during war demonstrated that new patterns of friendships can evolve when social barriers are taken down. People of diverse interests can find common concerns around a work situation. Around these interests propinquity permits and encourages the formation of intimate social contacts. Legislation and physical structure allow for this to occur but do not guarantee it. Much more is needed than opportunity.

Children can make contact outside their tightly knit families and communities. This may be a point of great concern or satisfaction, depending on your vantage point. To the family or community fearful for its existence, the easy availability of new ideas through school contacts is a threat. To the child it may mean freedom and an ability to come closer to the American norm and conformity. To the social worker it means change of patterns in a new generation and giving up the untenable patterns of the minority. The either-or view of this problem avoids facing the critical question as to the potential gain to the majority from the minority or deviant. Can the behavior of minority or deviant groups be preserved to the advantage of themselves and to society? Can we help them build on the strength they have in order to play a more active role in modern urban society? The current dogmas of land planning that affect minority groups may resolve this question to the detriment of our total society. Urban renewal provides a case in point.

Jane Jacobs is typical of some critics of urban renewal who point an accusing finger at the practice of tearing down some slums to replace them with sterile housing projects or dispersed living arrangements. She has been accused of having "too much nostalgia for the slums," and of preventing the development of "real plans" for the redevelopment of our cities. Many of these accusations, I feel are grossly misdirected. Studies of slum communities subjected to urban renewal give us an opportunity to understand something about the behavior of people living within them. The psycho-social mechanisms of slum life reported by Lindemann, Fried, and Gans in the West End project, and by Jane Jacobs and others meet not only the economic but the social and psychological needs of the slum inhabitants. These critics of urban renewal are calling not for a halt to slum clearance, but for planning that will weigh in its calculations the importance of patterns of life and the needs of the spectrum of groups who get caught up in the plans.

Much can be lost by a homogenization of society. Even the poor of the Negro slum have something positive to offer our larger American culture: the music of jazz, the warmth of the mother-child relationship, the potential for poetry, art, and for a wide variety of occupations should be built upon and not destroyed. Is wiping out a culture always more conducive to increasing human potentialities than building on the past strengths?

The kind of vitality found in the slums can be preserved in older communities by rehabilitation and community development and built into the new developments in our urban communities. Too often newly planned communities reject the values of this vitality in favor of a kind of design purity which feverishly excites only city planners and architects. City planners are *not* playing a game on a massive, terrestrial chess board, rearranging pieces so that the city looks magnificent in models, on paper, from the air. A vice president of the Prudential Insurance Company has appropriately observed that if the planners had little people to test out all their magnificent chess board models they might be able to determine whether living would be as pleasant, enjoyable, vital, and stimulating as postulated.

We do not have these little people for the big chess boards; we can only substitute research into human behavior. Simulation techniques and other kinds of analysis can be as useful as the little man. Primarily, though, we must acknowledge our own blind spots and recognize that various minority groups in our society have different patterns of living than we of the dominant middle class.

PLANNING URBAN SPACE FOR HUMAN WELFARE

Glenn and his mother Bessie are in a community that has many parallels in the United States. If their community were cleared, they would move elsewhere, and the physical blight would spread with little improvement of the total situation. As they are approached by agencies of social welfare, they retreat, setting up protections against the hostile world. They create a "culture of poverty" reinforced by the group they live with. Like "rate busting" in industry which is controlled by subtle pressure, the culture of poverty has many means of maintaining itself.

For Glenn's sake, urban renewal, city planning, and social welfare must be wed. City planning now considers the psychosocial needs of people secondary to other needs. These problems can perhaps be seen more clearly elsewhere as America faces up to poverty in the world. Yet, we will be unable to cope with that abroad unless we face our own.

Housing and building are not the whole answer when population explosions and poverty are widespread. People are rising up to fight against the imposition of outside plans upon them. Colonialism is being replaced by nationalism. Our own minorities are far from facing the extremes of the emerging nations, but they also are seeking some control over their own fate. Increasingly, their demands rise along with refusals to accept housing and urban renewal as it is currently defined. When we learn how to help these people to help themselves, we can begin to answer questions of space utilization. Clearly, the planner must decentralize the decision-making procedure in urban planning; perhaps community development as exemplified by Poston and others is the best current answer we now have to this problem, but it needs a new form, new tools, new skills, and people in order to meet urban problems.

Social or individual pathologies are not equated with space characteristics of cities directly. Rather, space can play a vital role in almost all aspects of human life, used in many different ways. Further, consideration of human needs can lead to more adequate utilization of space, and this space utilization is dependent upon the hierarchy of values expressed by those who make the decisions.

Currently, the decisions are primarily economic, and yet they affect the totality of human lives. Human factors and human questions are becoming more important and insisting on a different utilization of space. Those people responsible for the long-range planning of our communities must anticipate this new demand and adequately plan for it in the present.

Change, needs for closeness and propinquity, appetites for adventure and new experience and exploration are part of a wide variety of other human requirements. Consider, if you will, a recent ecological study of animal behavior that should be of vital concern to planners. Animals brought up in situations of high density become incapable of eating, sleeping, or procreating in relative solitude, and exhibit a wide variety of pathology. Density, with a tremendous increase in communications, interactions and, perhaps, "input overload" (too much incoming information for the organism to handle) can result in a breakdown of the individual. The breakdown may take a wide variety of forms: biological pathology, psychological abnormalities, and socially unacceptable behavior. Adult death rates and foetal and infant mortality may increase, and aggression may replace co-operation and play.

This finding in animals confirms findings on input overload in human individuals and groups. We must therefore protect ourselves as much from overstimulation as from isolation. Thus, the planning of our communities will need to avoid too much stimulation, choice, and information without respite. Although some individuals can find ways of protecting themselves against this, others can not. Too often society finds ways of drumming more information and experience into people than they can handle. How can space utilization provide a respite? A society which provides recreation, open space, and perhaps vacation retreats cheaply and close to centers of work and living offers such respite. A society which provides this resource to only selected segments of our population is failing to meet its responsibility.

Open space, when once it is experienced, can rarely be replaced. It provides for us that continuity with the past which our personal identity requires. The values of open space change, too. Wilderness areas now appear tame to our youth. They are turning, either actually or in fantasy, to adventures in newly available space: spelunking, parachute-jumping, free air dives, and scuba diving have become important ways of coping with the unknown and thus with their own selves. Perhaps the true reason for our massive space effort is the hope that outer space will provide enough room for this kind of adventure.

Behavioral and social scientists do not have all the answers about human needs and space; much more has to be done. The people planned for may have more of the answers, if we can find the techniques to extract them. The people in planning must try to evolve as broad a research base as they possibly can. Up to now they have been drawing on the experience of many disciplines; they should continue to do so. However, unless planners develop this broad base for current planning activities, and for the training of the many needed people, we will fail miserably. Our cities and communities will, in fact, continue in their crisis-ridden, haphazard development.

THE PHYSICAL PLANNING PROCESS

The case of Glenn—and of untold thousands like him—should bring front and center the need for a more effective psycho-social framework for planning the allocation of space.

The land allocation will have to reserve enough space to meet a wide variety of new needs. Physical planners will be forced to develop their plans in conjunction with social welfare planning. Where economic dimensions, engineering factors, and "pure" design have largely pre-empted the planning of urban space, planning to meet social and welfare needs will reshuffle the planner's strategies and his hierarchy of values by giving priority to the simple question—what are the human implications of planning action? Will a road splitting a community cause a social disruption which will result in a greater social cost than changing the highway pattern? Will a renewal project eliminate a slum only to aggravate the situation of those remaining? The notion of planning, furthermore, needs revision to include those planned for in the decision-making processes.

There is a need for the kind of planning that allows homogeneity within heterogeneous areas so that the needs of individuals and families can be coped with by people of similar background and experience in a smaller community within the larger heterogeneous communities. We need to think in terms of many kinds of communities making possible lively alternatives in living arrangements. A new "mind set" about our urban communities can increase the opportunities for finding a satisfying and productive way of life. It must acknowledge at least the following points:

1. Physical and spatial planning cannot be isolated from a broader concern with the needs of the community and its people. Consideration must be given to the complex relationships among space, buildings, institutions, industries, socio-economic class, organizations, social and physical mobility, play, health, welfare, and education.

2. Our use of space reflects the values of the part of our society empowered to make decisions. Some exploit these opportunities for personal benefit, or impose on minorities a way of life not compatible with their own traditions, values, or interests.

3. Utilization of space is only partially a reflection of physical structure and design. It is much more a function of the user's perception of his inner and outer environment, his way of life, values, needs, and customary patterns of behavior. Thus open space means freedom to some and fear and insecurity to others.

4. Membership in a privileged socio-economic class brings freedom, mobility, and an opportunity to control one's environment, frequently at the expense of adversely situated groups. So physical planning imposes most rigorously on those areas of the community inhabited by the lower classes, playing havoc with their ways of life, their roles in the larger community, and their opportunities.

5. New institutions must be created to meet those needs that the rising standard of living is bringing to the forefront. Future space utilization must anticipate these and other emerging needs.

6. Certain individual developmental needs related to nurturance—freedom, constraint, exposure to experiences, and opportunities for use of potentialities—are limited or expanded by certain patterns of living, which, in turn, are affected by the ways in which space is organized in our communities.

In the past, what has looked haphazard was, in fact, a functional development. Now our community is so large and complex that if we forfeit the opportunity to plan, the result will not be functional but destructive. Planning can only assume control of the future by mobilizing all of the skills and knowledge at our disposal; knowledge of the human being is the foremost of these.

Roland Artle is associate professor at the University of California, Berkeley, where he is teaching courses in managerial economics and microeconomic theory. This paper was co-sponsored by the Real Estate Research Program at the University of California, Berkeley. Mr. Artle's publications include two books, one of which, *Studies in the Structure of the Stockholm Economy* (1959), will be republished shortly. He is presently working on an econometric study of growth in California and on a mathematical model of planning. Mr. Artle was born in Sweden in 1926. He holds degrees from the Stockholm School of Economics, Sweden, and the University of Oxford, England. He has taught at Harvard University, the Stockholm School of Economics, and the University of Stockholm.

PUBLIC POLICY AND THE SPACE ECONOMY OF THE CITY

ROLAND ARTLE

WELL IN EXCESS OF 90 PER CENT of the United States economic activity is concentrated in that small fraction of the nation's land surface which we call urban. This tremendous concentration of productive and consumption activity exists by virtue of the extraordinary conditions of viability of the urban organism. One set of these conditions has to do with the anatomy of the city—its arrangement in space in ways to assure interaction among the multitude of consuming and producing activities that compose the urban economy. This is the set of conditions on which I intend to concentrate—the network of interaction which I call communication and in which I include both the exchange of information and the physical movement of goods and people.

First, I shall try to see how communication relates to the scheme of the urban economy and describe this in the form of a loose decision-model which can help us to understand and manipulate critical conditions and processes associated with urban development. Since I want to see this manipulation directed toward goals, especially the goal of efficiency, I shall explore some special problems associated with efficiency considerations in urban organization. Finally, I hope to cast around for some of the main processes and factors at work in the dynamics of urban growth and change.

THE ROLE OF COMMUNICATIONS

Workers in their homes busy watching closed circuit TV-screens, pressing buttons, and manipulating computers and microwave radio instruments, thereby guiding and controlling the operations of plants and factories located far away—such are the stuff of fantasy and science fiction and yet no more than extrapolations of a development that we have witnessed for a long time in our economic life and particularly in our urban economic life. This is the accelerating revolution in communications technology characterized by increased substitutability between different channels of communications. If such dreams were ever to come true, they would prompt great changes in the way urban economies function, and, consequently, in the spatial arrangement of the many kinds of activities on the urban scene. If people could carry out their jobs without leaving home, they would recreate at least superficially the relative self-sufficiency of the preindustrial household. Clearly elimination of the journey to work would give rise to great savings of human time. At the same time, the journey to work has been the single most important determinant in the dimensioning of our urban transportation systems—indeed, in the organization of our cities; the peak-hour concentrations of workers driving to their jobs or homes generate extravagant congestion costs for all users. If this flow of people could be replaced by a flow of information, we could substitute relatively inexpensive message-transmitting capacity for relatively expensive transportation capacity, and the bonds between work-place locations and residential locations would gradually weaken.

To city planners who have to make commitments in the form of long-range plans for freeways, rapid transit systems, and other large-scale investments, such dreams may seem more like nightmares. But, of course, that particular type of development may forever be confined to the world of dreams. The cost of decentralization necessary for the operation of such systems may be prohibitive. Other factors in the less remote future—such as a more widespread introduction of staggered hours of work and leisure to increase the rate of utilization of existing transportation networks and other facilities—may set the stage for some alternative path of development. Whatever course the actual development will take, it will be a manifestation of the search for new or cheaper ways of communicating within the urban economy which rests on the proposition that substitutions among different modes of communication are feasible.

Therefore, when studies of long-range development in urban areas focus narrowly on transportation dimensions, they may fail to comprehend some of the substitution processes in *communications* activity generally, for communication encompasses all point-to-point transfers, including shipments of goods and passenger transportation, in addition to transmission of energy and of messages. These processes, in turn, will deflect the future course of affairs and set new conditions for the future pattern of urban spatial organization.

To see how these communications phenomena enter into urban economic analysis, recall, first, that the economist often distinguishes three fundamental categories of economic activity. These are production, consumption, and capital formation of investment activity. In studies of a regional economy, such as an urban economy, he finds it necessary to recognize explicitly a fourth category, "foreign" or external trade, to account for the substantial portion of the production activity in an urban area which is geared to supplying customers outside the area and for the resources and other inputs used in local activity which originate outside the area. These goods and services flowing out of and into the area, are the "exports" and "imports" of the local economy.

We may think of local consumption, local investment, and exports as three *uses* of the products that are imported or created through local production. A fourth use is accounted for by the outputs of local firms which become the inputs of other local firms.

Since most of the economic units are spatially separated activities, the interaction between them takes the form of a multitude of point-to-point transfers of goods, persons, or information: the interaction between producers and users is analogous to the interaction between senders and receivers, so that the production or consumption activity that takes place at any particular site generates communications activity with other sites.

These relationships between producers and users can be neatly presented in the form of two-way "from-to" tables. The various categories of production activity are specified along one axis and the various user categories along the other, so that each "cell" in the table specifies the volume of the output flowing from the producer specified on one axis to the user specified on the other. Further, we may think of the associated communications activities as being recorded along a third axis in terms of some appropriate unit, such as the *transaction*. A transaction may be a shipment of goods from a manufacturer to a wholesaler's warehouse. It may be a telephone call or a flow of water through a pipe. Since transactions may differ greatly in the type and extent of *communications channel capacity* that they use, different operational units of transactions will accordingly have to be introduced. One unit of transaction will relate to such a channel capacity as a street, another to a telephone line, and so on. Thus, we end up with a set of tables—one for each type of communication channel studied—which provides a way of looking at the interrelation between production, consumption, capital formation, exports and imports, *and* communications activity in an urban area. We immediately note two kinds of substitutions among communications activities: substitution can occur *within* a table—a substitution of one set of senders for another, or *between* tables—a substitution of one kind of communication channel for another.

Communications activity, then, measured in terms of transactions or some other unit, is a fundamental economic category. It serves to indicate the nature and intensity of spatial linkages among economic activities. An understanding of these linkages and their changes is the key to an understanding of the distribution in the urban space of firms, residences, and other economic units: we are able, thus, to relate the spatial organization of the city to other and more fundamental economic relationships which we accept on theoretical grounds.

Economic analysis of urban phenomena and events, then, needs to recognize not four but five fundamental economic categories: production, consumption, capital formation, exports and imports, and communications. The failure to treat communications activity as interrelated with the other four economic categories has probably led so many analysts fallaciously to study urban economies in two essentially independent steps: first, an over-all economic study and, second, a study of the spatial organization of all activities.

The unique significance of communications activity in urban economic analysis stems from the fact that the responsibility to provide channels of communications is one of the crucial tasks of local, metropolitan, state, and federal authorities. This power to *provide channels* ranges from major decisions to construct rapid transit systems and freeways, to expand or improve water systems and sewage trunk lines, to allocate TV-channel capacities, all the way to decisions to route traffic only one way on a certain street. Related judgments involve various terminal and intermediate facilities, such as parking garages and other *nodes* in the communications systems. From the point of view of urban policy-makers, communications phenomena emerge in a strategic role. Governmental policies and decisions influence both the capacities and usage of communications channels. The policy alternatives may involve changing the capacity limitations of the parts of the communications networks—links or initial, intermediate, or terminal nodes. Or they may be charges, taxes, or subsidies on the use of these channels.

Return now to our set of "from-to" tables, or *model*, relating the major kinds of economic activity of the urban region—

production, consumption, investment, external trade relations, and communication relations. Now imagine that the broad classes of production and consumption are broken down into individual firms, agencies, and households, so that each is represented by a column and a row in each table. The "box" which is located at the intersection of the row for firm A and the column for firm B in the summary table represents the volume of A's output of goods or services which is purchased by (flows from A to) firm B. This same box in succeeding tables, then, will represent the volume flowing between A and B via particular modes of communication (or transportation). In short, these boxes will represent how two firms use communication opportunities to interact with each other; the columns identified by firm B will represent how the inputs to B's productive activities use the communication opportunities; the rows identified by firm A will reflect how A's output uses communication facilities to reach its destinations.

Now consider one additional dimension—there are costs associated with each flow, with each box, and we can think of a set of parallel tables which would identify the costs per unit of output of the flow from A to B via communications mode Z, while the master table of this new set would specify the market price of the flow item. Clearly then, firm A will be constantly aware of all the entries in its rows and columns in both the flow and cost tables and will make its production decisions on the basis of this information in its attempt to maximize its profits.

When, on the basis of such information, no firm or individual can change its present mode of economic activity profitably, an equilibrium is said to exist among the units. A kind of equilibrium of special interest to us here exists when no establishment can profitably change location, even though other changes in the productive relations are possible. Observe what happens when equilibrium is disturbed.

Suppose that firm A discovers that downtown traffic congestion is increasing its delivery costs to B and other customers in the outlying areas and rapidly making its present operation unprofitable. What kinds of responses are possible to *A*? First, he may pass along his increased costs to *B* as a price increase, an alternative which may be barred to him if, for example, there is stiff competition among producers of his item. He may substitute other transportation alternatives, such as slack-period delivery from the central business district. He may change the whole structure of his interaction costs by relocating outside the congested area, that is, he may substitute new investment for transportation costs. He has other possibilities, also, which would become apparent from an examination of the tables, but the central consideration here is the dependence of his response on a considerable array of alternatives which become manifest in the model in its exposition of the systematic relationships which exist between production, consumption, investment, external trade, and communication possibilities.

This model, as we have characterized it thus far in its disaggregated form, can amplify our understanding of how a firm such as *A* reacts to change in the economic environment of the city. If we condense it again, areawise, and put some test values in the cost tables to observe the response of the large classes of activity, we are using it as a *decision model:* the test values we insert can be the consequences of alternative government programs, say, in urban transportation improvement, whose impacts need to be understood and evaluated before a rational decision can be made.

A NEW ROLE FOR DECISION-MODELS

The phenomena which decision-makers influence or control directly I refer to as *instrumental* variables. Such variables have seldom been exploited for the implementation of long-range city plans by the planners, geographers, economists, and others who studied the future development of urban areas. Rather, the usual end product of metropolitan area studies—a set of forecasts of economic activity and population growth—resembles the meteorologist's weather forecasts in their implication that very little can be done to *influence* the course of events. This passive attitude may stem from a failure to recognize the potentials of economic planning for an urban area. Or it may simply be a reflection of the great difficulties involved in identifying the areas of choice which are open to the decision-makers. Whatever the reasons, planners can now play more active roles in urban development through the use of *decision-models*. A decision-model of the urban "space economy" can help them understand the consequences of such deep-seated changes as the tendency for both manufacturing and nonmanufacturing industries to become more and more "foot-loose" *within* urban areas (and possibly within the nation, as well), because new communications and production technology make them less dependent upon any particular demand or supply factors in their choice of location.

The great challenge in this field of research today is to develop increasingly sophisticated decision-models. In the past, analysis by diagram was a main tool in the study of urban spatial organization. While this makes for ease of exposition, it severely limits the further development of these particular studies. Urban economic analysis needs high-powered mathematical tools; verbal reasoning and diagrammatic analysis cannot possibly handle the complex relationships that characterize the urban economy.

Needless to say, instrumental variables are not confined to communications activity. Decision-makers on the urban scene— be they local or metropolitan governments—have an impressive variety of means at their disposal. These include administrative, legal, or "physical" measures, such as zoning, subdivision, open space preservation, public housing and other redevelopment projects, and construction and maintenance of public buildings and other facilities; and financial measures, such as charges, subsidies, and taxes. Here, to illustrate the usefulness of a decision-model, the implications for the urban spatial organization of various *possible* forms of taxation for production, consumption, capital formation, exports and imports, and communications could be analyzed. The fact that the real property tax is the largest single revenue source of municipal government for most communities—and for some communities the *only* tax revenue source—does not necessarily limit the attention of a decision-model to this particular tax element. The model should be designed to show the implications for urban organization of sales taxes, income taxes, taxes on value added in local business firms, or on particular inputs such as labor, since a primary purpose of any analytical model is to serve as a substitute for real-world experiments.

Although this brief paper can't spell out in detail how any particular urban decision-model should be designed and applied in the implementation of policy, some general points can be made. First, the emphasis upon instrumental variables does not imply that one naively assumes that the decision-makers who control these variables hold mastery over all urban economic development. On the contrary, it may be that the existing political structure and other factors, limit their influence. However, only through a framework cast in decision-model terms can the area of choice be identified, whatever it is.

Decision-models set up the problem as one of decision-making under conditions of uncertainty. The actual development that takes place is described as a set of *outcomes*. We express these outcomes in our economic categories—production, consumption, etc.—and, through these, in changes in the spatial arrangement of the activities. These outcomes are being viewed as determined by three sets of elements: (1) the *instrumental* variables, (2) certain variables determined by external conditions—"extraneous" variables, and (3) *stochastic* or chance elements. We can express our decision-model in a more compact form:

$$y = f(s, x, u),$$

where y is a set of variables describing the outcomes; s is a set of instrumental variables; x is a set of extraneous variables; u is a set of stochastic influences; and f is the set of rules describing the correspondence between the predetermined variables and the set of (dependent) outcome variables.

The extraneous variables (x) relate to changing economic and political conditions in other parts of the state, nation, and world, such as federal government activity in defense policy affecting the amount and regional distribution of defense contracts. These variables are "extraneous" in the sense that the decision-model could not spell out any repercussions upon these variables resulting from local changes. In forecasting, one may have to make guesses about the future course of these variables. Sometimes, it will be possible to formalize these guesses to derive values for the extraneous variables through *sub-models:* in a recent study of the Puget Sound Region we projected the future "exports" of the largest manufacturer in the region by means of such a sub-model. The stochastic variables (u) consist of residual elements representing those changes in the outcomes which could not be accounted for by the changes in instrumental variables or specified extraneous variables.

The symbol f denotes the ways in which the outcomes are linked to the instrumental and extraneous variables; these "structural relations" are determined through empirical research, part of which would seek to quantify the links between various inputs and outputs and between these phenomena and the transactions which are used to measure the communications activity. Other links that would intervene here are familiar to demographers, economists, and city planners: relationships between the size of the population and the number of households; relationships between the growth of the population over time (including migration) and changes in the number of persons in critical age groups (such as children in school ages and elderly people); relationships between household consumption of various commodities and household income; relationships between capital stocks—such as office buildings—and outputs; relationships between space and site demands of manufacturing and nonmanufacturing activities, residential activities, on the one hand, and land values, on the other. Some of these relationships are exceedingly complex, and additions to knowledge about them will come slowly. Current research in this area is following two main lines: simplifying the relationships that are being analyzed, and studying the "micro" relations or other "partial" relationships of individual firms or of limited areas such as in urban renewal projects. All relationships need not be formulated as equations. For certain problems, it is fruitful to use inequalities which set bounds on the variations of some dependent variables, such as limitations on channel capacities.

GOALS FOR CITIES AND URBAN SPATIAL ORGANIZATION

Let us jump ahead a little and assume that numerical values have been assigned to the extraneous variables. The question then arises: how should one assign values to the policy variables? This question is really not very meaningful, unless one can state goals or objectives for the subject urban area. Goal formulation is a most difficult problem which is compounded by the fact that conflicts among goals are bound to arise, no matter what criteria are selected—conflicts among the communities within a metropolitan area, a state, or the nation. What is good for the United States need not be good for San Diego or Seattle or Honolulu.

Five goals are sometimes cited for cities: safety, efficiency, convenience, stability, and beauty. Such very general goals elude measurement and compel us to work with "proxy" goals which are more measurable and which at the same time retain reasonable validity.

Generally speaking, we may distinguish between two approaches to the problem of goal specification and goal achievement. The first *optimizes* (maximizes or minimizes) some *index* of the community's welfare subject to various constraints. The goal may be to maximize the total income or the income per capita of the urban economy under study, or to maximize the growth rate of the area. Similar goals are to minimize the sum of all communications costs within the area, to minimize the sum of all communications costs and rents, to maximize tax revenue for the local governments involved. Such goals may be criticized as being too narrowly defined. Rather, it could be said, one should search for some more general index of welfare or well-being. One possibility would be to try to formulate a preference function for the community, through public opinion polls or attitude surveys. Although the prospects for the formulation of such a function appear dim, the difficulties are less formidable on the local than on the national scene, simply because the local choice situations appear more comprehensible. Such an index of community satisfaction would be a kind of super-goal that would contain the lower-level goals with appropriate "weights."

The second approach would specify a set of separate goals, which are not formulated as maxima or minima but as target values. For instance, one such goal may involve population density—density of the residential population in different areas of a local community as well as density of the working population in different areas. Here, there is no question of maximizing or minimizing densities, but rather of achieving or maintaining certain levels. Another goal of the same kind may involve the number of face-to-face contact choices offered to an inhabitant, as suggested by Karl Deutsch. A third goal is safety. If the goal were to provide maximum safety, certainly, much more could be done in any urban area. Rather, the goal appears to be one of maintaining a certain level of safety and protection for the residents. Thus, given such a set of goals, the decision-maker's task is one of adjusting the instrumental variables so that these goals are achieved. The present state of the arts makes this formulation of the goal problem more realistic if less ambitious. It also has the advantage that the decision-maker does not have to commit himself to optimizing according to any specific goal, relegating the other goals to the role of constraints. In our decision-model this kind of goal system requires that the number of goals coincide with the number of instrumental variables: if a local government tries to achieve ten different goals, it needs to have ten decision variables.

Among the more general goals, the goal of efficiency is seemingly most subject to measurement and, perhaps, therefore, easiest to work with. Besides, if any goal should be given priority, a good case can be made for efficiency. The sheer size of the proportion of economic activity taking place in the urban sectors means that the rate of economic growth of the nation is coming to approximate the average growth rate among its urban areas. Thus much can be gained or lost from even moderate changes in the efficiency of the urban economies.

Yet, as it turns out, the goal of efficiency may involve the thorniest problems of all. A decentralized economy such as ours contains thousands and thousands of decision-makers other than local or metropolitan governments—individuals, households, business firms, state agencies, federal agencies, trade unions, and other organizations. How do these units make their decisions? What goals do they have? Seemingly, the answers to such questions provide the clue to the problem of achieving, or at least maintaining, the goal of maximum efficiency in urban spatial organization. Assuming that these units behave rationally in the pursuit of some goal, say, maximum satisfaction, or maximum profit, then the goal of over-all efficiency would seem to be automatically maintained in a situation of general equilibrium among all the decision-making units, in which no individual or household or business firm or other unit has any incentive to change its present dispositions. Thus, the search for maximum efficiency in the allocation of urban activities over space seemingly becomes a problem of stipulating conditions under which general equilibrium prevails.

INTERACTION AND INDIVISIBILITY: THE UNSOLVED PROBLEMS

Several unsolved problems have a direct bearing on the efficiency goal, especially as it relates to the broad spatial organization of the city and to the underlying locational processes. They fall conveniently under two headings: problems having to do with the interaction between functionally linked but spatially separated activities, and problems having to do with indivisibilities—the economic characteristics of certain commodities which come in "lumps" of various sizes, such as a man or a blast furnace, and not in divisible flows, such as petroleum or water.

The existence of indivisibilities explains why returns to an economic activity increase or decrease with changes in the scale of operations, and why outside conditions (such as air or water pollution) can enhance or detract from profitability.

The difficulty in reconciling the effects of indivisibility with over-all efficiency in urban spatial organization stems from the fact that the costs and revenues facing the individual firm may guide its decisions—including its choice of location—in such a way that the net effects taken for *all* the firms and individuals together may be negative; indivisibilities, as it were, upset the price mechanism as an efficient allocator.

The problem of the interaction between spatially separated activities arises from the implication that the "profit" or "utility" of any activity at any location depends on the way in which *all other* activities are located. No study to date has been successful in comprehending these interactions as they relate to the urban spatial organization. A courageous attempt was reported a few years ago by Koopmans and Beckmann,[1] who tried to find a set of prices, associated with the goods and services produced in an area which would preserve an optimal locational arrangement of all activities, in the sense of allocative efficiency. When they permitted interaction between different activities, they were not able to find a system of prices which would sustain an optimal pattern of locations. In fact, they were able to show the opposite, namely that no such set of prices could possibly exist. However, they did not include in their framework the effects of inertia in locational assignments and patterns: it costs money and time for a firm to move to another location.

A main tool used in that study as well as in some recent large-scale urban transportation studies is *linear algebra*. There is something anomalous about this, since, except to a limited extent in so-called assignment problems, the linear theory is not

---

[1] T. Koopmans and M. Beckmann, "Assignment Problems and the Location of Economic Activities," *Econometrica*, vol. 25, 1957, pp. 53–76.

capable of dealing with indivisibilities, and, hence, with increasing and decreasing returns to scale, or with external economies and diseconomies—the very phenomena which location theorists consider basic in any attempt to explain why urban areas exist and continue to grow.

GROWTH AND CHANGE IN THE URBAN PATTERN: FACTORS AND TENDENCIES

The close association which these location theorists saw between urban growth and the shared economies which result from the clustering together of diverse economic activities has been enriched by the recent case study of the New York region.[2] The study stresses the central business district location as a means by which business firms dealing in *unstandardized* inputs and outputs can reduce uncertainty in their operations. It emphazies the role of the large city as a pool of facilities which the activities clustering there can tap at great speed as common facilities—the services of specialists, equipment, machinery, and other indivisible facilities. In the same vein, Ben Chinitz has explored another aspect of external economies and diseconomies in his comparison between New York and Pittsburgh.[3] He hypothesizes that New York, because of its multitude and variety of smaller business firms, is a better breeding ground for new entrepreneurs and a better environment for the supply of new capital, than Pittsburgh, with its relatively large and relatively less diversified business firms.

The New York study also illustrates how slowly locational patterns change. The cost of relocation, and sometimes prestige considerations and vested interests, may dictate a decision not to move. But at the same time, the study points to the long-range tendency of certain types of industry to move out from the downtown core. When its products become standardized,

[2] E. M. Hoover and R. Vernon, *Anatomy of a Metropolis* (Cambridge: Harvard University Press, 1959).

[3] B. Chinitz, "Contrasts in Agglomeration: New York and Pittsburgh," *American Economic Review*, vol. 51, May 1961, pp. 279–89.

a firm may adopt mass-production techniques that call for a shift to a one-story plant to facilitate handling and continuous processing. This may force the firm to seek a new location in the periphery of the urban area. A move of this kind is often facilitated by a reduced dependence on nearness to railroad sidings and other fixed points. Some banks and insurance companies whose paper-handling and record-keeping activities are similar to the procedures of standardized, mass-producing plants have been affected by the same locational tendencies. The advance of high-speed data-processing equipment may eventually reduce their dependence on the large, in-town supply of relatively unskilled female clerks, and a downtown location will then be much less significant. Thus, decentralization of at least part of the operations of various manufacturing, commercial, and financial activities has not only become feasible but economically attractive.

On the other hand, the New York study also lays stress on a tendency towards further concentration of certain activities in the downtown core of large cities. Involved here are the central offices of large companies, advertising agencies and law firms, certain government agencies and financial institutions, and other top-level decision-makers. These are all activities for which, as yet, no substitute has been found for the face-to-face contact.

The tendency among plants and large-scale nonmanufacturing activities with standardized operations to move out from central areas and to some extent away from cities may indicate that in the future need for mass transportation facilities to the city core may actually be less than it is today, even if the urban economies continue to grow. A similar situation was suggested earlier as a possible outcome of drastically increased substitutability between different channels of communications. We could probably find some other and perhaps more substantial material which would also suggest that the future rate of capacity utilization of certain urban transportation channels, such as rapid transit systems, will be lower than the assumed rate which today might serve as a basis and justification for decisions to go ahead with the construction of such systems. However, there is another angle to this problem that has to do with the *range of choices* open to the consumer or resident in an urban community. Lewis Mumford expressed this well when he suggested that ferry traffic should reopen on the San Francisco Bay. The average American consumer is privileged in having a far wider range of choices than the consumer in any other country of the world, whatever criteria one applies. One possible exception to this statement is of course in urban transportation, where the American might in fact have no choice but to use his car. Even if it turned out that he did not use the rapid transit system so much as the planner had expected him to, it might be that the very existence of the system would enhance his welfare, because it increased his range of possible choices.

But decisions about transportation systems, like other important decisions by the community which affect the structural conditions within which firms, agencies, and individuals carry on their economic activities, need to be played through for the whole gamut of effects and impacts on the urban economy. Otherwise, we will have no way of knowing whether inferior goals are being realized at the expense of more general considerations of the community's well-being. At the very least, two propositions need to be kept front and center in our considerations about the growth and development of the urban region:

1. future states of the urban region will be compounded of the interaction of instrumental with extraneous variables, and current decisions will affect, even if they can't fully direct, the shape of the future; and
2. policy-making requires the systematic generation and evaluation of alternatives, and especially an awareness of the substitution possibilities among urban economic relationships.

Production, consumption, investment, external trade, and communication relations are the active elements shaping the organization of cities. The decision-model is, in effect, a strategy for building these considerations into the processes by which the future of urban communities is being determined.

. . . . .

In the preparation of this paper, I received many helpful suggestions and comments from friends. I feel particularly indebted to Lowdon Wingo, Jr., and Robert Arnold.—R.A.

CHARLES M. HAAR is Assistant Secretary for Metropolitan Development in the Department of Housing and Urban Development. He is on leave from Harvard Law School, where he is professor of law. He is a member of the faculty, Littauer School of Public Administration; of the Faculty Committee of the Joint Center for Urban Studies, MIT-Harvard; the American Bar Association; the American Institute of Planners; and the American Academy of Arts and Sciences. He has been a consultant to various governmental agencies, and has participated in President Johnson's Task Force for Urban Affairs and Housing. He was Chairman of the Task Force for the Preservation of Natural Beauty. His publications include: *Land Planning Law in a Free Society* (1952), *Land Use Planning* (1959), *Federal Credit and Private Housing* (1960), and *The Golden Age of American Law* (1965).

THE SOCIAL CONTROL
OF URBAN SPACE

CHARLES M. HAAR

THE FUTURE COURSE OF SOCIAL CONTROL of urban space inevitably requires speculation, euphemistically called making informed guesses. My purpose here is to explore those legal policies and institutions which threaten to interfere with the rational development of metropolitan land uses. Concomitantly, the aim is to highlight those policies which foster desired development, as well as to consider the legal and institutional arrangement—including the creation of new techniques—that can best attain community ends.

By way of preface, I pose the following general proposition for discussion: the continued sway of outmoded legal institutions will not be the cause of any irrationality in the long-run trends of urban space patterns.

This proposition does not deny the rigidity of law at any given point in time. To the contrary, such rigidity is the essence of the legal structure. Every law represents the decision of society concerning a particular problem in a particular climate of conditions and ideas. But the decision is rarely unanimous; hence the need to clothe it with the dignity of law. The function of law is to effectuate that decision, notwithstanding the opposition of dissenting elements in the society.

But the rigidity is not fixed for all time. As pressures for change build up, the rigidity dissolves and a new accommodation results which subsists until a new pressure becomes sufficiently great to force another change in the law. In short, at any point in time, law is predominantly static; over a period of time, it is predominantly, and inevitably, dynamic.

The thesis, while acknowledging both aspects, emphasizes the dynamics. It asserts that this country's legal climate is such that any strong and persistent pressure or need will make or force accommodation. Naturally certain critics contend that the thesis that law adjusts to life rests simply upon the unfounded optimism of a Pangloss. Its fundamental soundness, however, is borne out by innumerable footnotes in legal history. Time after time, seemingly immutable doctrines have come into conflict with apparently unyielding social pressures, and out of those frictions there have developed new, reconciled relations. This is the fact of the present; it is the promise of the future.

PAST EXPERIENCE

Land Use Control May Prevail

In the early 1900's the institution of private property—as then expounded—was still girded with the legal rules which, earlier, had led Blackstone to conclude that the "public good is in nothing more essentially interested than in the protection of every individual's private rights." The twentieth century, however, lacked faith in the identity of public and private interests. The principle that private rights in property were impregnable against invasion even "for the general good of the whole community" conflicted with the increasingly general belief that property rights could be subordinated to the health, safety, morals, and general welfare of the community. Judicial decisions, which are often behind but seldom completely out of touch with prevailing views, articulated the lines of battle. Numerous decisions that invalidated the zoning ordinances of many localities embodied the philosophy of *Spann* v. *Dallas* [1] that "the right to acquire and own property, and to deal with it and use it as the owner chooses as long as the use harms nobody, is a natural right. It does not owe its origin to constitutions. It existed before them. It is part of the citizen's natural liberty—an expression of his freedom, guaranteed as inviolate by every American Bill of Rights." *Ignaciunas* v. *Risley* [2] added an economic overlay, warning that "men will not undergo the labor and hardships necessary to the acquisition of property if they find that the ownership and enjoyment thereof is not to be protected."

Contrary decisions focused on "the increasing complexity of our civilization and institutions" which was asserted as justifying an increased emphasis on the "general welfare" component, as opposed to the health and safety basis of the power.[3] One court concluded that "So thoroughly has the value of zoning been demonstrated that no longer is the constitutionality of the principle open to question."

Though an accurate prophesy, this was, in 1925, an inaccurate description. The very next day the Maryland Supreme Court handed down a decision decreeing zoning unconstitutional. The *Ignaciunas* case was decided in New Jersey later the same year. The voice of Blackstone was finally silenced in 1926, by the now historic decision of the United States Supreme Court in *Ambler Realty Co.* v. *Village of Euclid,*[4] which laid to rest, decisively and for all time, any doubts as to the constitutionality of regulating land use through zoning.

The institution of private property and the related rules of law so far as they had been interpreted as barriers to this manifestation of legislative power, gave way. The immediate change, and perhaps the most dramatic one, was in those states where, before *Euclid,* zoning had been deemed unconstitutional. The change did not, however, end there. Private property survived

---

[1] 111 Tex. 350, 212 S.W. 513 (1921).
[2] 98 N.J. L. 712, 121 A. 783 (1923).
[3] *Miller* v. *Board of Public Works of Los Angeles,* 195 Cal. 477, 234 Pac. 381 (1925) and, a few years earlier, *Carter* v. *Harper,* 182 Wisc. 148, 196 N.W. 451.
[4] 272 U.S. 365 (1926).

and, happily, gives every indication of remaining a viable institution; but it has undergone many permutations as the implications of *Euclid* were spelled out in the years following 1926.

Land Use Control May Yield

A conflict situation may result in defeat for a planning control. Take, for example, provisions such as those of the New Jersey legislature limiting under some circumstances the width of land which subdividers could be required to dedicate for road purposes. Such legislation appears to run counter to the solution, worked out over many years, for present road needs, over-rapid obsolescence, and minimizing public costs. Some may consider such legislation an obstacle to the rational use of urban space. Others may take an equally dim view of a recent amendment to Massachusetts subdivision control law, expressly negating the right of localities to require subdividers to dedicate land for recreation or school purposes. That right, which had been exercised in Massachusetts until adoption of the amendment, is still deemed *intra vires* the enabling laws of many other states, and a vital tool in the control of land uses. They may, of course, be wrong, in which case the Massachusetts amendment should not spawn new irrationalities. Or they may be right as to the impact on land uses, but less wise than Massachusetts in the relative scaling of values, undervaluing the freedom of property and overvaluing the optimum physical development. It may also be, however, that the change in Massachusetts law is regressive both from the point of view of land uses and the broad view of the welfare of the society as a whole.

It is comforting to remember the importance attached by some planners, concerned about open space needs, to a requirement that developers dedicate 5 per cent of proposed subdivisions as a condition of plat approval. Experience under such rigid requirements has substantiated the fears of planners opposed to them. Municipalities found that too often they had been given land unsuitable for any public use, they had lost tax revenues, and taken on legal responsibilities for care and maintenance.

Most planners do not need to be reminded that the future may vindicate what earlier appeared to be regressive action or unduly stubborn resistance to change. Present and past do not always see things in precisely the same light. Indeed, the differing discount of time is the very rationale for planning. A control may seem highly desirable to many public-spirited persons in and out of public office; and even members of the judiciary who declare its invalidity may do so reluctantly. Nevertheless, later generations, with the benefit of hindsight, may applaud that check. To them the irrationality may seem a small price to pay to preserve intact some other value. Or, possibly, to them the result will not seem irrational.

Land Use Control May Be Modified

Moreover, even assuming the controverted planning proposal is "right" or at least "best," the alternatives are not enactment of the disputed measures versus irrational land use. To state it challengingly, and perhaps overdramatically, I can conceive of no goal in regard to urban space which is obtainable by one means and by that means only.

Were not this the case, official mapping statutes would have fallen victim in the fight for specific performance of a contract for the purchase or sale of real property. An early New York case is a good example of the process. Scott, the reluctant purchaser, based his defense on the fact that the subject property was the bed of a proposed street as projected on a map filed by the city under the official mapping statute eliminating any right to compensation for improvements made after the date of the filing, and which therefore constituted a lien on the property. The Court of Appeals rejected defendant's contention that the official map was a lien rendering plaintiff's title unmarketable, but it did so on the ground that "a law [which] deprives the owner of the beneficial use and free enjoyment of his property, or imposes restraint upon such use and enjoyment, that materially affect its value, without legal process or compensation, . . . deprives him of his property within the meaning of the Constitution." [5]

As any lawyer would be quick to note, a strict construction of the decision in *Forster* v. *Scott* had no legal power to affect the validity of the myriad of official mapping acts then on the statute books. No public official or body was represented in or a party to the suit and consequently none was bound by the decision. Moreover, in 1936 the Court of Appeals, reviewing its forty-three-year-old decision, read it narrowly in light of the facts—particularly the fact that Forster's entire lot lay within the bed of the street as mapped—and held that the act was invalid *as applied,* and not invalid *on its face.*[6]

Judge Lehman, speaking for the Court in 1936, may have been correct in his interpretation of the *Forster* case. But the fact remains that it had been otherwise understood, and that this contrary understanding was a very real and important force in determining the fate of such statutes in several states for close to half a century.[7]

The reversion to the legal status *quo ante* those statutes was only temporary. New statutes were adopted. Like the old, they had the effect of eliminating compensation for improvements made in the bed of mapped streets. The New York act does so indirectly, through the interposition of a permit requirement controlling the right to improve, rather than directly, by deny-

[5] *Forster* v. *Scott,* 136 N.Y. 577, 584, 32 N.E. 976. Perhaps nothing conveys the tenor of the opinion and the attitude of its subscribers more clearly than their opening volley: "this case is governed by a few principles so well settled and understood that they are elementary, and nothing can be added to their force or application by illustration or extended discussion."

[6] *Headley* v. *City of Rochester,* 272 N.Y. 197, 5 N.E. 2d 198 (1936).

[7] See, e.g., *N.Y.C. & HRR RC* v. *Priest,* 206 N.Y. 274 (1912), holding invalid a similar statute enacted in 1807, partly in reliance on the precedent provided by a broader reading of *Forster* v. *Scott.* Nor were the repercussions confined within state limits. A Massachusetts court cited it as sole authority for its view that a similar official mapping statute, enacted in 1891, of that state was unconstitutional in *Edwards* v. *Brurton,* 184 Mass. 529 (1904). It also helped to persuade the Delaware Court to a similar result in *Kittinger* v. *Rossman* (12 Del. Ch. 276, 112 Atl. 385).

ing damages. But, more important, it also provides for relief where strict enforcement would eliminate any possibility of reasonable benefit from the ownership of property. This modified act was upheld by *Headley* v. *City of Rochester, supra.* Despite the suggestion by an intermediate appellate judge that the *Headley* case is not conclusive on the question of constitutionality, it has generally been accepted as such authority since it was decided twenty-seven years ago.

No Increase in Rigidity

Nor is there any indication of increasing rigidity. One notices a recent instance of this sort of accommodation in three Massachusetts decisions dealing with a proposed enactment for an urban renewal development, the highly publicized Prudential Center. The initial opinion stated that the enactment would violate the Constitution in two respects.[8] One vice was that the developer, a private corporation, was to be given advantageous tax treatment. The other was that the public purposes to be served—the prevention of blight already incipient, an increase in tax ratables, and the development and dedication of a certain portion of the area for unquestionably public uses—were inadequate to justify the public purchase of land "to be turned over or sold to private persons for private use." Five years later the court said that the second proposed taking of the same land failed to satisfy the two constitutional objections set forth in the 1955 opinion.[9] A comparison of the two opinions indicates that while the legal barrier remained, it no longer had the same impenetrability: this second opinion is, in effect, a manual of legislative drafting to guide a third and solid enactment. It points out that the preamble does not declare urban renewal to be a public purpose, that it makes no use of the fact that the site was in the path of city growth, that it does not recite facts

[8] Opinion of the Justices, 332 Mass. 769, 126 N.E. 2d 795 (1955).
[9] Opinion of the Justices, 341 Mass. 738, 167 N.E. 2d 745 (1960).

which might exist "disclosing a condition" affecting adversely the inhabitants as a community, and finally, that the bill does not provide for a regulation or review of earnings.

The legislature obligingly took its cue, and in August, 1960, the court found a third enactment unobjectionable.[10] The latest version declares the existence of blight, decadent, and substandard areas, the need to eliminate them, and the inefficacy of existing legislation. It subjects the developer to continuing regulation and limits the profits which may be earned by the project. The tax provisions were kept intact.

These legislative changes are substantial but it is uncertain whether the different judicial result can be fully explained by these statutory alterations. The 1955 opinion sees as "the main difference between the area we are now considering and such other tracts that the location of this tract makes it more prominent than many others, and this is hardly a difference in principle." Referring to the same area, the August 1960 opinion sees as one of the "public advantages to be considered . . . the elimination of grave doubt as to the future use of a great area, now largely vacant or occupied by a nearly obsolete, unsightly, railroad freight yard; covering over a railroad right of way; improvement to neighboring properties; the encouragement of prompt action unlikely to be undertaken by private enterprise in the foreseeable future; stimulation of other building and opening a new opportunity for urban growth at what might be a time which is appropriate but of short duration; and new facilities made available to public use." [11] Thus even in the short period of time which had elapsed the needs of the community appear to have modified the views of the court.

EVALUATION

The thesis that law accommodates to life promises that changes will occur. However, the above cited illustrations dem-

[10] Opinion of the Justices, 341 Mass. 760, 168 N.E. 2d 858.
[11] 168 N.E. 2nd at 869.

onstrate that time and content qualify this promise. Change is inevitable, but the rate of change is not predetermined. It may come quickly. But it may come only in the long run, which may be very long indeed (for as Keynes commented, even before the atomic age, we will all be dead in the long run). The pace of accommodation seems to be accelerating, however. Ten years elapsed between the first zoning resolution and *Euclid*. In the case of New York's official mapping statute it had taken the quite considerable time of thirty-two years. However, in Massachusetts the process was telescoped into a matter of five years.

The promise is limited also as to content. When the change does occur, the thesis does not offer any assurance that it will conduce towards greater rationality in the use of urban space. The precise changes that take place, and the length of time needed to bring them about, will depend, among other things, on urgency of the need, the strength of impeding values of institutions, the extent to which the proposed solution is an innovation, the relative strength of the interests which would be affected, and, by no means unimportant, the co-operativeness, vigor, and ingenuity of the legal and planning professions.

Notwithstanding the qualified nature of the thesis, its implications for the future of land use controls in achieving rational development of that resource are optimistic. For if it does not depict our legal institutions as a fully automatic vehicle to Utopia, neither does it depict them as iron laws which react to every change instituted by man so as to prevent improvement. On the contrary, it holds out hope that, given intelligence and energy, our legal institutions will assist toward our goal.

While the thesis will not of itself bring about desirable legal changes, it can be made to play a significant role in the process. By understanding the relevant forces that impede and enhance our efforts to utilize urban space we can channel our efforts to achieve maximum result with a minimum expenditure of time and energy.

THE PROCESS AT WORK

Theory and history aid in evaluating the current scene. Presently many areas experience active fermentation, but the multifarious nature of the problem compels a selective examination.

Not all of the omissions are deliberate. While some of the forces at work are quite obvious, others are barely discernible, and certain forces may only become known in the future when more facts are brought to light and their interrelation is studied. Similarly, some facilitating measures could be taken now, and techniques, combinations, and approaches still unthought of will no doubt be devised.

Preview of Study

Private land use activities are most obviously regulated by overt and direct exercise of governmental powers. These include many basic tools of land use controls and may be primarily legislative (e.g., zoning), administrative (e.g., subdivision controls), or judicial (e.g., rule against restraints on alienation or the nonenforceability of covenants).

Less obvious, perhaps, but increasingly significant are the measures having an indirect impact on development patterns. Included in this category are such matters as the availability of government credit, the possibility of a direct subsidy or of tax concessions, any one of which may determine not only whether a site or area is developed, but, if it is, what form it will take. Here the legislative and the administrative branches of government dominate the scene, almost to the exclusion of the judicial.

The last category to be considered is what might be called the *de facto* as opposed to the *de jure* controls. Under this rubric are actions of various groups which are likely to have a discernible influence on the development of urban space: for example, insuring policies of title companies, credit policies of private lending institutions.

Direct Controls

Zoning. A pervasive tendency in zoning is toward greater flexibility. One manifestation is the proliferation in the number of use categories and of height and bulk specifications. The original breakdown of uses was little more than a tripartite division into residential, industrial, and commercial. This is a far cry from the minute detailing of all conceivable kinds of residential, industrial, and commercial uses that are set forth in a modern zoning enactment, such as the long, detailed New York City ordinance adopted in 1961. That ordinance—resembling the Internal Revenue Code in breadth and complexity of detail— requires 255 over-size pages to contain its provisions intended to streamline the much amended resolution of 1916, as well as bring it into line with current concepts.

Another manifestation is the fairly new technique of classifying in accordance with *performance standards,* i.e., by the impact of the actual user, rather than by class of industry, process, or product. This bids fair to supersede the older classification scheme. At present, however, the two are more likely to be used conjunctively, as in the New York City ordinance. In it, classification by some uses in effect creates a presumption only; performance standards, set forth elsewhere, actually control.

Still another indication of flexibility is the greater use of licensing techniques in conjunction with the self-executing statute. The number of special uses, admissible into specific districts but only upon the discretionary grant of an application for a permit, has risen over the years. Other new techniques have come into play, such as flexible zoning or floating zones— the creation of districts which, instead of being mapped in advance are delineated by amendment upon petition or application—have gained rapidly in popularity.

In part, these changes merely mirror the growing complexity of our civilization. If industry becomes more specialized, a dynamic law will tend to reflect this by listing more uses. An increase in scientific knowledge will give rise to new forms of control as well as to new industry. Unless there is some cataclysmic disaster, the impetus toward greater complexity will probably continue. This, in turn, will create a pressure on zoning and other laws to become correspondingly complex.

But to some extent the desire for flexibility, particularly as manifested in greater reliance on the licensing approach, may stem from a loss of confidence or from feelings of modesty with respect to the potential of planning. The planner is thereby relieved of the burden of prophesying and prescribing development over which, after all, he wields only negative powers. His powers are still negative: he can prevent a particular development in a particular place but he cannot order it. However, his powers no longer need be exercised in advance without knowledge of particular circumstances.

Some planners suggest that the pressure for flexibility in the form of floating zones comes from residents who are willing to admit uses regarded as basically undesirable neighbors, but only to the extent indicated by the locale's tax situation. They want to retain maximum control over such admissions and feel this would be achieved by exerting pressure on a planning commission given discretionary power.

Of these developments, only the licensing techniques have thus far been judicially reviewed to any appreciable extent. Whether because of differences in the means used to achieve flexibility, in the degree of flexibility sought, in the court's attitude toward flexibility, or to some combination of these, reactions have been various. In *Rockhill* v. *Chesterfield Township*,[12] the enactment overthrown was in form a conventional zoning ordinance designating permitted uses, and uses which could be permitted by grant of an exception. However, it created only a single district in which only two uses—agricultural and certain residential—were permitted as of right. All other uses, except for a few specifically excluded, were subject to the licensing requirement. *Huff* v. *Howard County*,[13] a Maryland case, construes the New Jersey court's opinion, hold-

[12] 23 N.J. 117, 128 A. 2d 473 (1957).
[13] 214 Md. 48, 133 A. 2d 83 (1957).

ing the Chesterfield Township ordinance invalid, as resting on the inadequacy of the standards set forth in the ordinance to guide its administration. The Maryland dissent underlines other language in the New Jersey opinion indicating the vice was viewed as more fundamental and not susceptible of cure by legislative doctoring.

The Maryland court also split as to the proper interpretation of *Rodgers* v. *Tarrytown*,[14] New York's leading case on flexible zoning. That case upheld an ordinance creating a garden apartment classification for zones to be designated within a single family residential district upon application. The Maryland dissent emphasizes the fact that both uses affected were residential and hence could reasonably be found compatible. The majority stresses broader principles enunciated by the New York court. The *Huff* case itself upheld an ordinance permitting an admixture of restricted manufacturing and residential uses through the device of floating zones.

These precedents are all ignored in *Eves* v. *Township of Lower Gwynedd*,[15] the most recent decision on the subject. It involved an ordinance creating a floating industrial zone to be periodically delineated within the larger residential district from time to time on application by the developer. The Pennsylvania court saw the ordinance as an attempt to zone on an *ad hoc* basis rather than in accordance with a comprehensive plan as required by the state's enabling law, and hence invalid.

In this area of the law, as with most land use controls, the initiating force is the legislature. The courts have the essentially negative function of review; they may kill but they can not create. The first step must obviously be to overcome the inertia of the legislative body. The planner, not the lawyer is the logical source of the necessary impetus. The lawyer's role *qua* lawyer is to prescribe for the problems which may be encountered in court once the legislature has acted. One ancient prescription of general applicability is to pour new wines into old bottles. If a new technique can be dressed up to look like

[14] 302 N.Y. 115, 96 N.E. 2d 731 (1951).
[15] 401 Pa. 211, 164 A. 2d 7 (1960).

an old one, it may ride to safety on the precedents upholding the old technique without submitting to an examination of its own merits. More often than not, the court will perceive the substance beneath the form, in fact it will be forcefully thrust on the court, if the lawyers in the case are earning their fees. Within limits though, it probably has value, if only in providing the court with a make-weight for its decision.

The *Huff* majority, for example, quite clearly felt that the compatibility of particular uses was a legislative question and that the legislature had properly exercised its judgment in that regard. This view, rather than the analogy to special exceptions —a traditional, hence acceptable, form of safety valve—pushed the decision to a favorable outcome.

Similarly, the Pennsylvania court was fully aware of, although it chose not to cite, the New York decision on the Tarrytown ordinance, which was discussed at length by the brief of the attorney for Lower Gwynedd. Whether or not one agrees with all the strands of the court's reasoning or with its result, one emphasis of the opinion can be studied with profit from the point of view of gaining judicial acceptance for floating zones, for other devices to increase flexibility, and for innovations generally. The court was quite obviously concerned with several species of possible unfairness which might result from the Lower Gwynedd ordinance. Among others, it saw a danger of discriminatory administration in the application procedure and a danger of incompetent administration in the by-passing of an "expert" body. That its concern may have been excessive or unwarranted on the facts does not alter the fact that courts generally are concerned with considerations of fairness and reasonableness.

Many judicial fears on this score can be allayed by the master plan. Of course, if the master plan for the area is locational— a type of preliminary zoning map—its usefulness for this purpose will be limited. If, however, it consists of applicable principles and relevant goals which are to guide the subsequent districting in a way that can be understood by the court, its existence may prove decisive. It would be evidence that the zones though not fixed were nevertheless the result of planning.

It would be evidence of a sufficient guide for and limitation on administrative discretion. It would furnish a guide for judicial review.

In order to perform this function the master plan needs to bear in some form the imprimatur of the local legislative body. For in limiting the administration's discretion to grant or deny applications, it would conversely limit the property owner's rights and thus constitute a restriction on those rights. Many of the restrictions of individual liberty—in the Smithian sense of encompassing rights in property—are rationalized on the political theory of democratic government. This requires as indispensable basis that the restriction be imposed by elected representatives.

It has been suggested that the reasoning in *Rockhill* v. *Chesterfield Township* [16] by its emphasis on use districts, constitutes a threat to the future of performance standards. This may be a real danger if the delegation in an enabling act or constitutional provision is in terms of use districts. In other jurisdictions, the adoption of performance standards may be somewhat slowed by the inertia of a judiciary which has come to equate zoning with use districts of the conventional kind. But the potential of this technique to provide objective standards for reasonable classifications and impartial administration augurs its acceptance. It would be surprising if any reasonably well drafted ordinance were held invalid.

Subdivision controls. Typically, subdivision ordinances are administered pursuant to rules and regulations promulgated by the administrative body. Individual negotiations and compromises are a hallmark of this form of land use control. Consequently, there has not been any occasion for a thrust toward flexibility paralleling that in zoning. To the contrary, there are indications of a reverse tendency. For example, both New

[16] See, e.g., the recent report to the Massachusetts legislature asserting that, because of abdication on the part of legislative bodies or overzealousness on the part of appointive planners, planning commissions were in fact wielding powers properly exercised only by elective bodies.

Jersey [17] and Massachusetts [18] have recently amended their respective Acts to circumscribe more narrowly the discretionary power of planning commissions. Originally little more was required of the subdivider than his dedicating for streets the land designated on the plat or perhaps on an official map covering the sites. That requirement has procreated with the same fecundity as the use classifications of the zoning ordinance. Today the subdivider must contemplate the possibility of having to dedicate land for educational or recreational purposes, in addition to that for street purposes. He must also contemplate having to improve the property to be subdivided, *inter alia,* by grading and paving streets and walks, by installing lights, a whole water system, and sewers.

Additional conditions are likely to be imposed upon rural areas entering the transitional stage to urbanism so long as our standard of aspirations continues to rise. At the same time a far lesser countermovement appears to be in progress. The same Massachusetts legislature that limited the discretion of planning commissions also prohibited them from requiring a subdivider to dedicate land. New Jersey's amended law for the first time limited under some circumstances the width of land which might be demanded for street purposes. Whether this is a temporary reaction or a long-term limiting factor is not yet discernible.

Among the most important non-legal forces at work have been increasing population and its concomitant increased urbanization, a rising standard of living, practical exigencies of financing needed improvements, wasted resources resulting from abandonment of subdivisions after partial improvement by the municipality. The strength of these forces can perhaps best be gauged by the small amount of resistance laws like those just mentioned have encountered from the courts. The same forces can probably be counted on to secure judicial acceptance for changes and additions to these laws.

Nevertheless, in particular cases, courts have refused to sanction conditions because they conflicted with judicial concepts

[17] N.J. Stat. Ann. 640:55-1.20 (1953).
[18] Mass. G.l., C. 41 (1958).

of fairness and reasonableness. With respect to subdivision controls this appears to mean that the conditions imposed should be justifiable by some approximation to a calculus of social costing. The test, according to *Pioneer Trust & Sav. Bank* v. *Village of Mt. Prospect*,[19] is whether the costs sought to be imposed on the subdivider are "specifically and uniquely attributable to his activity which would otherwise be cast upon the public."

This Illinois case also illustrates that the test is not one which can be mechanically applied. It sustains the developer in his refusal to donate 6.7 acres for school and playground purposes, for which, concededly, there was a pre-existing need aggravated by the 250 residential lots added by the new subdivision. The court's reasoning is fair warning to counsel of that state on both sides, but particularly to counsel for the planning authority which has the burden of proof, that the record must assist the court in computing social costs:

> The agreed statement of facts shows that the present school facilities of Mount Prospect are near capacity. This is the result of the total development of the community. If this whole community had not developed to such an extent or if the existing school facilities were greater, the purported need supposedly would not be present. Therefore, on the record in this case the school problem which allegedly exists here is one which the subdivider should not be obliged to pay the total cost of remedying, and to so construe the statute would amount to an exercise of the power of eminent domain without compensation.[20]

In some other states, the courts, although apparently understanding and approving the principle in abstract, seem confused as to its applicability to the concrete facts of particular cases. In *Ayres* v. *City of Los Angeles*,[21] one of the conditions upheld over the objection of the developer was that he dedicate land to widen a road adjacent to the subject property. The road was a heavily traveled main artery. Its widening had been contemplated prior to, and *a fortiori* independently of, the proposed

---

[19] 22 Ill. 2d 375, 176 N.E. 2d at 801 (1961).
[20] 176 N.E. 2d at 802.
[21] 34 Cal. 2d 31, 207 P. 2d 1 (1949).

subdivision. The new development would add twelve lots, ten for single family residential purposes, and one each for business and religious use. It seems highly unlikely that a subdivision of such small size would generate sufficient traffic to add any significant burden to the already existing volume of traffic. If *Pioneer Trust & Sav. Bank* was correct, *Ayres* was wrong and the developer should not have had to pay more than a proportionately small fraction of the total cost of widening the road.[22]

The law in this area is thus still not entirely clear. Hence, an ordinance authorizing conditions the burden of which was clearly disproportionate to the activity might be upheld if the facts fell within one of the more confused spots. But even where, as in *Ayres,* the result may be thought to be wrong, the principle of social costing appears to be accepted. An ordinance violative of it would, therefore, be begging for trouble.

Two New Jersey cases demonstrate that the courts' concern for fairness is not limited to social costing. The law of that state provides for tentative plat approval which vests in the subdivider a right to the continued existence for three years of the general terms and conditions on which the approval was granted (N.J.S.A. 40:55-1.18). In *Klein* v. *Hilton Acres,*[23] the court construed this statute to protect the subdivider against an upgrading of minimum lot requirements. In *Levin* v. *Livingston*

---

[22] Compare *Gruber* v. *Township of Raritan*, 68 N.J. Super. 118, 172 A. 2d 48 (1961) (subdivider may not lawfully be required to dedicate land for school purposes, because the provision of education is the responsibility of the entire community through its municipal government), with *Midtown Properties, Inc.* v. *Madison Township*, 68 N.J. Super. 197, 172 A. 2d 40 (1961) (minimum lot acreage requirements may be upgraded to control population density and thereby reduce the financial burden on it for schools and other essential municipal services). *Quaere* the soundness of the rule which emerges: a municipality may not protect general funds by placing the cost of education on the developer responsible in a sense for the need, but the municipality may accomplish the same object by keeping the developer out. See also *Haugen* v. *Gleason*, 359 P. 2d 108 Oreg., 1961, and *Rosen* v. *Downers Grove*, 19 Ill. 2d 448, 167 N.E. 2d 230 (1960), which hold that subdivision controls may not be used as a means of obtaining tax revenues. Partly this can be explained on the ground of *ultra vires*. But that is only a part of the explanation. Reasonable and fair in the realm of taxation no longer mean identical taxes. While our notions on this subject have become more sophisticated they have not yet reached the point where it is regarded as fair to tax a person on the basis of the size of a subdivision he proposes to make.
[23] 165 A 2d 819 (1960).

Township,[24] the issue was whether specifications for street pavements were similarly insulated against change. This time the court held that they were not. It explained that "compared to the basic conditions of development layout, an upgrading of the type of street pavement is a relatively minor item to the developer which it is not unfair to change when balanced against the future public benefit to be derived from the enhanced requirements." Only with final approval did the subdivider acquire protection as to such changes. We may quarrel with the courts' decisions on the facts of the two cases but the court's attempt to prick a fair line between justice to the individual and the rest of the community is clearly the right focus to bring to bear on the problem.

Fortunately, if one may judge from reported cases, crude and blatant unfairness is rare in this area, but when it does occur, no uncertainty attends the outcome, as, witness, *Knutson* v. *Seberger.*[25] The court found in that case that the developers had to

> lay . . . out streets and alleys and construct . . . sewers and other utilities through a continuing process of consultation with town officials. During this construction there was a change of city engineers and several changes in plan and specifications were required and submitted. After 15 months, with many delays occasioned by these negotiations, the construction was completed, but on final examination of the "plat" as developed, the commission "disapproved" it. A government which exercises such police power over the property of its citizens without any fixed standards which are known to the citizen and the enforcing officials, is government by men, and not by law.

Restraints on alienation, rules against perpetuities and accumulations. This last group of direct controls differs from the two preceding categories in that first, these are not only administered but formulated by the courts, and, second, they are not brand new, but hoary or venerable (depending upon whether the spokesman is for or against them). The rules against perpe-

[24] 173 A 2d 400.
[25] 160 N.E. 2d 200 (Ind. 1959) 202.

tuities, the rules against accumulation, and the rules against restraints on alienation are all fairly persuasive indices that the slow case-by-case adjudication of the courts is not necessarily more productive of satisfactory solutions in this area than the relatively rapid legislative approach of enactments aimed at comprehensive coverage.

The policy of the common law emerges clearly enough. It is to prohibit all sorts of restraints on alienation. The reason, too, is not hard to discern. Land is the one ultimate resource of the community. It should be alienable so that the person who owns land but does not have the skill to develop it properly can sell it to someone who is ready and able to put it to a more intensive and automatically higher and better use for the community.

But the body of case law which has grown up is a labyrinth in which even astute, experienced lawyers can lose their way. Read through the marvelously intricate attempt of the American Law of Property to draw all the refinements among restraints on legal life interests, restraints on legal fee simples, restraints on equitable interests, forfeitures and disabling restraints, and the myriad variations that have sprung up in all the jurisdictions. It is easy to conclude that the courts have decided case-by-case often on peculiar reasons and frequently without thought to the whole pattern of the field. Moreover, although the rules dealing directly with restraints exist side by side with and are logically related to indirect prohibitions such as rules against perpe-tuities, little or no thought appears to have been given to this interaction. Thus, notwithstanding all the rules against perpe-tuities, a house which generations ago was restricted to 14 feet in height to protect a view of the cows grazing on the Boston Common can today, despite the able efforts of generations of conveyancers, be kept to that same height. The generality of courts have also been remiss in continuing to view each piece of land as unique, for we live today under a system where land is becoming more homogenized and perhaps equivalent to other factors of production. Because the courts have failed to consider the side factors that might test the wisdom of what they and the lawyers are doing, the case law is logically inconsistent and acts at cross purposes to its alleged goals of assuring the best use of land.

Inconsistency and mockery of the declared policies of the court may trouble the lawyer. The average citizen may be more concerned with whether these policies accord with empiric studies and with the land use policies and goals articulated by other land use controls and by the other commitments of the community to planning of land and of housing. He would doubtless applaud as wise the conclusion of *Gayle* v. *York Center Community Cooperative*[26] that if "accepted and economical considerations dictate that a partial restraint is reasonably necessary for their fulfillment such a restraint should be sustained." In this case the validity of the state law to permit nonprofit corporations to own co-operative housing was held dependent on the restriction on membership transfers. Of course, the Illinois Supreme Court had to pay lip-service to the old doctrine by determining whether the restraint would violate the policy of the doctrine, to wit, keeping property in the same family and concentrating wealth. In this instance it was able to say that it would discourage retention by one family by encouraging people to liquidate interests, and hence was a permissible restraint.

The importance of private and doctrinal land controls in day-to-day conveyancing and in the day-to-day world of lawyers, mortgagees, and developers may soon result in pressure for over-all review of this area and its co-ordination with other land use controls.

Indirect Regulatory Mechanisms

The classification of controls into direct and indirect is not intended to bear any relation to efficiency. Even as a neutral line for discussion purposes it is at best fuzzy. Zoning, for example, has been classed here and is generally regarded as a direct control. But it could just as easily be classified as an indirect con-

[26] 171 N.E. 2d 30 (Ill. 1961).

trol; as a barrier to some irrational development activity, zoning may result in development being channeled into desired areas, but it exerts no directive force. Incentives, planning and government developmental activities, on the other hand, may be very potent forces in stimulating desired activity.

Incentive controls. Incentive controls bring into play government's powers to tax and to spend. They are laws relating to metropolitan land uses which neither order nor direct action, but seek to achieve it by a conditional offer of some benefit. The benefit induces action; the condition regulates its form. This category includes guarantees, low interest loans, subsidies, grants-in-aid, tax advantages, and technical assistance. The basic idea is not new. The guarantee, for example, was used by the federal government during the depression of the thirties to help small home owners secure mortgage money. But it is only during recent years that the whole battery of techniques has begun to be used on a large scale in furtherance of planning proposals relating to housing, highways, and other matters affecting urban shape. Some idea of the magnitude of what is involved is conveyed by the fact that on the federal level alone the President's message to Congress for 1962 reported $320 million of actual expenditures in 1961 for housing and community development. This amount was expected to increase to $545 million in 1963. The program objects include urban renewal, open space, transportation, public and private housing.

These controls operate between levels of government as well as between government and individuals. One important influence in the direction of greater use of incentive controls is the tripartite structure of our government and the respective functions and financial strength of each level. The federal government has been getting an ever larger share of the tax dollar. The states and their subdivisions have been charged historically with responsibilities for schools, roads, such public housing as was constructed, and the like; demand for such construction has increased far beyond the financial capacity of the states. Hence while they may resent what they regard as federal intrusion in this area they are not in general reluctant to accept federal financial aid. The delicacy of intergovernmental relationship renders it more expedient for the federal government to act indirectly and to protect its investment by strings and conditions, rather than to attempt to take over direct control of these functions.

Analogous interrelated pressures are at work between government and private enterprise and conduce toward the same result. Politically also, it is far easier to confer a benefit subject to conditions than to achieve the same result through the overtly coercive force of police powers.

Looming over all the questions of future institutions and future land use controls are the implications of the military budget. But the significance is probably greatest for the incentive controls, which consume tax revenues, available for other purposes, either by redistributing them after collection or by not collecting them in the first instance. Should the cold war grow colder or, worse yet, wax hot, increased amounts of government funds will be channeled there. Urban renewal, housing, and land policies would take a subordinate position in any competition for the tax dollar with such exigent political goals as victory in a hot or cold war. Other competitors for tax funds would have a like influence on the future use of incentive controls: a substantial shift of public resources to that other space program, the new frontier of air and satellites, would be likely to result in less allocated to land use development.

Another limiting force may be the continued existence of the problem of race relations. Incentive funds may be reduced if one camp in the Congress attaches conditions unacceptable to another camp large enough to defeat the measure. Available incentive funds may remain idle if, as is now happening to some extent, localities opt to forego their share of federal urban renewal funds rather than give up segregationist racial policies which acceptance would entail.

The legal picture by contrast is one of expanding frontiers for the use of incentive mechanisms. One pressure springs from the fact that, however far we are from Blackstone, the prevailing philosophy of the bench which reflects that of the country at large is still individualistic. Another complementary pressure has grown out of disillusion with laissez-faire and the free market as a means of promoting the general welfare. More efficacious police power measures inevitably entail restrictions on the liberty—in the broad sense which encompasses property rights—of the individual. Thus they normally encounter a resistance which is overcome only by the urgent and continued pressure of manifest necessity.

It may perhaps be argued that while, in theory, housing, zoning, and subdivision controls are a direct control almost of a rationing and licensing nature, in practice, mostly by the process of overzoning, sometimes through variances, exceptions, generally lax administration and inspection, they have not operated as such a curtailment of property rights. But the argument becomes less persuasive the closer we move towards fine pinpoint zoning, performance standards, floating zones, detailed handling of subdivision problems, the granting of broad discretions, spot rehabilitation, and the like. By contrast, control through incentive and subsidy may be regarded as permitting liberty of action. A system of government control which operates through the indirect effects of fiscal and monetary policy can be regarded as impinging less on the individual than do direct controls.

These considerations may explain the modification of those doctrines limiting the use of incentive controls where the alternative was resort to police powers. Thus public use, a requirement for the valid exercise of the eminent domain power, has been judicially transmuted from the restrictive public purpose or employment to public advantage or benefit, with benefit being given a broad rather than narrow construction. The Massachusetts Opinion of the Justices in 1955, that where justification for a redevelopment plan was sought in existing conditions there must be a full-blown residential slum, reflects a more restrictive view which was the earlier consensus. Its survival is attested to by decisions such as the Opinion of the Justices in Maine, considering a bill to condemn land for industrial development, and

Hogue v. *Port of Seattle*,[27] in Washington, reviewing a bill to take legally blighted lands, also for industrial development. Both decisions hold that the exercise of the power may not be justified on the public benefit to be derived from industrial expansion. The Washington decision additionally rejects the elimination of blight-productive defects in legal title.

These decisions, however, are contrary to the tide of judicial opinion toward the broader horizons opened by the United States Supreme Court decisions in *Berman* v. *Parker*.[28] Among others, Connecticut, Illinois, Massachusetts, and Pennsylvania courts are part of the new judicial consensus that holds that the elimination of blight—whether residential, industrial or un-developed—and the provision of industrial areas satisfy the re-quirement of public use.

A less significant limiting doctrine suggested by a Massachu-setts opinion is that when the evil is one which can be cured by use of the police powers, a public purpose basis is lacking for the exercise of eminent domain powers. While no longer the view there, if approved elsewhere, it may prove fatal to desirable programs. In Florida, this alternative power was one of the many reasons offered for the invalidation in the *Adams* [29] case of that state's first urban redevelopment statute.

Even in the more favorably disposed states, the inclusion of provisions safeguarding the public interest will facilitate ap-proval in borderline cases. Thus the courts of Massachusetts and Illinois have given considerable, if not decisive, weight to profit limitations in projects involving expenditure of public funds in connection with a development to be owned and operated pri-vately. Such slight restrictions should not impair the effective-ness of the tool, and may in fact have quite the opposite effect. To the extent public confidence is increased by allaying or fore-stalling suspicion of a give-away, the expansion of the program becomes that much less of a political gamble. It may also be

[27] 341 P. 2d 171 (Wash. 1960).
[28] *Berman* v. *Parker*, 348 U.S. 26 (1954).
[29] 60 So. 2d 663 (Fla. 1952).

decisive in determining the outcome of public referendums, such as that in Alexandria on a proposed shopping center.[30] There the vote was adverse to the project. The opposition, reportedly due to the provisions for development by private enterprise, might have been overcome by greater tangible emphasis on the public aspect of the undertaking.

Planning controls. Planning activity can be a direct control where the regulatory measure is made part of the plan; a direct control once removed where the regulatory measure controls individuals, but the plan controls the regulatory measures; or an indirect control where it influences, but does not coerce, development decisions.

Where incentives exercise control by changing the attractions of a specific development, hortatory planning exerts control by revealing already existing attractions. Rather than dictating what the planner deems to be desirable—which seems to be a common misconception among laity—the aim of planning may be to eliminate the inefficiencies of the market mechanism. The survey and plan thus provide a basis for rational decisions, and thereby foster rational development. Public planning collects and pulls together a host of information about economics, population, industrial tax space, and the rest which is not available to the ordinary entrepreneur—especially in a field like real estate where small business predominates. The effect may be to expose certain gaps in the existing fabric of land and housing to a man looking about for a field in which to produce.

By projecting probable development, the master plan furnishes a clue to the future of an area and, therefore, to the risk involved in making particular kinds of investments in that locale. The educational process of the plan, the sense of participation in the values of the community on whose resources the plan is to operate, and the setting of a general framework to maximize individual choice in the operations of the market mechanism are the means. This type of reconciliation of public and private

[30] See Haar, *Land-Use Planning: The Use, Misuse, and Reuse of Urban Land* (Boston: Little, Brown, 1959), p. 444.

purpose makes appropriate General Motors' use of the word "planning" in its planning division at the same time that, in the public field, a misconception sometimes fostered by planners themselves makes its use by a Conservative Ministry of Town and Country Planning almost improper.

If the level of planning activity is lower than desirable, it is not because legal barriers prevent it from rising; it is that the state laws which enable planning activities permit rather than direct. The laws exert no compulsion upon a city which does not choose to prepare a master plan for itself, or to join with other localities in the preparation of a regional plan. Even gentler prods of self interest are used sparingly. Urban renewal and redevelopment acts very frequently require the preparation of a plan before the benefits of the act can be had. But regulatory powers are generally not conditioned on or co-ordinated with any planning. Most zoning enabling laws do require a "comprehensive plan." But the overwhelming weight of judicial authority is that the requirement of the zoning law does not refer to the master plan of the same state's planning law, and, moreover, that it may be satisfied by the zoning ordinance itself. Thus zoning, the oldest land use control and the one still most widely employed, may be exercised without a guiding master plan, or, what is even more absurd, in disregard of such guidance where it is available.

At least one state, New Jersey, has taken a contrary view as to subdivision controls. The terms of the relevant enabling act do not specifically subject the delegation to a condition that its exercise be preceded by preparation of a master plan. Nevertheless, the condition has been inferred by courts which did not even have the question thrust on them. While this may render its dictum in legal jargon, the fact that the court reached out for the question may reflect its lack of doubt as to the proper answer.

Logically, the failure, even in New Jersey, to reach a parallel conclusion as to the relation of zoning and planning may seem indefensible. But subdivision control powers are generally delegated in the same act or at the same time as planning powers, whereas zoning powers usually precede both. In view of this embarrassing time sequence, it is hard to see how the courts could have reached any other conclusion with respect to zoning, and harder still to see how they could rationalize overruling their established precedent. If this should be changed—as does seem desirable—the onus is on the planning profession to make the necessity known to legislators.

As long as enabling acts are permissive, the potential benefits of planning will often remain unrealized. But the most disappointing experience has been with regional planning laws. In Wisconsin, for example, three years after the state legislature had authorized regional planning, not a single regional commission had been formed. Most of the reasons for planning inactivity on the smaller local level probably apply to the larger area of the region.

In addition, there is the obstacle of local government's jealousy of its power. Local government has accepted the idea of regulating the present use of land, transforming harmful areas, and planning future beneficial development. Thus far, at any rate, there is no evidence of similar acceptance of the idea of metropolitan government. Despite the pleas of several intellectuals and a few of the elite leaders such as the Regional Plan Association group in New York, the core's suburbs continue to exercise what land use measures have been delegated to them under state enabling legislation in at best a roughly co-ordinated fashion. Only the emergence of a greater common menace seems to induce voluntary co-operative action. This was recently demonstrated in Ohio. There the ordinarily home-rule-minded municipalities acted together through a regional planning association to oppose the greater danger of incursion into their powers by a commission having state-wide jurisdiction. But such emergency coalitions tend to disintegrate once the original raison d'être no longer exists.

Here again the difficulties in the way of a judicial solution make it unlikely that one will be found. Some years ago the New Jersey courts appeared to be making an effort in this direction. The foundation was laid in *Duffcon Concrete Products* v. *Borough of Cresskill*,[31] which presented the question of whether

---

[31] N.J. 509, 64 A. 2d 347 (1949).

a municipality had power to exclude all industry from its boundaries; the court deduced this power from the statutory direction
to encourage the "appropriate use" of land. While the municipal
zoning enabling act under which the case arose limited its sights
to the area of the municipality, the court took a broader view.
"What may be the most appropriate use of any particular property depends not only on all the conditions, physical, economic
and social, prevailing within the municipality and its needs, but
also on the nature of the entire region in which the municipality
is located and the use to which the land in that region has been
or may be put most advantageously." This was in 1949. In 1954
the credo was reaffirmed in the battle of the boroughs reported
in *Borough of Cresskill* v. *Borough of Dumont*.[32]

Then, in 1955, *Pierro* v. *Baxendale*[33] presented the court with
an opportunity to start building on the foundation, in determining whether the defendant community acted within the
scope of its power in totally excluding motels. Instead, a majority of the court put its decision on the narrow ground that an
ordinance permitting rooming and boarding houses, but excluding motels, was not *per se* invalid as discriminatory. The regional
implications are spelled out by the dissent. It points out that
the inference of the legislative history of the enactment "ac-
knowledge(d) a legitimate public need that must be denied
because lax operation of such facilities gives rise to police problems of supervision, a 'burden' to be borne by the neighboring
communities."

In *Pierro* the majority's opinion, far from rejecting a regional
approach, is tinged with regret that the issue was framed in a
way as to make regionalism irrelevant. With *Fanale* v. *Hasbruck
Heights*,[34] the circle is completed. The court clearly implied
that it regards as absurd the notion that a municipality might
have to "accept uses it believes to be injurious, in order to satisfy
the requirements of a county."

This line of cases illustrates two points. First, that concerted
action by a professional organization of planners, analogous to

[32] 15 N.J. 238, 104 A. 2d 441 (1954).
[33] 20 N.J. 17, 118 A. 2d 401 (1955).
[34] 26 N.J. 320, A. 2d 749 (1958).

that undertaken by the American Civil Liberties Union in its field of interest, may be as important as getting legislation enacted. In *Duffcon Concrete Products,* which contains probably the best judicial statement on regional planning, the court had the benefit of an *amicus curiae* brief filed by the Joint Council of Municipal Planning Boards in Essex County, New Jersey. The court's sophistication on the regional issue almost certainly owes much to that source. In none of the other cases did a regional organization attempt to educate the court as to how the *Duffcon* regionalism, which planners had helped to create, bore on the particular facts and issues before it.

The second point is that the doctrine of *Duffcon* is fine as an article of faith but, given the best will in the world, it was still only an attitude and not a guide to an answer in particular cases. If, in addition, the court had a master plan for the region, framed by the proper public body, it would have both the will and the means. It is doubtful whether the court can or will, or for that matter should, make the planning decisions which would properly be part of a regional master plan. Until some means are devised for requiring the preparation of such plans and for getting them before the court whenever regional questions are present, legal impetus to regional planning will be minimal.

Nevertheless, and even without changes in state legislation, the future will almost unquestionably see a substantial increase in planning, locally and perhaps even more regionally. A tremendous impetus is being given to such activity by the federal government aid programs which stress the necessity of planning, and, often, planning on a regional scale. Thus the President's 1962 Message to Congress requesting federal aid for urban mass transportation attributed "key importance" to "area-wide transportation planning and comprehensive development planning for metropolitan and large urban areas."

For this increased planning activity to result in proportionately greater indirect controls, the plans, including the underlying factual survey, must be generally available. This is not always the case, and often the unavailability is advertent, perhaps due to vestiges of the view of some early planners that the plan was purely a tool for the commission. To function properly, it had to have the utmost flexibility, and hence was certainly not to be enacted into law, and, for preference, it was not even to be a public document. This is a planning concept, not a legal one, and the initiative for any change must properly come from the planners.

The legal impact on the situation is slight. The theory has been advanced that designations on a plan of future public acquisitions of private property constitute a cloud on the title to the earmarked property. In *Moglingner* v. *Marion Co. Planning Commission* [35] where this theory was urged, the court gave it very short shrift. It is significant to the evaluation of the decision that the governing enabling act gives the master plan a quasi-constitutional role. It provides in substance that any municipal action involving the construction of, or authorization to construct, improvements usually covered by subdivision controls, is to be deemed *prima facie* contrary to the public interest if it departs from the master plan. If the provisions of such a master plan do not cloud title, the more typical, largely hortatory plan would *a fortiori* not cast a beclouding shadow.

Others fear that such designations may produce blight because the owner who knows his property is to be acquired for public purposes lacks incentive to expend money to keep it in good repair. To the extent that these dangers exist or there is a fear that they do, safety is being purchased at a needlessly high price. The benefits of a publicized plan without legal or factual blight can be had by the simple expedient of stating the plan in terms of principles and goals, rather than general locations.

Another desideratum is that public development adhere to the plan. The private developer in making his decision is hardly going to give much weight to the prophesies of a plan which experience has shown to be wrong in the very area where accuracy might most reasonably have been anticipated. Thus when, as is reported in a California case, the local authorities pick a site for

[35] 236 Ind. 298, 140 N.E. 2d 220 (1957).

public construction different from that recommended by their own plan, the self-fulfilling power of the plan with regard to the private sector is also weakened. The California court upheld the action of the municipality on the ground that the question was one governed by home rule rather than general law. It might with equal plausibility have held that although the question was within the home rule powers the municipality was bound by its own decision, as stated in its master plan, until it followed the prescribed procedure for changing that decision. It would nevertheless be a much harder result to reach because the court probably viewed the municipality's decision as a political matter and reversing it would be contrary to a very strong tradition.

Control through development. Government development is both the most forthright of controls and an important indirect control. The government operates largely in spheres the private sector finds unprofitable to enter—schools, parks, roads, and selected forms of housing. New York City alone has over $1 billion invested in schools and a like amount in housing, redevelopment, and renewal projects. By way of perspective, the private construction boom in New York City amounted to $1 billion from mid-1940 to mid-1950, while during the same period the city spent about twice that amount for schools, hospitals, port facilities, parks, bridges, libraries, and other facilities.

The indirect control results from the inevitable repercussions in land uses, both publicly and privately owned, and on the whole setup of the metropolitan areas. For example, a highway program may remove land from the tax rolls, displace families, pump more cars into central cities, and constitute competition for a transit system already weak. But the same program can result in vast areas of slums being razed; federal aid may be made available for access roads and to channel traffic into and around the heart of the city; capital expenditures can provide catalytic agencies for private urban renewal investments.

One important factor in determining the amount of government development activity is the rate of population increase. A rapidly growing population makes demands for more schools, roads, park and recreation space; in short, more of all the goods and services traditionally furnished by government. If at the same time the standard of living is rising, the demand will be for new services as well. The extra-legal limiting factors are in general the same as those operating on incentive controls.

Legal institutions enter the picture at several points. One is with respect to compensation, a field of law which is, to put it most kindly, both confused and confusing. How much the government must pay to acquire the property it proposes to develop has a direct effect on how much development it can undertake. Part of this same question is how much property the government may acquire. If it may condemn in excess of its needs, it may be able to capture the increment its activities add to the value of surrounding properties. The effect is the same as a reduction in the cost of the project site. But, some jurisdictions hold this economy is beyond the pale of the Constitution. It may be that nothing short of an amendment to the Constitution will be able to effect a change.

The other point of contact is producing a most interesting legal accommodation. An attempt is being made, mostly in the context of open space, to reduce public costs by restricting purchases more closely to what is needed. The effort is resulting in the invention of new interests which can be carved out of the fee simple absolute. These include development rights, popularized by the British 1947 Planning Act, and conservation easements, which is California's contribution. Massachusetts has taken this idea and woven it into an interesting new combination with zoning and tax controls. A 1957 act authorizes the owner of land zoned for agricultural, forest, or open space use to apply for classification for tax purposes as open land. This entitles him to a tax rebate of 90 per cent during the first three years, 70 per cent for the next seven years, and 50 per cent during the remaining years that the land is so classified.

These concepts should encounter little difficulty in the courts;

in fact, quite the reverse—particularly in jurisdictions where excess condemnation is prohibited. Although the emphasis of the newly carved-out rights is on public interests and that of excess condemnation is on the individual, both lead to the conclusion that the taking should be the smallest possible which permits achievement of the public end in view.

Some courts might be sympathetic to an argument that a taking of development rights, where the owner would be severely limited in the use he could thereafter make of his property, constitutes in substance taking of the entire fee. A more realistic danger is that the jury would be so persuaded and would render its award in accordance. This would completely defeat the purpose of the act to economize the use of public funds. It would also increase compensation inequities by giving the owner a windfall to the extent of the value of the rights retained by him.

Apart from how much is taken, the governmental exercise of the power to condemn has been singularly free of restraint in this area. An unusual instance occurred recently in *Progress Development Corp.* v. *Mitchell*,[36] which prohibited a municipality from condemning certain property. The ostensible purpose of the taking was to acquire the land for a public park, a traditionally accepted use of the power. Notwithstanding this, and notwithstanding also multitudinous precedents holding that the court will not undertake to examine legislative motive for an otherwise legal act, the ground of the decision was that the legislature's real purpose was to frustrate the owner's plans to construct a racially integrated housing project. This is, hopefully, an aberrational case in that the legislative powers of government will not often become the tool of local prejudices. The decision has a much wider import if viewed as another manifestation of the court's generalized awareness of racial implications even in actions which on the surface appear to be entirely unrelated to such issues.

[36] 286 F. 2d 222 (1961).

Private Policies

Although not generally regarded as such, many private acts or policies are in effect semipublic enactments affecting land use. The line between private and public is by no means rigid; variations occur from day to day and from place to place.

Covenants and conditions. Covenants are one of the earliest forms of land use control known to the common law. Agreements to use property for residential purposes only were lawful when the weight of authority still regarded zoning as unconstitutional. And since, under proper circumstances, such agreements would be enforced by equity, their provisions in a very real sense were law as to the convenanting parties. With the final validation and increasing use of zoning, resort to covenants probably declined. Now, however, there appears to be a resurgence brought about by the use of such agreements to control development of large subdivisions.

One criticism of the law of covenants has been that it permits one generation to fetter too severely the power of succeeding generations to deal with land. A remedial measure recently adopted in Massachusetts sets up two categories of agreements: (1) those imposed as part of a common scheme, i.e., private planning, and (2) others; it then establishes the period of their legal duration and provides for their recordation. It also prescribes the test to be applied by the courts in litigation seeking to enforce a covenant. Enforcement is to be denied unless the claimants actually benefit substantially by reason of it. Within the framework of the new statute, an able and experienced conveyancer, however, will probably be able to achieve the same objectives and with a degree of certainty not possible under purely case law regulation. Nevertheless, the provisions as to enforceability may tend to facilitate a more rational land use pattern.

The Massachusetts test of enforceability adopts the common law rule. Courts of equity in many jurisdictions have refused to enforce restrictive agreements that have outlived the conditions under which they were appropriate, and no longer serve a useful purpose. The criteria used by many of the cases are very much those of planning. What is the neighborhood affected? How long does it have to be in a use inconsistent with the covenant to be deemed a change in use? How does one know what is a "predominantly residential" purpose if that is the wording of the covenant? How does one decide what the traffic generation impact on a building is so that a present covenant for quiet no longer serves any useful purpose?

This area so clearly smacks of city planning considerations that in England the Lands Tribunal has been given jurisdiction over it, concurrent with the traditional jurisdiction of courts of equity. By statute, the tribunal is authorized to discharge restrictions not only when they have been rendered obsolete—the common law doctrine—but also when they impede the reasonable use by one without conferring "practical" benefits on the other. Money damages may be awarded to compensate for any losses suffered thereby.

A basic question under our present legal structure is whether the judiciary or an administrative agency should make decisions concerning change in neighborhood, new needs, technology, and interrelationships of land use. If the decisions are to be made by the courts, private developers, who usually launch the arrangements, will also have the power to initiate proceedings looking to change. What criteria are to be applied to deciding the particular case and how can the results be correlated with what is happening in the administrative and planning branches of government? What, for example, should be the relationship of covenants to zoning? The old zoning ordinances often confer immunity on existing covenants. This may not give rise to much conflict under the cumulative type of zoning ordinance. But with the growing use of exclusive zoning ordinances providing for noncumulative uses in particular districts, conflicts are bound to grow apace. Will the courts say that the private power to dispose of land should prevail? Or will the contract right be put on a higher level of immunity from the reach of the police

power, as was done so strongly by the New York Court of Appeals
in the prior lien case of *Central Savings Bank* v. *City of New
York?* [37] Many of the zoning ordinances do not even purport to
deal with covenants. If zoners live apart from the world of real
property, and blissfully do not provide for recording variances
or exceptions in the registry of deeds, and if planners survey,
analyze, and project existing conditions of traffic and industrial
uses, but utterly ignore the pattern established by conditions,
determinable fees, covenants, and easements, what should be the
court reaction? Should it say that this was not thought of by the
agency and therefore it has to supply an artificial legislative in-
tent, or should it assume that the zoning was meant to override
the particular restriction in issue? What weight should a court
give to the existence of a zoning ordinance? Should it simply
disregard the zoning as not relevant for its common law adjudication? Should it regard zoning as conclusive upon it? Should it
simply be regarded as evidence? Nor is this a tedious unraveling
of alternatives; these are all views that have been taken by different jurisdictions. The problem from the point of view of achieving rational land use is not legal doctrine, but procedure. These
and similar issues are raised in litigation between two private
parties, with no representation of the public considerations.
Often the zoning ordinance is simply ignored or not argued by
counsel. Planning principles may similarly not be brought to the
court's attention. Yet such private litigation has tremendous
land use effects. It may, for example, modify an entire zoning
pattern either by starting new nonconforming uses, by encouraging further deviation from the plan, or by not permitting the
kind of development which would be the most rational and best
organized for that particular district. [38]

The need for much more thoughtful reformulation of related
planning and property controls is apparent in the land disposi-

[37] 279 N.Y. 266, 18 N.E. 2d 151 (1938).

[38] Nuisance litigation raises the same issue. If a use permitted by a zoning
ordinance is nevertheless claimed to be a common law nuisance by a legislator,
what weight should the court give to the ordinance? How does public legislation
of land controls, in general, fit in with the "private" side of the legal system
where the courts are formulating what John Chipman Gray in his *Casebook on
Property* described as the law of the "proper place"?

tion contract pushed on to the stage by urban renewal. In order to obtain detailed control of design, open space, and shape and placement of buildings, generalities of a zoning ordinance have proven inadequate. Detailed covenants and easements therefore have come into play. Assurance of the type of developer, the positive implementation of an architectural plan, non-speculation in redevelopment futures also require a resort to new property controls. What is the relationship between a zoning ordinance, which has to be in accordance with a comprehensive plan, and the redevelopment plan which has to be in accordance with the comprehensive plan or a master plan? What if the redevelopment plan is amended from time to time? What if the zoning ordinance is revised from time to time? How can we fit in the one lesson learned from land use controls—that time keeps wearing away at man's intentions, that one generation needs a power of appointment over the preceding one's assets, and that technology and man's knowledge are always expanding as are his desires? Since both the redevelopment plan and the zoning ordinance are adopted by the local legislative body, is it simply a question of the more recent one prevailing should the two conflict? Conflicts are likely to arise, for the subsidy element in urban renewal means a demand for greater public controls, such as density or open space standards which in a zoning ordinance would give rise to claims of a taking of private property.

Private institutional policies. Just as covenants represent the primarily private counterpart of public planning enactments, the policies pursued by title companies are in some respects an important private counterpart of public enforcement in this area. In fact the zeal of title companies may exceed that of public enforcement, as in the period following the widespread invalidation of official mapping statutes. Contemporaries report that even after these decisions title companies were refusing to insure titles which violated the integrity of an official map.

For some reason, however, the title companies adopted a contrary approach to violations of zoning or subdivision laws; an exception to them is part of the "boiler plate" on every insurance binder. It is small comfort, as some Massachusetts land owners discovered, to find that you have a perfect "title," but cannot make the intended use of the land because it would violate the subdivision law. A similar unsatisfactory result may obtain with respect to bulk uses control, especially in the new guise of flexible floor area ratios; often the same open land is counted for the floor area ratio for two different parcels so far as the deed of chain of title is concerned, without cognizance being taken of the planning significance.

A recent pamphlet by the Home Title Insurance Company indicates that conservative conveyancers are increasingly aware of the necessary intertwining of private and public land use controls. Considerable impetus was given this development in Denver by a requirement to record all nonconforming uses. The result was swift enforcement through the action of mortgagees. Mortgagees—and after all, it is credit which is the life-blood of land development in this country—generally and their attorneys, too, are beginning to be more aware of the significance of subdivision and other land use controls.

This may have a great deal of significance in enforcement— that constant bugaboo of planning controls. It could greatly reduce the need for planning and building inspectors and local district attorneys as the enforcement arms of a government planning system. Policing by way of title and conveyancing may raise serious issues as to delegation of power to private groups, but its effectiveness in the day-to-day ordering of men's affairs can be little doubted, and the precedents of easements, covenants, and the like should ease acceptance.

A GLANCE AT THE FUTURE

This survey of selected land use controls depicts an over-all situation which in one sense might best be described as unexciting. A planner may wander through the entire domain and, unless he owes as much to Cervantes as to AIP, he would not meet with as much as one legal dragon belching forth proposal-consuming flames. This is not attributable to the fact that the selection is a mere fraction of the whole, because in this respect at least, it is a fairly representative sampling.

Private property, which not very long ago might have seemed nearly, though never quite, dragonesque, is now a relatively tame creature—civilized, if not socialized. A proposal portending substantial new restraints might show that there is still some fight left, but at present no great battles are being fought, only minor skirmishes.

Even as to these skirmishes how much constitutes a real, if lesser, conflict between planning on the one hand and legal institutions on the other depends on how planning is defined. If, for example, every proposal to control land use automatically enters the ranks of planning, the instances of conflict would add up to a very large figure. Using this method of classification, the Michigan case (that already mentioned of *Progress Development Corp.* v. *Mitchell*), vacating a condemnation because its purpose was found to be unlawful discrimination, would be dignified as conflict. While no empiric inquiry to ascertain the number of planners in sympathy with that attempt has been made, such a survey undoubtedly would show them to be an insignificant minority.

If, on the other hand, a proposal for controlling land use must have the unanimous support of the planning profession before legal veto of the proposal ranked as conflict, the picture would be one of perfect but meaningless rapprochement. Since our goal is the creation neither of a fool's paradise nor of a planner's inferno, the only reasonable approach seems to be to require some substantial consensus, short of unanimity. For present purposes, "substantial" is as precise as we need get.

With this as the yardstick, some tensions are discernible, more are inevitable. If suitable land were so plentiful that each individual could have all he desired without conflict with any other person, there would be no need for a law of real property. But where land is scarce in relation to demand, decisions must be made as to who gets what, and when, and the body of law grows because it is needed to assist in this decisional process.

Obviously the supply of suitable land in this country is less than the demand, but how much less is the subject of continuing dispute. Many people are fond of stating that the U.S. population could be sheltered at a figure of twelve houses to the acre in the state of Kansas. Others answer, "Who wants to live there?" and point to the shortage of land in metropolitan areas. The evaluation is complicated by the fact that neither element in the equation is a constant, a fact sometimes overlooked when inventorying supply. Right now, for example, we are in the process of discovering uses for urban space which lay idle because of lack of technological know-how and creative imagination. In the air space over the Franklin Roosevelt Drive in New York City there have recently risen high-rise luxury co-operative houses. A motel is rising in the air space over the New York Central's freight yards on the west side of the same city. The changes in living-working patterns wrought by the automobile after the First World War may be dwarfed by changes brought about by the airplane or some device not yet born.

Nevertheless, present indications are that demand will outrun supply. Our population, contrary to predictions made in the 1930's, continues to grow. Metropolitan centers have been further swelled by the continuing flow of people from the rural areas. These people will need housing; their demand for goods and services will increase the pressure for business and industrial space.

Another factor making for increased demand is a rise in aspirations and standards of living. This can be expected to continue for the next generation, although the precise extent depends on how successful we are in eliminating cyclical fluctuations in the economy. Some minority groups may enjoy more than pro rata increases as artificial barriers come down.

This situation makes for a growth in the law because scarcity is simply a shorthand way of saying that some needs are not being satisfied. These may be expected to create the pressures which are a major wellspring for proposals dealing with urban space, proposals to rearrange relations, to modify existing rights and duties. Every remedial law—and these formal enactments must come into being or the proposals will remain just so much talk—displeases someone. Such measures, therefore, contain within themselves the potential of conflict. Part of that potential will never be realized, but part will. Thus, it can be assumed that the near future will see many legal innovations attempted, with the usual proportion gradually gaining legal acceptance.

Incentive Controls

Prominent among the legal innovations will be more extensive resort to incentive controls: guaranties, low interest loans, subsidies, grants-in-aid, land assembly, tax advantages, and technical assistance. This means that positive aspects of development will be emphasized; above all, it signifies state and especially, since it is the fountain of credit, federal entry into the land use control field on a far larger scale.

One reason for this development is the dispute as to the scope of the police power, a dispute which goes back into common law history, probably even to the time where "The memory of man runneth not," but is not perceptibly nearer solution for all its years. The police power was the issue in the struggle which accompanied the introduction of zoning, and it emerged triumphant in the debate among planners and lawyers as to the proper theory on which to base land use controls. Proponents were vindicated by the same Supreme Court which had invalidated minimum wages for women as an undue interference with property rights.

Today the most disputed subject matter is open space, whether park, playground, recreation, or simply undeveloped land. The effort to achieve it through the police power has taken many forms. In *Osteicher* v. *Wolcott*, an Ohio case, the technique was simply withholding subdivision approval. In *Forston Investment Co.* v. *Oklahoma City*,[39] the device was a condition precedent to subdivision approval that a fee be paid into a general park fund. In a recent New Jersey case, the device

[39] 17 Okla. 473, 66 P. 2d 96 (1957).

was zoning the subject land for park, recreation, and school purposes.[40] In all these cases, the courts expressed their sympathy with the open space objective and the concern for the common weal which inspired the government action. But they were also in accord that the police power could not constitutionally be utilized for the task.

Most recent attention has focused on development rights, with some planners arguing that such rights can be acquired or, more accurately perhaps, frozen through the exercise of the police power. The issue has not yet been presented to any court in this context. Even if, in a development rights case, the judiciary could be persuaded that the foregoing cases were distinguishable, and need not be followed as a matter of authority, the issue would remain a question of policy. Compensation allows greater, more intimate, and additional individual controls. There is a growing recognition that the money lubricant needs to be added to the machinery of land use controls in order to achieve greater flexibility. More important, perhaps, the affluence of our society may make subsidies and controls for the benefit of upper income groups politically palatable under a "filtering down" philosophy. Compensation also accords more precisely with accepted notions of fairness. In other words, even though a court would regard a control as a proper regulation under the police power, in fairness to the individual as well as on grounds of acceptability to the community it is appropriate to redress and spread the loss. Thus the recently proposed Pennsylvania law of open space, combining zoning and eminent domain, represents a legislative decision not to drive regulatory aspects too far. To a large extent this approach, if adopted, will be made possible by moving away from the limited property tax base through appropriations and subsidies by the state or federal government.

The considerations applying to open space resemble those mounted in the early years of zoning, but it has long been recognized that at some point differences in degree become, for practical purposes, indistinguishable from differences in kind. Thus

[40] *Angermeir* v. *Sea Girt,* 27 N.J. 298, 142 A. 2d 624 (1958).

the older regulation, even ignoring the effects of inflation on the values of real property, had a far deeper and wider bite, and the public, if it had had to pay the cost, would have prevented imposition of the control. This is probably not true as to development rights.

Each legal accommodation is bound to raise fresh problems. In the context of willingness to pay, the issue will arise of whether the benefits of planning traceable to the restriction should not be recaptured from those who benefit by planning. This, in turn, can be analyzed in another fashion: instead of paying through eminent domain—a burden on the general taxpayer—should not the cost be assumed by that district which is going to benefit primarily from the control? We can anticipate conflicts between the benefited neighboring group and the general taxpayer. There may be newer techniques aimed at recoupment, excess taking, and incremental taxation. As awareness grows of who is subsidizing whom, we can anticipate the invention of new kinds of transfer mechanism and new subsidies.

Mandatory Controls

However much incentive controls are expanded and improved, direct controls will continue to play an important role. The mandatory planning control of tomorrow will be a quite different animal from its predecessors of 1916–26. As has already been noted, mandatory control is now in a process of change. Two lines of development stand out, and both tend in the direction of greater flexibility. Carried to the extreme, the result could be that every change of use must be preceded by administrative authorization reminiscent of English development permission, with a transition of the zoning system to a licensing system through such techniques as special exceptions, special use districts, and floating districts. The reactions of the courts that have had occasion to consider this line of development have varied. A fairly favorable climate of judicial opinion appears to exist in Maryland where *Huff* v. *Howard County* [41] was decided, and in New York where *Rodgers* v. *Tarrytown* [42] is law. How far these precedents can be pushed is still conjectural. Not only were both decisions by sharply divided courts, but the *Tarrytown* decision contains language which a later court could seize upon to limit its authority. Slow and extremely cautious procedure seems to be indicated.

Elsewhere, the courts have signalled not merely caution, but retreat. In New Jersey and Pennsylvania barriers have been erected beyond which, for the present at least, this development may not legally proceed.

The other vulnerable area of mandatory controls emerges when the concepts of racial, religious, and perhaps economic equality run counter to the use of controls to upgrade residential areas, provide parks, or gain other planning goals. The relationship between planning controls and discrimination, since the Supreme Court's decision in the School Cases, has been subjected to increasing judicial scrutiny. Coming after some years during which attention focused elsewhere, these issues tend to appear more novel than they are. Such early leading cases as *Spann* v. *Dallas* [43] bottomed their opposition to the then infant control in very large part on the grounds that zoning was or could be used to perpetuate racial discrimination. And *Buchanan* v. *Warley* [44] condemned in 1917 a zoning ordinance making it unlawful for a white person to reside in a block where the residences were occupied by Negroes and for a Negro person to reside in a block where the residences were occupied by whites.

The verdict of the intervening years has been almost without exception in favor of the planning controls. The decisions never rejected the values of racial equality, equality of housing opportunity, and the like; the rationale was rather that the particular control did not entrench on them. *Town of Harrison* v.

[41] 214 Md. 48, 133A 2d 83 (1957).
[42] 302 N.Y. 115, 96 N.E. 2d 731 (1951).
[43] 111 Tex. 350, 212 S.W. 513 (1921).
[44] 245 U.S. 60 (1917).

Sunny Ridge Builders [45] is fairly typical. In issue was an upzoning from ½ to 1 acre minimum lots, which, the petitioners argued, would create an economic barrier which none but the wealthy would be able to surmount. The court vigorously asserted the impropriety of such a barrier as a planning goal. It upheld the zoning, however, pointing out that the subject area contained some of the most desirable residential sites in the community.

Today the result might well be different. The reason is not a shift in values. Rather there appears to be a heightened awareness of the realities of the situation, and a willingness to face up to them rather than to skirt the issue by resting on the theoretical or possible effect of the challenged action. This view, or renewed consciousness, is not limited to zoning, but probably will soon permeate the entire gamut of land use controls.

Here again there is a twofold question. One view is that if the control can be justified as advancing any proper planning goal it should be upheld regardless of its actual, probable, or intended purpose. But doubtless many planners would shun association with any measure motivated by discrimination.

The division in the planning ranks may well be such as to eliminate those controls from the category of conflict by definition. But even so, the new judicial sensitivity to discriminatory implications casts doubt on the propriety of far more defensible controls. These include most obviously zoning, but also all controls which have any tendency toward the prohibited effect, however innocent their purpose.

Real Property Devices

Still a third major innovation probably will occur in development of new legal concepts based on property conveyancing. New, more precise interests in property will be created—California's conservation rights and Minnesota's development rights point the way—making it possible for governments to acquire

[45] 170 Misc. 161, 8 N.Y.S. 2d 632 (1938).

only that which they deem necessary and to compensate more often those injured by the acquisition. Experiments will be made in combining estate concepts, new and old, partial police power, eminent domain, and special tax theories, in enforcement of planning controls through the machinery of property conveyancing rather than through public government. There will be greater attention paid to the joint venture, to the relation between public and private energies. It is because of this spirit of experimentation, this willingness to regard the law of property as simply a tool which this age, like past ages, must reshape to meet its needs, that the American common law of property will probably continue to satisfy the needs of contemporary society.

Reviewability: The Legal Framework for Reasonableness

All three of the developments, by pushing hard the theory of controls, frame sharp issues for judicial review of land use decisions and of public and private relationships. An important factor in the resolution of many of them may be a suspicion that the new developments are probably more susceptible of abuse than the older controls by regulatory law. While the bulk of controls will continue to be upheld, some will not; the problem is to identify the factors which will determine validity. Some are quite clear.

In subdivision controls the rule has been fairly well crystallized that subdivision approval may be conditioned on the developer's assumption of the social costs occasioned by his activity. Similarly, in zoning it is now relatively clear that exclusionary zoning is not *per se* unreasonable and therefore illegal although specific instances might be. But as to other, newer issues, the courts have not yet had an opportunity to work out rules to determine legality. Hence the only determinant is the judicial distillation of what is reasonable in the circumstances. Since precise rules have not yet crystallized, these new issues will be handled in the common law fashion; generalized but accepted notions of reasonableness and fairness will furnish crude guideposts to future decisions.

Those aspects of fairness and justice denoted by equality of treatment and impartiality of procedure can be regarded as law ends which on occasion clash with physical planning ends, but essentially they are values shared by a consensus of society and expressed in a statute or decision. But even the state courts, which retain greater scrutiny than the federal courts, seem reluctant to interpose the Constitution against proposed solutions of urgent metropolitan problems. In fact, the constitutional role, which the layman tends to stress as the prime manifestation of United States planning law, has become so narrowed since the end of World War II that it is a minor constraint to the planner. One by-product is the need for a substitute for the tests of constitutionality that so often have been substituted for considerations of wisdom. But the typical judicial stress of balancing property rights against planning need underlines a major point. At the constitutional level law tends to focus on the relation between means and ends—in fact, the classic definition of the police power is "whether the means employed . . . have a substantial relation to the public welfare." This concern with a testing of this relationship feeds into a concern over the intermeshing of goals so that even at the level of the legislative draftsman this search for co-ordination, which I have earlier referred to as rationality, is a natural inquiry into any planning proposal.

However, the planner, as much as the lawyer, has tended to rely too much on court review. Judicial invalidation of an enactment does not mean a reactionary brake; judicial vindication is not necessarily a victory for wise planning. The positive contribution of the restraints upon imprudent action has sometimes obscured the fact that judicial processes are somewhat helpless to induce rationality or even, at technical points, to review it. Given properly stated objectives, courts can be relied upon to review challenged actions to ascertain consistency with the avowed purpose for delegating the power being exercised. But it would be unrealistic in the extreme to rely on judicial review to ascertain whether the avowed purpose of one measure is in harmony with the stated goals and objectives of other inter-related measures. It is a job beyond the competence of the judiciary—beyond the scope of the type of knowledge an adversary system can present to a court, as well as beyond the remedies which a court can formulate or enforce. These difficulties are infinitely greater when the interacting measures are the product of different legislative bodies, whether on the same governmental level, as two cities, or different levels, as the federal government and municipalities. Equally important, both courts and legislature would almost certainly regard such judicial review as a rank usurpation of legislative powers by the judiciary. Hence, the ultimate conclusion: the pressing need is the guidance of a plan formulated and adopted by the local legislature, or, on the regional level, by the state legislature.

Developing New Legal Accommodation

Stated objectives are probably desirable for all laws. For most land use controls they are a virtual necessity because the governing laws are in the first instance enabling laws on the state level. Recently, too, the federal housing legislation may properly be classified as enabling acts, encouraging certain land use activities by conferring not constitutional power but that more important source of action, financial power.

Without policy statements we lack a satisfactory guide for formulating regulatory statements—the do's and don't's that have direct impact on the individual's actions. Also, as the federal highway program shows, without policy statements we lack a standard by which to evaluate the effects of the regulatory measures; and lacking that standard we often fail to make any effort at evaluation.

If the plan is recognized simply as a guide to the planning commission of a general and flexible kind which does not even have to be written, much less adopted by the legislature, the impact on constitutional law, property rights, and on people's expectations can be dismissed as *de minimus*. Where this largely self-defeating approach is dropped and the master plan is given authority in the direction of human energies, constitutional law becomes important. If the projection of the master plan is a touchstone for a proposed urban renewal plan, for determining whether a whole program for open space is legitimate, or for testing a zoning or subdivision regulation, what it says at the outset is of great importance to the property developer and to the lawyer. If the master plan is simply gazing into the future with no means available for effectuation, then its proscriptions may constitute a taking of land without compensation. Is the alternative thrust on the city that it may not plan for this area unless it has the funds ready to acquire the affected property? This highlights again the advisability of having a master plan that states the important principles and not the specific locational aspects of planning. A statement of principles would give flexibility, furnish a guide for testing land use controls, and avoid the necessity for immediate land taking which can curtail usefulness of the master plan.

Elsewhere I have discussed the role of the master plan as an impermanent constitution.[46] In considering the future of social control of land use, stress must be placed on the master plan's relationship to the federal government. Although discussions of land use controls emphasize direct actions oriented toward housing and land policy and the local units of government in which these powers are constitutionally vested, these controls must always be perceived within the context of federal government policy. What is the attitude of the Federal Reserve Board? Or the Treasury Department? What of the Employment Act of 1947? The whole attitude toward government taxation and spending, and the pursuit of those linked goals—high employment, high rates of growth, and reasonable price stability—have an impact not only on the rate of development of land and housing, but also on the type of development. The FHA Title 203 program is the driving force behind the spread of sub-

[46] Haar, "The Master Plan: An Impermanent Constitution," *Law and Contemporary Problems,* vol. 20 (1955) p. 353.

divisions. The glass and aluminum filing boxes sprouting on Madison Avenue may shift, with different types of capital controls and fiscal and monetary policies, to other types of construction. A change in the tax policy which now favors the home owner over the home renter may also cause different types of land uses, different types of developments, and different places of development within the metropolitan region.

The key to rational policy is to integrate local master plans with federal economic and monetary programs. In addition to greater awareness of economic development on the part of the planner, this entails greater recognition by the federal government of the peculiar role of housing as a stabilizer in the economy, and of its particular vulnerability to credit controls. Thus, should the federal government establish a secondary mortgage bank, comparable to the Home Loan Bank System for savings and loan associations or the Federal National Mortgage Association dealings with the FHA and VA mortgages, the new enterprise would loose a host of pressures for development of the type and in the location which it deems desirable. Those pressures would release pent up energies by making capital available in an industry where equity financing is almost unknown. They would influence the use of some local land use controls, and hasten the obsolescence of others. This attempt to integrate direct controls and local master planning with federal policies affecting land is indeed a complex undertaking. But the choice is not between action and no action; the need is to recognize implications of actions that will be taken. Fiscal and monetary measures will be passed; their effects must be assayed. In several aspects the protections cast by the federal government activity in terms of quality of personnel, standards, subjection to public criticism and openness of procedure, and internal review are better than on the local level and can provide useful prototypes.

These activities of the federal government constitute a field traditionally immune from judicial review. Yet as bounty and privilege increase, issues arise of depriving people of livelihood, and of simple administrative decisions determining the fates of cities. And here is a crucial institutional vacuum to be filled by new mechanisms of internal review by federal urban agencies, by greater willingness by Congress to spell out its delegation of authority in relation with local and regional master plans, or by courts to accepting responsibility for working out standards. This means again a greater emphasis on definition and articulation of policy by the federal executive and legislative agencies so that a reviewable standard can be given to the less expert body that is entrusted with reviewing this policy.

The result of inattention to framework by the legislative and administrative branches has been confusion and hesitant implementation. Judicial respect for legislative findings of fact and disregard of legislative motive as irrelevant point up the "empty bottle" nature of existing tools. The tool is created first, policy is later provided by each user and may vary from user to user and from the declaration of policy attached to the tool by its creators. Opening of the flood-gates of discretion by the newly evoked, more sophisticated land use control devices raises serious institutional challenges if private property, in the Bentham sense of expectations, is to continue as the engine of land development. One of the important obstacles to success in such an endeavor is nonjudicial in origin: the failure of planning measures to incorporate adequately stated objectives. Without a general objective against which particular action can be judged, administration may not be even-handed and may have a patchwork pattern of policy implementation. It is also difficult to check arbitrary execution of the law, by either judicial or administrative review. Here the formulation of the objective is a matter of clear legislative statement. The judiciary, too, can play a role in prodding the legislature by refusing to enforce laws which lack adequate standards.

In the future social control of urban space there will undoubtedly be experimentation not only in the form of the plan and the controls but in the government instrumentalities charged with their administration. The changes in law brought about by urbanization and industrialization are not confined to property law alone. The development has parallels in many fields of law. For example, the injured employee now looks for redress to the administrative paraphernalia established under workman's compensation acts instead of, as formerly, the law of torts administered by judicial machinery. Antitrust laws, a factor to be considered in every business contract negotiation, are now delegated to an administrative agency. The legal relations of organized labor and its employers come within the purview of still another agency.

This suggests that the court system begins to be regarded as an unsatisfactory mechanism for original decision when the law undertakes to regulate in some detail the everyday and fairly routine action and interactions of large numbers of people. Multitudinous questions of a relatively narrow compass are inevitable, which may explain the appeal of a streamlined procedure administered by experts in the field. This force is already at work in the area of land use law and can be expected to accelerate rapidly. The result, as in labor law or workmen's compensation, will doubtless be more administered law.

On the other hand, the master system, under which water law adjudication has been handled in Massachusetts, suggests judicial competence. There are also traditional judicial dealings with basic land policies in fields as diverse as nuisance and restraints on alienation, as well as in determining the continued viability of covenants. With a codification of the standards pieced together from the cases, a repeal of inconsistencies, and a testing of doctrine by the needs of the new urbanism, fresh starting points for judicial decision could be set. In short, here is an "agency" that can be reformed out of the common law materials to handle these new, intricate planning controls.

The English Lands Tribunal furnishes an interesting and instructive model. There the bench consists of lawyers, expert appraisers, real estate people, and surveyors. But the organization is that of a judicial tribunal, with presentation of cases and arguments by attorneys. The testimony before the Franks Committee indicates that this new entity has functioned well, that its task has been most adequately discharged, with respect gained from planners and lawyers alike. In this country, the housing courts are an effort to concentrate controversies over housing, building code, and zoning matters, much as the Land Court in Massachusetts and other states is directed at giving expertise in the land conveyancing and title areas to judges now made specialists by that best of teachers, experience. All disputes primarily involving issues touching land development could be channeled there. In addition, the traditional courts might certify questions which have or may have important consequences for land use development although arising in cases more appropriately tried before some other tribunal.

The preparation of the policy guide might be one of the functions assigned the new institution, if it is modeled not on purely adjudicatory lines, but on the example of the federal administrative commissions which perform also in a legislative capacity. It could be undertaken by the legislature itself by the developing of more definite standards and by the interplay of tribunal decisions and further legislation. Or, depending on the particular conditions of the state, this policy formulation could be delegated to an administrative agency.

Such an agency, if given statewide jurisdiction, might for example lay down some type of zoning policy for the metropolitan areas, isolating those functions which are more than intra-community concern, in much the same way as we have developed—true, with struggle and occasional ambiguity—the concept of intrastate and interstate commerce on the national level. There is no need for these agencies to zone directly. They would simply view the housing and land needs of the metropolitan region in broad perspective and set up standards whereby local ordinances could be judged. The commissions themselves, with an ultimate right of appeal to the courts, could decide when this type of local activity has begun to conflict with state policy.

· · · · ·

Present urban problems can be analyzed solely in terms of particular fact clusters, for example: What is the best planning machinery for the region? Are gray areas eradicable? Do planning officials, generally non-elective, exercise more power than is consistent with democracy? Is flexible zoning better or worse than traditional zoning? This analysis may be adequate where the aim is amelioration of a particular evil. But the goal of rational development aspires to more and thus requires a different analysis. "Rational," in this context, implies that the goals and their consequences are known and that policies are adopted and reviewed in the light of that knowledge. Furthermore, rationality implies the articulation and harmonizing of the relationships of these goals and policies. This approach is not a substitute for fact studies; it is a framework for their analysis. The lack of such a framework is a serious aspect of the urban problem facing American society; its construction is one of the most interesting challenges in an area replete with them.

In this hammering out of a framework for goal clarification and alternatives, there will be a need for (1) local master plans of generalized statements of objectives, to which public developments and public controls over land uses must accord; (2) an articulation of federal policies and programs—those within a future Department of Urban Affairs as well as those without—which affect the pattern of metropolitan land uses; (3) a stress on the private dynamics of land development so that planning and controls can tap those energies which build and develop cities; (4) new relationships between private controls judicially administered through common law channels and public controls; and (5) new state-wide agencies both for administration and adjudication.

Law is only one profession which faces this challenge. In conjunction with other concerned groups, a legal framework can be devised for planning which can express the community consensus on planning objectives and means. This framework can also provide a system for articulating and testing these objectives and means as well as make possible community acceptance of proposals for attaining a rational utilization of urban space.

HENRY FAGIN is a professor in the Department of Urban and Regional Planning, University of Wisconsin. He was executive director of the Penn-Jersey Transportation Study from its launching in June 1959 through August 1962. For seven years prior to this he served first as planning director and then as executive director of New York's Regional Plan Association. In 1958 he was Ford Rotating Research Professor in Governmental Affairs in the Department of Political Science, University of California, Berkeley. His recent publications include "Problems of Planning in the Suburbs," in Part V of *The Suburban Community; Planning and Community Appearance* (co-author); and "Planning Organization and Activities within the Framework of Urban Government," Chapter 7 in *Planning and the Urban Community*. Mr. Fagin was born in New York in 1913. He received his B.Arch. degree and his M.S. in Planning from Columbia University.

SOCIAL FORESIGHT AND
THE USE OF URBAN SPACE

HENRY FAGIN

WITH A KEEN SENSE OF TIMELINESS Resources for the Future has
brought together this set of essays by scholars, planners, and ad-
ministrators concerned about the future use of urban space.
Broad areas of consensus among the authors are punctuated by
sharp conflicts, divergences of opinion, and contrasting values.
I shall make it my responsibility to ask, "What do these reflections add up to?" and to offer in answer some observations of
my own which have been stimulated by these essays.

I have spent some time pondering the form of these remarks
—the form to impose on what has been discussed so as to syn-
thesize and interpret the whole. The function of form is to aid
perception. The more complex the elements to be grasped, the
greater the need for a simplifying form.

To discuss the future use of urban space, I have chosen as
format: three professions, two issues, and one prediction. The
three professions are medicine, economics, and the law; certain
of their insights as to what is happening to our culture will set
the stage for the ensuing discussion of issues. And then, having
opened somewhat more questions than will be answered this
year or next, I shall end with a judgment about the next

crucial political development toward a better use of social foresight in determining the use of urban space.

MEDICINE

In his essay Dr. Leonard J. Duhl challenges professional planners when he writes: ". . . man is conquering outer space before he is master of his earth space."

It is Duhl's view that economics, transportation, design, and engineering now dominate planning for the use of urban space, but that the psycho-social dimensions should transcend all other considerations. Physical and spatial planning cannot be done in isolation from a much broader concern with the needs of the community and its people. The ecological interrelationships of space, buildings, institutions, industries, socio-economic class, organization, social and physical mobility, play, health, welfare, and education make it urgent that we understand these relationships *prior* to any decision about space. On the simplest level we must ask: what are the human implications of planning action? Will a road, for example, split a community and cause a social disruption that will result in a greater social cost than revising the proposed highway pattern?

Duhl is fundamentally correct. To the present, I have not come across anyone in any planning office who has ever faced this crucial type of question and produced an answer based on the facts.

Duhl's suggestion is that planners begin with authentic studies of the social and economic needs of the community's people, proceed next to the design of social and economic programs, and only then turn to the preparation of plans for the physical and other changes required to reinforce these programs. Once stated, this sequence seems self-evident. Add the concept that these three steps are phases in a continuous cycle, and we have a definition of the planning process truly deserving the designation "comprehensive."

A year or so ago, Nathan Glazer shocked some of his friends

by writing a kindly article about Los Angeles—a western prov-
ince sometimes referred to as "600 suburbs in search of a city,"
and currently as "a great big slurb." Recently, Jane Jacobs
issued a ringing defense of the good old *eastern* slums. In this
one respect, evidently, Duhl is something of a conformist. He
writes, "These slum communities have attractions for many
groups that cannot be surpassed by anything we now have on
our planning boards." But then in suggesting what *might* be on
the drawing boards, Dr. Duhl draws on his experience as a
psychiatrist to state something that has extraordinary implications for planning. "Social welfare services which offer the possibility of a changed way of life have their attractions, but
involuntarily changed behavior can be costly to the individual
concerned. A variety of apparently unrelated pathologies may
develop which on careful evaluation can be traced to the impact
of a forced change in life style."

The real objective, Duhl reminds us, is not to change the
buildings (though this sometimes may be necessary) but to
change the people: change them not in the usual sense of trading them in for a more socially acceptable set but in the sense
of allowing them to change themselves—and to do this through
their own personal involvement and development. Thus, he
makes a key link between personal development and community
development, asserting that they are inseparable parts of the
same process. Duhl remarks that the planner, in his reorienta-
tion of the planning process, must achieve decentralization of
significant sectors of the decision-making. I would suggest two
directions for this decentralization: one, to the residents directly involved in neighborhood change; the other, to the people responsible for social and economic programs.

The most thoughtful among our physical planners would
argue with Duhl, if at all, in terms of who should be responsible
for carrying out the planning process he prescribes. They have
recognized for many years the need to study the community's
social and economic evolution to determine the requirements of
its physical environment. They accept also the responsibility
for indicating the prospective impacts of the physical measures

they propose upon the social and economic aspects of the community. But most planners draw back from professional involvement in the recommendation of measures purely in the socio-economic realm. They are loath to undertake studies very far removed from a *direct* and demonstrable relationship with the physical environment; and they rarely involve themselves in thinking about non-physical solutions except to the extent that these are needed as an adjunct to proposals for altering the physical environment.

I myself grant some validity to this orientation as a prudent, self-imposed limitation in the direction of professional specialization. But I am greatly concerned about the gap that results from the implied withdrawal from comprehensive responsibility. I stand with Duhl in his plea for some professional planners to address themselves to the whole scope of the problem that faces the man in the street.

ECONOMICS

Economics is the second profession focused on the topic of urban space in order to enrich the background considerations. Roland Artle has been studying the levers by which urban development might be guided. He has been working on mathematical decision-models. These models are sequences of analytic steps designed to say "what will happen if." They trace the probable effects of carrying out various possible programs. They assess the potential impact of what are called decision variables —that is, the elements that the people who make decisions directly influence or control.

In order to construct an economic model of the urban area, Artle suggests the need to trace through the inner workings and interactions of five fundamental categories of urban economic activity: production, consumption, investment, transactions with other areas, and communications. He (and Melvin Webber and Lowdon Wingo as well) puts special stress on communications as a fundamental activity, attributing to it a vital strategic role in the shaping of the metropolis. In a key passage Artle says:

"The unique significance of communications activity in urban economic analysis stems from the fact that the responsibility to provide channels of communications is one of the crucial tasks of local, metropolitan, state, and federal authorities. This power to *provide channels* ranges from major decisions to construct rapid transit systems and freeways, to expand or improve water systems and sewage trunk lines, to allocate TV-channel capacities, all the way to decisions to route traffic only one way on a certain street."

Wingo develops this point about the key influence of transportation in the course of describing the interactions among three regional sub-systems: (1) the *activities* of living and making a living as these occur and change at specific geographic locations; (2) the *patterns* of land use, which express the spatial relationships among the activities; and (3) the *transportation and communications* flow, which link the activities into a system of interactions. Wingo suggests that changes in the mix and nature of urban activities, together with changes in transportation and communications, produce the long-run changes in the geographic arrangement of activities—the pattern of land uses.

Artle, in further describing levers on development, points out that governmental policies and decisions influence both the capacities and usage of communications channels. Hence, policy alternatives may involve changing the capacity limitations of the various parts of the communications networks or changing the charges, taxes, or subsidies on the use of these channels.

The instrumental variables that decision-makers have at their disposal to influence or control development have seldom, he avers, been exploited for implementing long-range city plans. Most metropolitan area studies result in a set of forecasts of economic activity and population growth and resemble a weather forecast by implying that very little can be done to influence the course of events.

Roland Artle is, I know, following with great interest the program at the Penn-Jersey Transportation Study, where the whole approach to method is based on a *regional growth model*.

This is in fact a decision-model in Artle's sense, designed specifically to anticipate the long-term behavior of the region's people in response to alternative sets of policies that might be adopted and programed over time. As Artle states, such an approach has few precedents—and, may I add, a truly appalling number of potential pitfalls. Be this as it may, the only thing riskier than depending on our new methods, I think, would be to depend on our old ones. After all, a familiar, much used pitfall is not inherently less worthy of avoidance than a brand new pitfall.

A most intriguing section of Artle's essay deals with the possible use of the decision-model to manufacture solutions as well as to simulate consequences. He distinguishes two approaches to the manufacture of solutions.

One approach is to optimize—that is, maximize or minimize—a certain index that reflects a number of goals: for instance, to maximize the total income per capita of the urban economy under study; or to maximize the growth rate of the area; or to minimize the sum of all communications costs within the area; or to minimize the sum of all communications costs *and* all *rents;* or to maximize tax revenue for the local governments involved.

His other approach would be to specify a set of goals, which are not expressed in a combined index but are kept separate. These goals are formulated not as maxima or minima to be discovered but as fixed target values to be achieved. For instance, one such goal might involve population density—to achieve or maintain certain levels. Another goal might involve a specified number of contact choices offered to an inhabitant within a fixed distance and travel cost: for example, access to five potential jobs appropriate to the individual's skills or access to three regional shopping centers within a half-hour and a dollar of travel cost. "Thus," says Artle, "given a set of goals, the decision-maker's task is one of adjusting the instrumental variables so that these goals are achieved." What a prospect *that* idea opens up! But it does, perhaps, beg the question to which I shall return later: How are the goals to be generated in a society that assumes a pluralism of values and a pluralism of choosers?

THE LAW

In addition to the special insights of the psychiatrist and the economist, the symposium on urban space was fortunate in having the observations of a legal mind. Charles Haar has concerned himself with problems of planning for the use of urban space almost continuously since the 1940's.

Recurrently, in the course of my career as a professional planner, a planning board and I have arrived at a plausible solution to some problem only to conjure up the same disconcerting, ritualistic phrase: "It's good, but is it legal?" I might answer this by paraphrasing the central thesis of Haar's essay: If it's *really* good, it's really legal.

"The thesis that law accommodates to life," writes Haar, "promises that changes will occur . . . [but] time and content qualify this promise. Change is inevitable, but the rate of change is not predetermined . . . When the change does occur, the thesis does not offer any assurance that it will conduce towards greater rationality in the use of urban space." Professor Haar makes very sure, by the way, that the burden of rationality falls on the planners, not on the lawyers.

"Notwithstanding the qualified nature of the thesis," he continues, "its implications for the future of land use controls in achieving rational development of that resource are optimistic. For if it does not depict our legal institutions as a vehicle to Utopia, neither does it depict them as iron laws which react to every change instituted by man so as to prevent any lasting improvement. On the contrary, it holds out hope that given intelligence and energy our legal institutions will assist toward our goal."

Haar contributed another invaluable observation in what he calls a *calculus of social costing*. After warning that any extension of social controls of urban space will have to be designed to respect "judicial concepts of fairness and reasonableness," he states: "With respect to subdivision controls this appears to mean that the conditions imposed should be justifiable by some approximation to a calculus of social costing. This is deducible from *Pioneer Trust and Savings Bank* v. *Village of Mt. Prospect.* The test laid down there is that the subdivider may be made to bear those costs resulting from or necessitated by his activity.

In this case, the court sustained the developer "in his refusal to donate 6.7 acres for school and playground purposes for which, concededly, there was a pre-existing need aggravated by the 250 residential lots added by the new subdivision." However, in reaching its decision the court made it clear, "particularly to counsel for the planning authority which has the burden of proof, that the record must assist the court in computing social costs."

This suggests the question: If social costing can relieve the owner of part of the *cost* of facilities on his property made essential by his development activities, can social costing also justify a more carefully estimated sharing in the *benefits* of public facilities built in developing areas to make the land more accessible and to furnish it with off-site utilities? Will our communities begin to devise financial mechanisms for recouping to the public a larger portion of the incremental values created by public works when new areas are opened to development? At present, these increases funnel almost exclusively to the particular individuals who now happen to hold title to the benefited lands. I shall return to this matter later.

ISSUE NUMBER ONE: WHAT CONCEPT OF PLAN-MAKING?

Looking back over the observations of doctor, economist, and lawyer, it is clear that they have made a considerable contribution to the thinking of those of us who are professional planners. But now I come to two issues that have concerned all authors of the symposium papers, including those who are planners.

The first of these is the changing nature of the plan-making concept itself. Some of the questions that have arisen are: By what methods will the planning be done in the years ahead? How can we plan for an ever-changing process of urban action and interaction? What should be left to the free play of private choice and what should be the subject of deliberate social foresight? Is governmental planning to be defined inclusively to encompass all disciplined decision-oriented research leading to public action, or more narrowly to include only research necessary for authentic development of physical plans and their implementation?

As to the essential *scope* of social foresight, let us reread Dr. Duhl: "A variety of apparently unrelated pathologies may develop which on careful evaluation can be traced to the impact of a forced change in life style." And again, "Where economic dimension, engineering factors, and 'pure' design have largely pre-empted the planning of urban space, planning to meet social and welfare needs will reshuffle the planner's strategies and his hierarchy of values by giving priority to the simple question— what are the human implications of planning action?"

Echoing this theme is a remark made by Frederick Gutheim: ". . . the aim of the designer is to structure life and not merely to shape its external appearance." I might, and in fact do, quarrel with the implied *role* of the designer, but not with the bold scope advocated.

Admittedly, this is a tall order. Melvin Webber sensed the immense difficulty of the challenge when he wrote me: "The task becomes much more complex than we have hitherto understood it to be. The locational planning task is to find that spatial arrangement that will optimize human interactions and the conduct of human activities, while simultaneously allocating mineral, land, and other resources in some optimal fashion for the production processes. This becomes so complex a job as to defy my efforts to comprehend what it means, much less to discuss it effectively."

I speak with particular sensitivity, perhaps, to the question here raised as to whether the technology of planning is capable of being transformed to handle the sweeping scope suggested above. It is fundamental to the Penn-Jersey Transportation Study program, in which I was engaged for three years, that we do develop such a capability—a capacity to relate alternative programs for modifying the physical environment to the total environment in which we operate.

The central mechanism through which the program seeks to do this is its *regional growth model;* and this is one application of Artle's decision-model to which I alluded earlier. The Penn-Jersey Study is working with perhaps one-half billion bits of recorded information about its large bi-state urban region—information covering physical, social, economic, and political aspects. An intricate series of submodels is being designed for operation on high-speed computers for the purpose of simulating regional change over a long period of years in response to one or another of many sets of conditions, policies, and programs that might be assumed as operative at various future dates. The mere line-by-line inventory of the sets of variables in card and magnetic tape files takes the pages of a volume half an inch thick.

Penn-Jersey is aided by some astonishing new devices that can help make the data comprehensible: an automatic card-fed data plotter, for example, that makes maps with up to 10,000 dots in six colors in two hours per map—or plots whole transport networks with assigned traffic volumes in a matter of minutes.

But, let me make emphatically clear that the complex mathematically based mechanism for simulation called a model will not do any *fundamental* thinking. It will only provide mathematical computations made at very great speed—somewhere in the neighborhood of a quarter-million additions or subtractions every second. It will enable the study group to investigate relationships of an order totally beyond the analytic capacity of a decade ago, or even of the quite recent day in 1959 when Britton Harris of the University of Pennsylvania and I began to lay out the Study's detailed research program.

Beyond helping us to analyze relationships among existing

factors, computers can also be used to reveal how some future imaginary region would operate. But we have to do the imagining first.

To a degree, then, we can play with inputs and extrapolate all sorts of intriguing outputs, but basically it is only by the inspired use of the human imagination that we develop the hypotheses worthy of test.

In the words of Gutheim: "What the designer contributes to the process of city building, then, is not only the final form of a concept of the city given him by others. He also contributes valuable hypotheses, perhaps to be tested by research before execution, but in any event leading to the creation of new and alternative modes of urban life as well as urban forms which, once realized, research can confirm. This is not simply to contend that art is experiment, but to argue that it is the only creative element in the city building process. The rest is measurement, analysis, projection, effectuation."

With our new glimpse of how to harness contemporary technology to aid planning, I firmly believe we have reached a new stage in the evolving technology of decision-oriented urban research. Henceforth, it would be frivolous to approach planning for the use of urban space in the simple fashion of yesterday, when we isolated two-dimensional or, at best, three-dimensional patterns from the many-dimensioned reality of human life.

ISSUE NUMBER TWO:
HOW WILL URBAN SPACE BE USED?

The second vital issue is the probable nature of the future urban region. We have been living through more than half a century of inconclusive debate over desirable urban structure. A great many years ago, Sir Raymond Unwin wrote his classic *Nothing Gained by Overcrowding;* and today Stanley Tankel could well have called his paper in this series: "All is Lost by Undercrowding."

In addition to Tankel's warnings, which grow out of intimate experience with the world's most extensive metropolitan region, three other viewpoints—those of Catherine Bauer Wurster, Lowdon Wingo, and Melvin Webber—are well worth emphasizing.

Mrs. Wurster recalls the traditional function of a city—one which brought together a wide variety of people who engaged in many kinds of specialized but interdependent activity. The essential functions of its government were to resolve the people's differences in the common interest and to provide their necessary services. The city was a little world. Today a whole array of developments has weakened the tight-knit, articulated form of the city. Chief among these one might cite electric power, the telephone, radio and television, the automobile and truck, the pipeline, and especially the general rise in productivity which, by reducing work days in the week and hours of work in the day, also reduced the premium on home-to-work propinquity. As to a new form to replace the old, the suggestions have been many.

Mrs. Wurster suggests a new conceptual framework within which to ponder the essential differences among alternative urban structures. She believes that the trends and issues in metropolitan patterns of land use and communication may relate primarily to a pair of variables which can be loosely considered co-ordinates.

One is the gradient from extreme dispersal to extreme concentration. This is the obvious metropolitan dichotomy: the tendency of certain functions to spread out horizontally over huge areas while other functions pile up in a central place. The major force behind dispersal appears to be the desire or need to maximize "private" space values, a push that has been facilitated by automobility and the increase in aspatial and long-distance communication. Concentration, on the other hand, indicates dependence on a location with close-knit physical linkages at the expense of private space. This may reflect purposeful choice, as in the case of office skyscrapers, or a considerable degree of compulsion, as in the case of low-income and minority immigrants.

The other variable is more difficult to characterize in simple terms because the issue, although fundamental for all metropolitan planning, is seldom clearly posed. Indeed, the continuing controversy between the "decentralists" and the Big City defenders comes down to this question: What is the physical scale at which a significant degree of integration can, or should, take place among the various specialized elements and functions of a regional complex? Specialization implies interdependence, with more or less coherent organization at one or at several levels. The question is where, and at what scale, and for what purposes.

This pair of variables, viewed as co-ordinates, suggests a wide range of theoretical choices for future form and structure. In practical terms, however, an assessment of current trends, countertrends, and the forces behind them leads to the selection of four possibilities, though these would not all be equally possible everywhere.

Mrs. Wurster names the first of these *present trends projected;* the second, *toward general dispersion;* the third, *toward a concentrated super-city;* and the fourth, *toward a constellation of relatively diversified and integrated cities.*

During the past year the Penn-Jersey Study has been at work designing the first round of regional policy alternatives to be tested in its regional growth model. I have found it fascinating to see the degree of correspondence between alternative form concepts developed there and Mrs. Wurster's four prototypes. Indeed, her distinctions may prompt the Study to restate several of its alternatives in a different way in order to gain deeper significance.

In his essay, Lowdon Wingo uses a different approach to the issue of the future evolution of the urban region but produces a concept reasonably within Mrs. Wurster's framework. Wingo's judgments about the probable trends in the nature and mix of urban activities and in transportation and communications technology lead him to conclude ". . . that new organizational factors are beginning to dominate the form and organization of American cities. . . . The growing accumulation of capital in transportation facilities coupled with the increasing substitution of information flows for material flows is gradually dissipating many of the advantages of economic togetherness."

What he believes may happen is that marginal activities gradually will be spun off from the center of the city as sunk capital can be written off, with the lion's share of new activities finding locations away from the center. The urban core, however, will probably continue for some time to attract activities with peculiar communication and transportation needs. ". . . eventually we will come to a new urban pattern—no longer the centrally articulated, classical city, but a loosely knit, weakly centered, low density urban region spread over a wide hinterland."

Wingo sees three main problems in moving from now to then: (1) how to program the redefinition of our central areas and their conversion to a lesser role without catastrophe; (2) how to adjust urban transportation to the demands for private automotive travel between highly dispersed places; and (3) how to manage the use of land in the new patterns—and especially the interstitial lands that will separate the more desirable lands attracting urban development.

One can glean some reassurance for the future of metropolitan areas from both Catherine Wurster and Lowdon Wingo, but Melvin Webber foresees some rather drastic changes in the form that urbanization is likely to take. "The spatial patterns of American urban settlements are going to be considerably more dispersed, varied, and space-consuming than they ever were in the past—whatever metropolitan planners or anyone else may try to do about it. It is quite likely that most of the professional commentators will look upon this development with considerable disfavor, since these patterns will differ so markedly from our ideological precepts. But disparate spatial dispersion seems to be a built-in feature of the future—the complement of the increasing diversity that is coming to mark the processes of the nation's economy, its politics, and its social life. In addition, it

seems to be the counterpart of a chain of technological developments that permit, if they do not demand, spatial separation of
closely related people."

"To date," declares Webber, "very few observers have gone
so far as to predict that the nodally concentric form, that has
marked every spatial city throughout history, might give way
to nearly homogeneous dispersion of the nation's population
across the continent; but the hesitancy may stem mainly from
the fact that a non-nodal city of this sort would represent such
a huge break with the past. Yet, never before in human history
has it been so easy to communicate across long distances. Never
before have men been able to maintain intimate and continuing contact with others across thousands of miles; never has intimacy been so independent of spatial propinquity. Never before
has it seemed possible to build an array of specialized transportation equipment that would permit speed of travel to increase
directly with mileage length of trip, thus having the capability
of uniting all places within a continent with almost-equal time
accessibility. And never before has it seemed economically feasible for the nodally cohesive spatial form that marks the contemporary large settlement to be replaced by some drastically
different form, while the pattern of internal centering itself
changes or perhaps dissolves."

Having reviewed these several lively points of view on key
issues of future urban form—including Webber's happy hint
that the issue of urban form may quietly go away while we are
figuring out what to do about it—let us consider how social
foresight is likely to be applied in future years to determine the
use of urban space.

SOCIAL FORESIGHT

Let us start by recalling Haar's concept of a calculus of social
costing. This idea emerged from a consideration of how far to
go in requiring private land developers to provide the public
facilities that become necessary when their own business activ-

ities convert raw land into communities of people. The proposed calculus would distinguish between the cost of providing new community facilities directly occasioned by particular new projects and the cost of providing any needed additional capacity in these facilities to serve the needs of general growth in the area as a whole. The social costing would charge new development its distinct share of the costs of new municipal facilities and services, but no more.

Interestingly enough, an editorial in the *New York Times* early in March, 1962, came at social costing from an opposite tack:

"The 1953 decision to take flowage easements instead of title to the land at Federal flood-control reservoirs was one of the strange natural-resource errors of the last Administration.

"Little or no savings resulted because, as a Congressional investigating committee found out, it cost about as much to secure the easements as to buy the land outright. But the riparian owners who collected the easement fees and kept title to the land reaped a windfall at public expense. The value of the land boomed because of the public investment in the reservoir. The favored few were permitted to sell, lease or develop the lakeside sites for cottages, fishing resorts or other private purposes. Meanwhile the public was denied full access to the lakeshore.

"The present Administration has now returned to the policy that prevailed before 1953, that of acquiring enough of the surrounding land to permit full development and public use of the man-made lakes created with public funds."

The juxtaposition of these two complementary conceptions about values socially created suggests the question: What if we were to apply the principle not just to the new values created by man-made lakes but more broadly to the new values created by other key developmental activities of government—for example, highway construction or the public provision of utilities to serve an erstwhile undeveloped area? Suppose, as has been increasingly suggested of late, the idea of the public role in urban renewal were to be applied not only to obsolete central areas but also to outer areas being developed for the first time?

In urban renewal, government takes title to land by purchase or condemnation; designs the uses appropriate to the land in the context of broad considerations of the general welfare; improves the land where appropriate with new or widened access streets, parks, or schools; and sells or leases such parts of the land as are suitable for private development at the market value of the land *after* it has arrived at its new status.

If undeveloped land made accessible by new freeways were handled in similar fashion, what new possibilities would emerge from the resulting relationships between public action and private action? Would suburban and non-urban patterns of land use be as profoundly affected as urban development patterns have been where renewal concepts have had impact? Would we find, as we have in urban renewal, that we had discovered dramatically improved ways of engaging the energies of our essentially mixed economy toward the creation of a better human environment?

The test of such an approach to development, I think, is likely to occur first not within the United States proper, but rather in the lands aided by our resources—places that can afford no other approach to the development of new communities. Perhaps the feedback of this concept, tested abroad, will be a vital reward to us for our programs of aid to others.

One last point should be made by way of a kind of prediction. It has become clear to everyone that urban development no longer can be considered the *exclusive* responsibility of any single level of government—or "extension" of government, as Luther Halsey Gulick would put it to avoid any suggestion of hierarchy. The federal government, the states, the counties, and the municipalities all engage in region-shaping programs, and all are deeply concerned with the outcome of their innumerable interacting influences. One by one, the officials initiating comprehensive urban transportation studies, like that in the Penn-Jersey region, have found it utterly necessary to create new intergovernmental structures to bring all the governments involved into regular deliberation, negotiation, and collaborative decision on region-shaping issues and programs. And such is the logic of the inseparability of the elements of urban existence that transportation considerations are leading inexorably to a recognition of the need for more effective intergovernmental decision-making processes involving the other key elements of regional existence as well.

I think we can look forward confidently to the early emergence of new intergovernmental arrangements for the co-operative handling of urban development programs, in which the full gamut of governmental extensions—local, county, state, and federal—will collaborate toward making the best use of urban space. We have at long last reached the time of invention, decision, and action in working toward the better handling of metropolitan affairs.

Moreover, such is the importance of coherence, regularity, and finality of decision in metropolitan matters that we probably are talking about a new, truly legislative function and not merely a place of episodic bargaining when we explore organizational inventions at the metropolitan extension.

To sum up the contributions to the symposium which produced these essays on the future use of urban space:

I agree with Leonard Duhl that the central attention of planners will shift from land development to human development, that changes in the physical environment will come to be planned integrally with changes in the social and economic environment, and that what we call citizen participation will be transformed from a means of persuasion into a major force in community development.

The law, as Charles Haar assures us, will find one way or another to make possible those changes that are truly essential.

The formidable technical problems that must be surmounted to clarify the issues of urban change and to spell out the consequences of policy alternatives will be solved with the help of the decision-models sketched for us by Roland Artle, aided by a growing understanding of the interactions among urban activities, transportation, and communications traced here by Lowdon Wingo and Melvin Webber.

But no mechanical substitute will ever be found for the creative act that lies at the heart of planning: the invention of imaginative alternatives generated by the mysterious and wonderful processes of the human mind seized by a passion for excellence, beauty, and human betterment—alternatives illustrated by the invigorating and contrasting visions of Wurster, Wingo, Webber, Tankel, and Gutheim.

And finally, I affirm that our society will invent political means for working with the forces of contemporary life to fashion a human environment of true splendor. When our astronauts at last communicate with the creatures of other worlds, they will do so not as refugees from a shattered globe but as emissaries from a proudly remembered homeland.

INDEX

A

Accumulations, rules against, factor in land use control, 193–95
Adam, Henri-Georges, 105
Aesthetics in urban design, 104, 106, 109–11, 119–22; need for research in, 129–30
Alberti, Leon Battista, 126
Alienation, restraints on, rules against, factor in land use control, 193–94
Ambler Realty Co. v. *Village of Euclid,* 177–78, 183
Amsterdam, 115
Annapolis, Md., 126
Architectural Review, quoted, 34
Architecture:
  Modern movement, opposing wings of, 103–4
  Role in urban design, 64, 104–6; illus. fol. 122
Arnold, Robert, 172
Arp, Jean, 105
Artle, Roland, 20, 154–72; summation of thesis, 234–37, 240, 248
Atlanta, Ga., 33
Augur, Tracy, 118
Automation. *See* Technological advances
Automobile *(see also* Freeways):
  Advantages over mass transit, 16–17, 40
  Contribution to low-density urban growth, 45–46, 81
  Effect on urban design, 119–22
  Incompatibility with urban concentration, 85

Possible successors to, 40; effect on urban growth, 41
Ayres v. *City of Los Angeles,* 191

B

Bacon, Edmund N., 106, 121n
Barbican area of London, 121; illus. fols. 122
Bauhaus, 94
Beckmann, M., 168
Berenson, Bernard, 111
Berman v. *Parker,* 130, 199
Bernini, Giovanni Lorenzo, 108
Blackstone, Sir William, 176, 177, 197
Blessing, Charles A., 106
Bone, James, 123
Borough of Cresskill v. *Borough of Dumont,* 203
Boston, Mass., 8, 13, 27, 28, 48, 51, 146
Brasília, 115, 138
British new towns. *See* Great Britain
Broadacre City, Wright's, 93, 105, 120, 125, 127; illus. fols. 122
Buchanan v. *Warley,* 219

C

Calder, Alexander, 105
California:
  City planning in, 96
  Conservation rights, 207, 220
  Legal decision relating to land use, 205–6
  Urban growth in, 48, 97, 117